Petrit Halilaj
An Opera Out of Time

Nationalgalerie
der Gegenwart

Hamburger
Bahnhof

Für die / For the **Nationalgalerie –
Staatliche Museen zu Berlin**
herausgegeben von / edited by
Sam Bardaouil & Till Fellrath

SilvanaEditoriale

Nationalgalerie
Staatliche Museen zu Berlin

Inhalt / Content

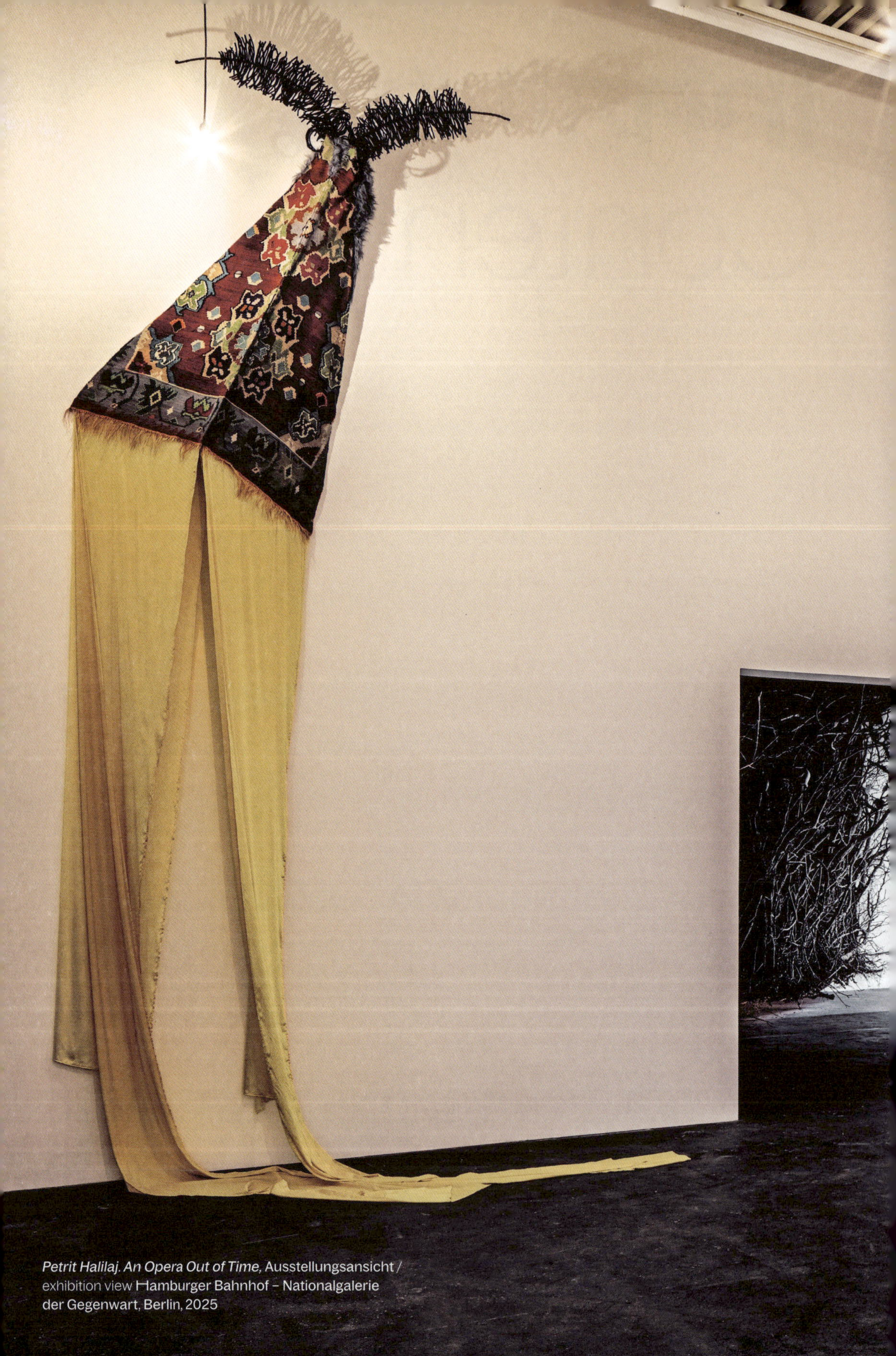

Petrit Halilaj. An Opera Out of Time, Ausstellungsansicht /
exhibition view Hamburger Bahnhof – Nationalgalerie
der Gegenwart, Berlin, 2025

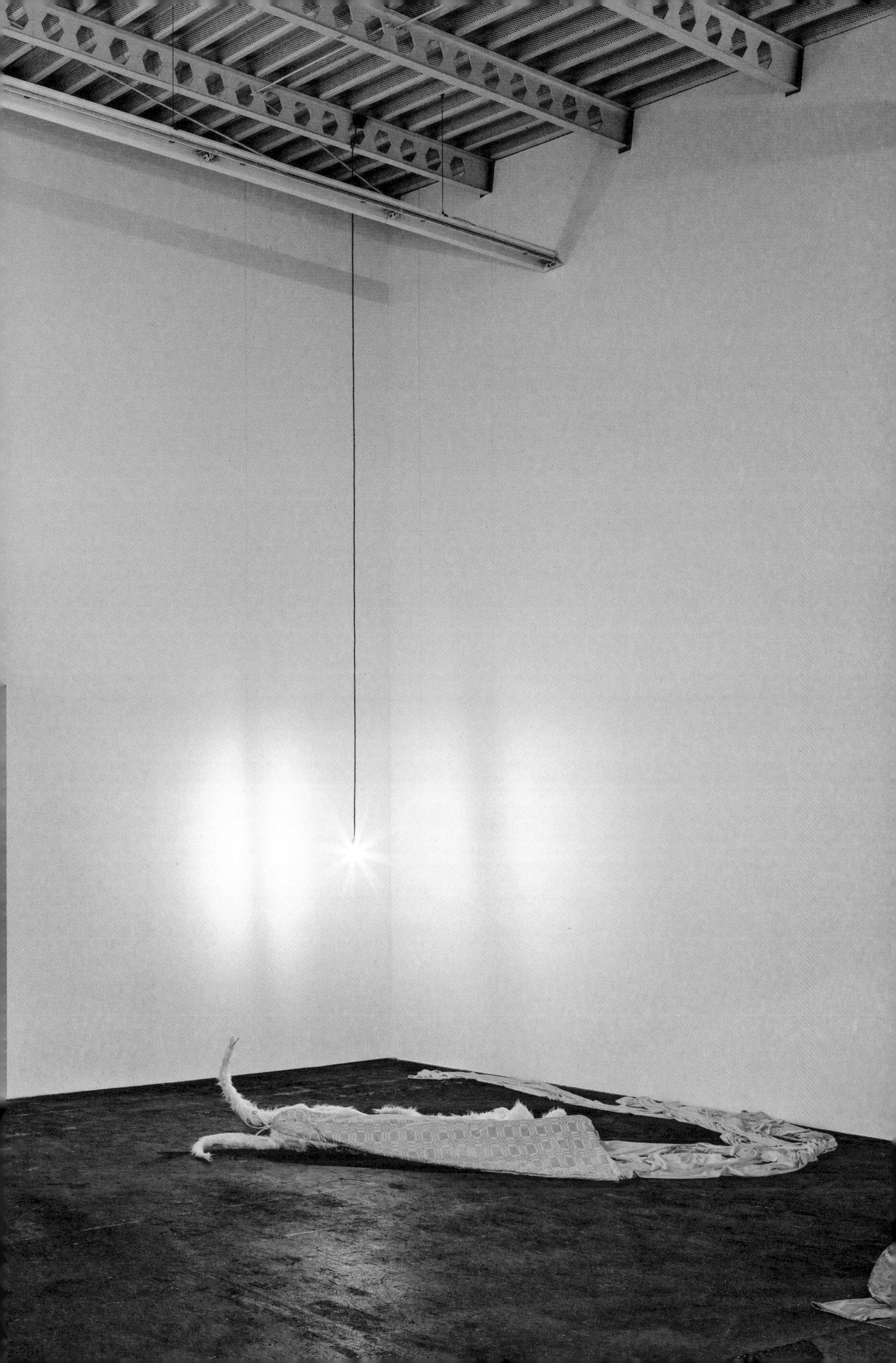

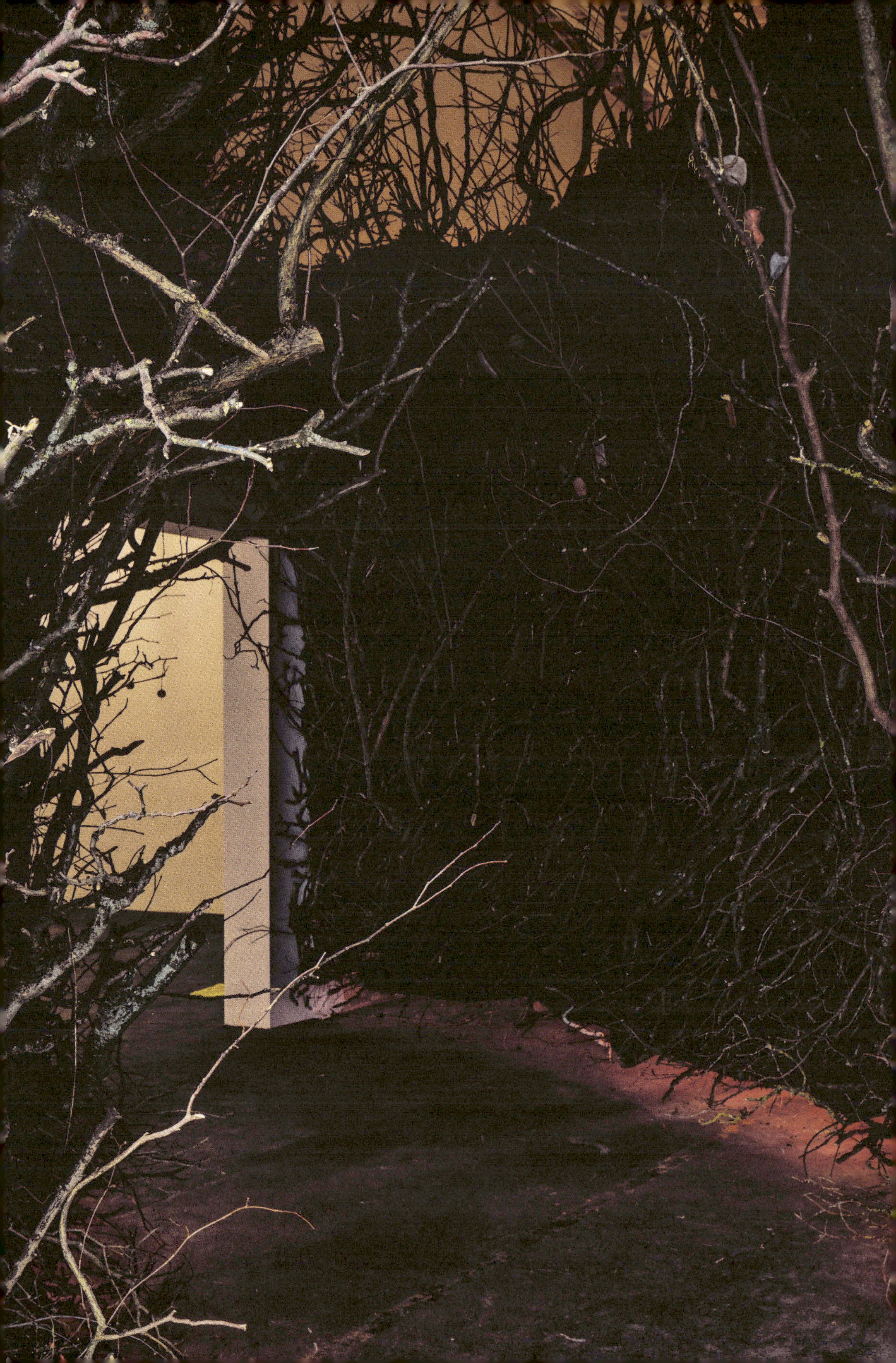

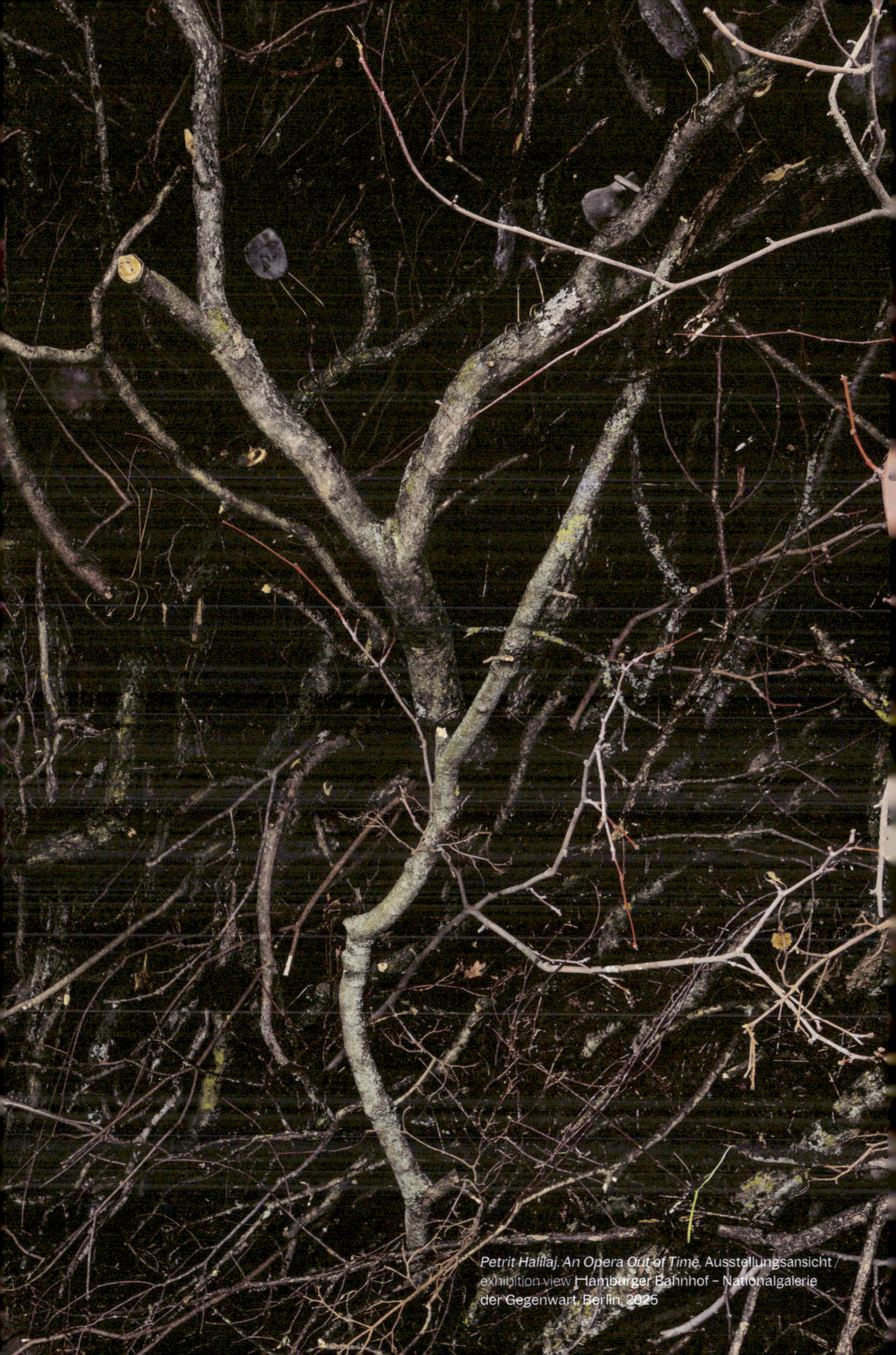

Petrit Halilaj, An Opera Out of Time, Ausstellungsansicht /
exhibition view Hamburger Bahnhof – Nationalgalerie
der Gegenwart, Berlin, 2025

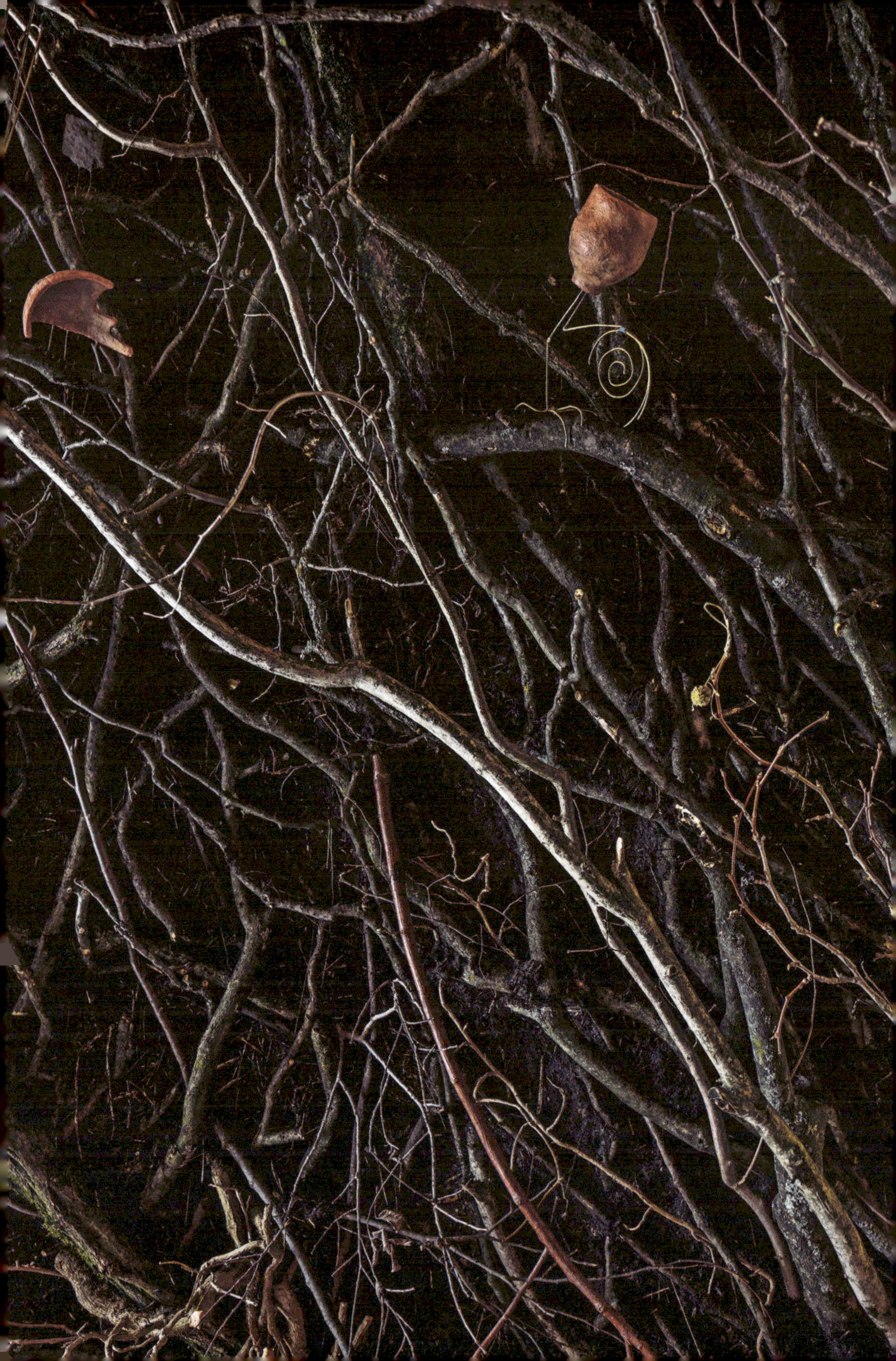

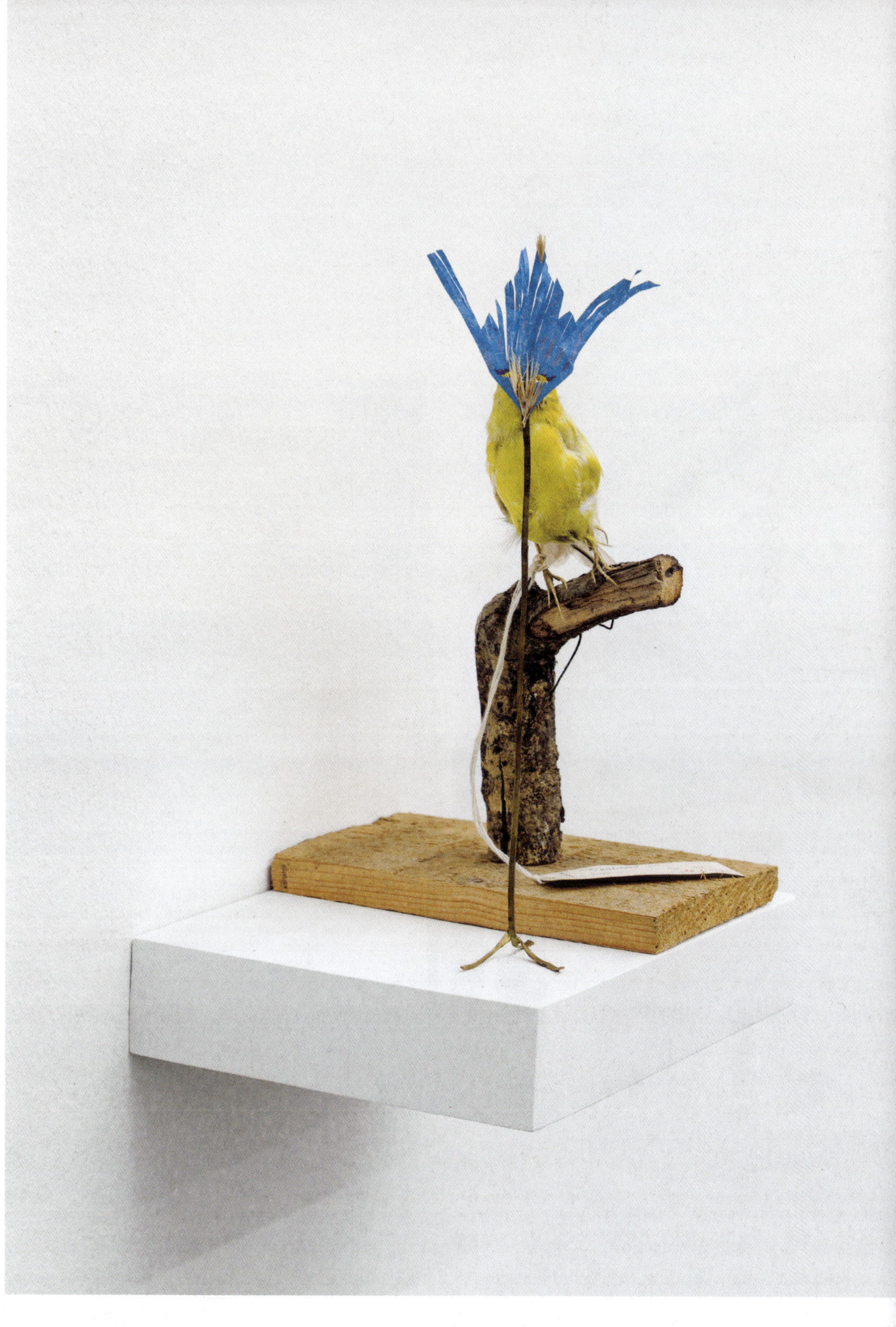

Petrit Halilaj. An Opera Out of Time, Ausstellungsansicht /
exhibition view Hamburger Bahnhof – Nationalgalerie
der Gegenwart, Berlin, 2025

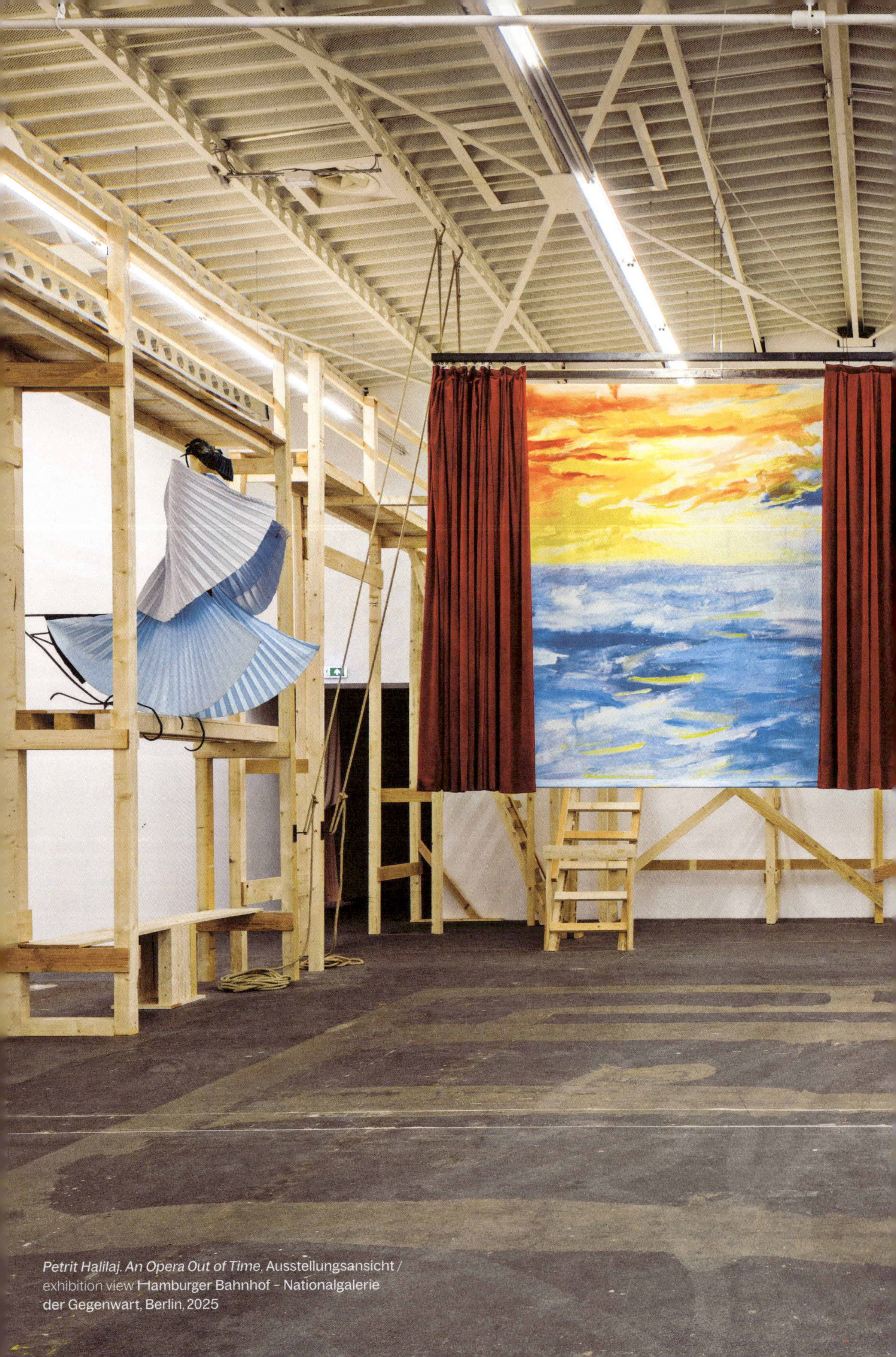

Petrit Halilaj. An Opera Out of Time, Ausstellungsansicht /
exhibition view Hamburger Bahnhof – Nationalgalerie
der Gegenwart, Berlin, 2025

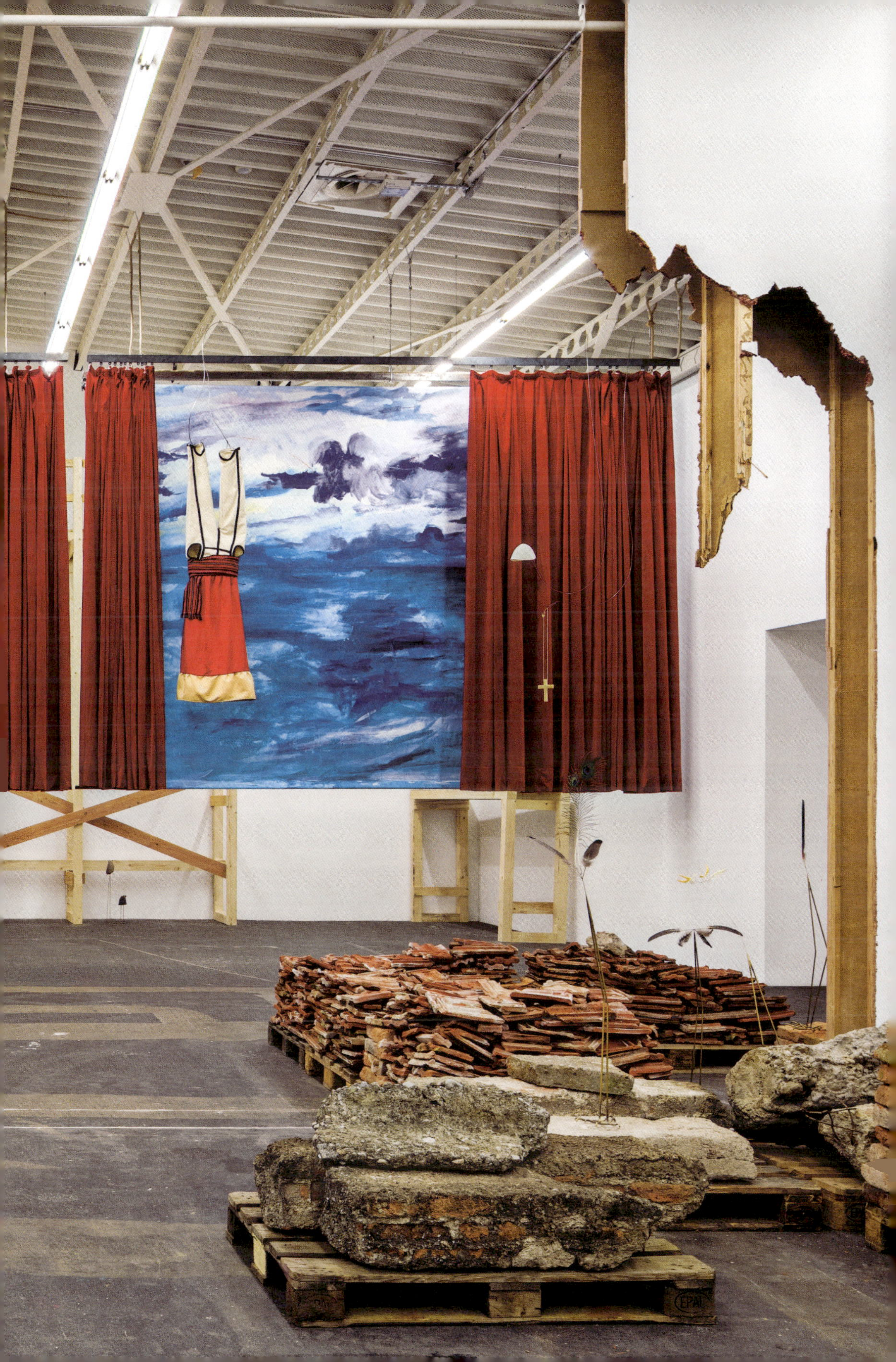

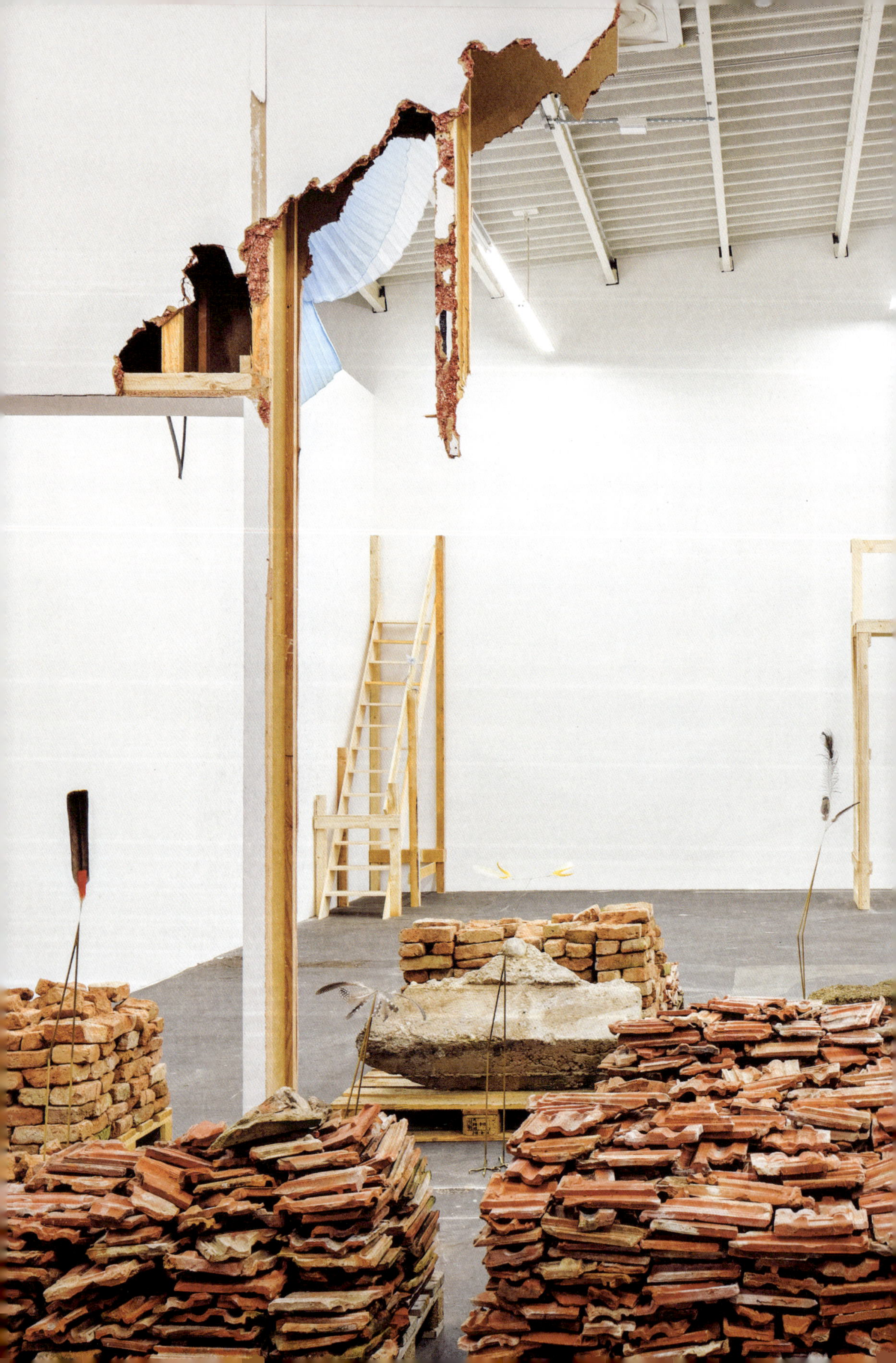

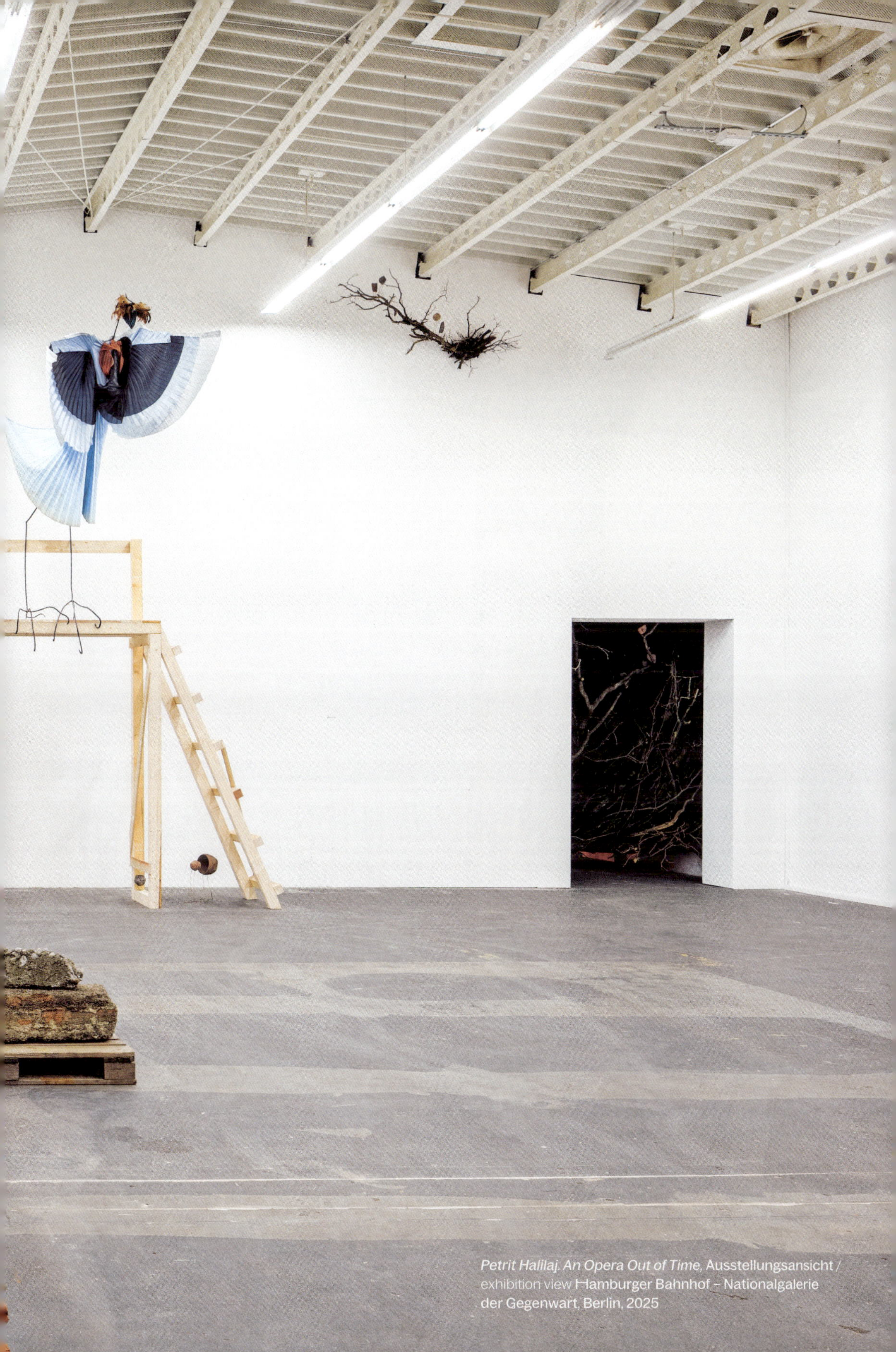

Petrit Halilaj. An Opera Out of Time, Ausstellungsansicht / exhibition view Hamburger Bahnhof – Nationalgalerie der Gegenwart, Berlin, 2025

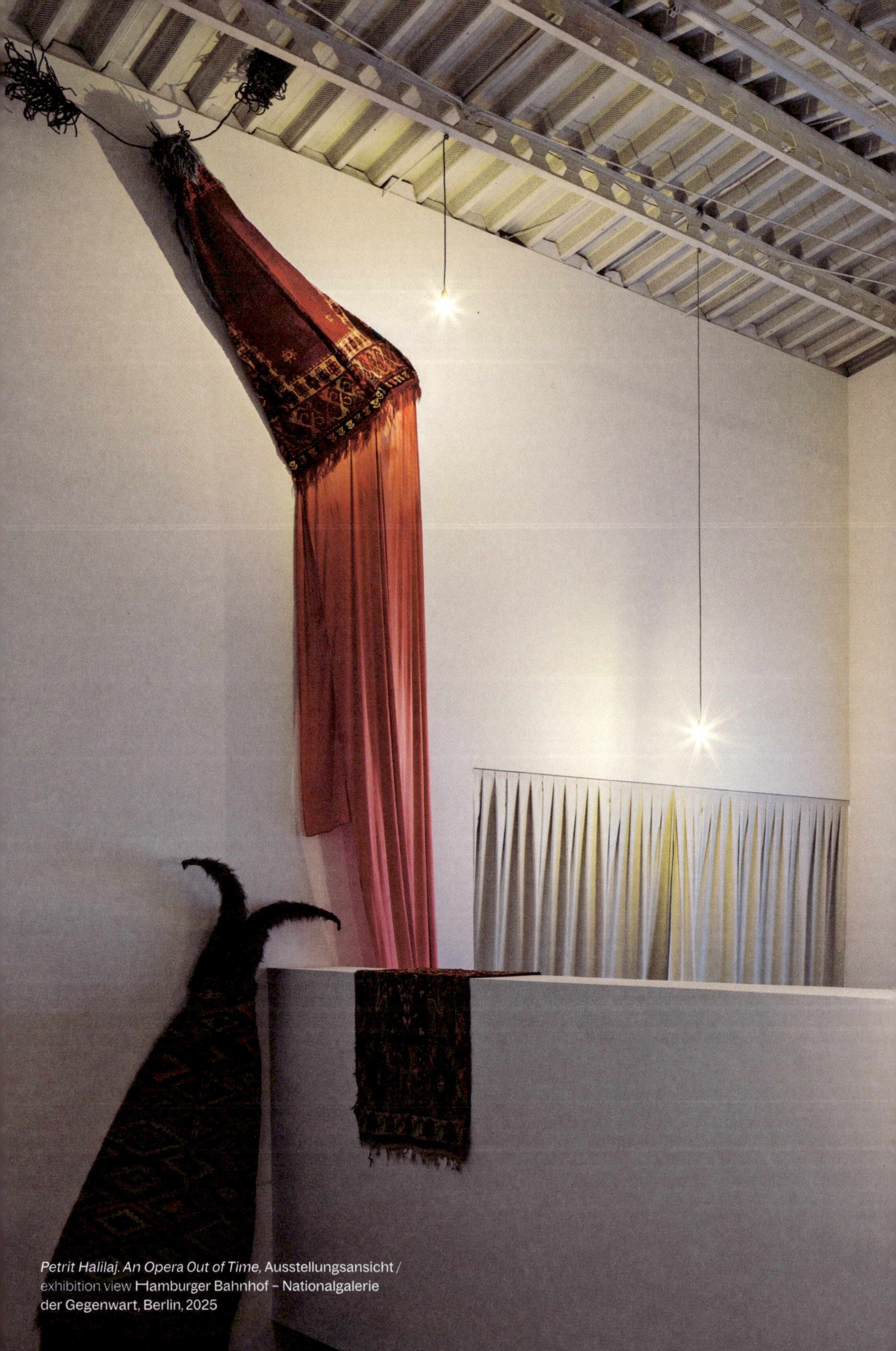

Petrit Halilaj. An Opera Out of Time, Ausstellungsansicht /
exhibition view Hamburger Bahnhof – Nationalgalerie
der Gegenwart, Berlin, 2025

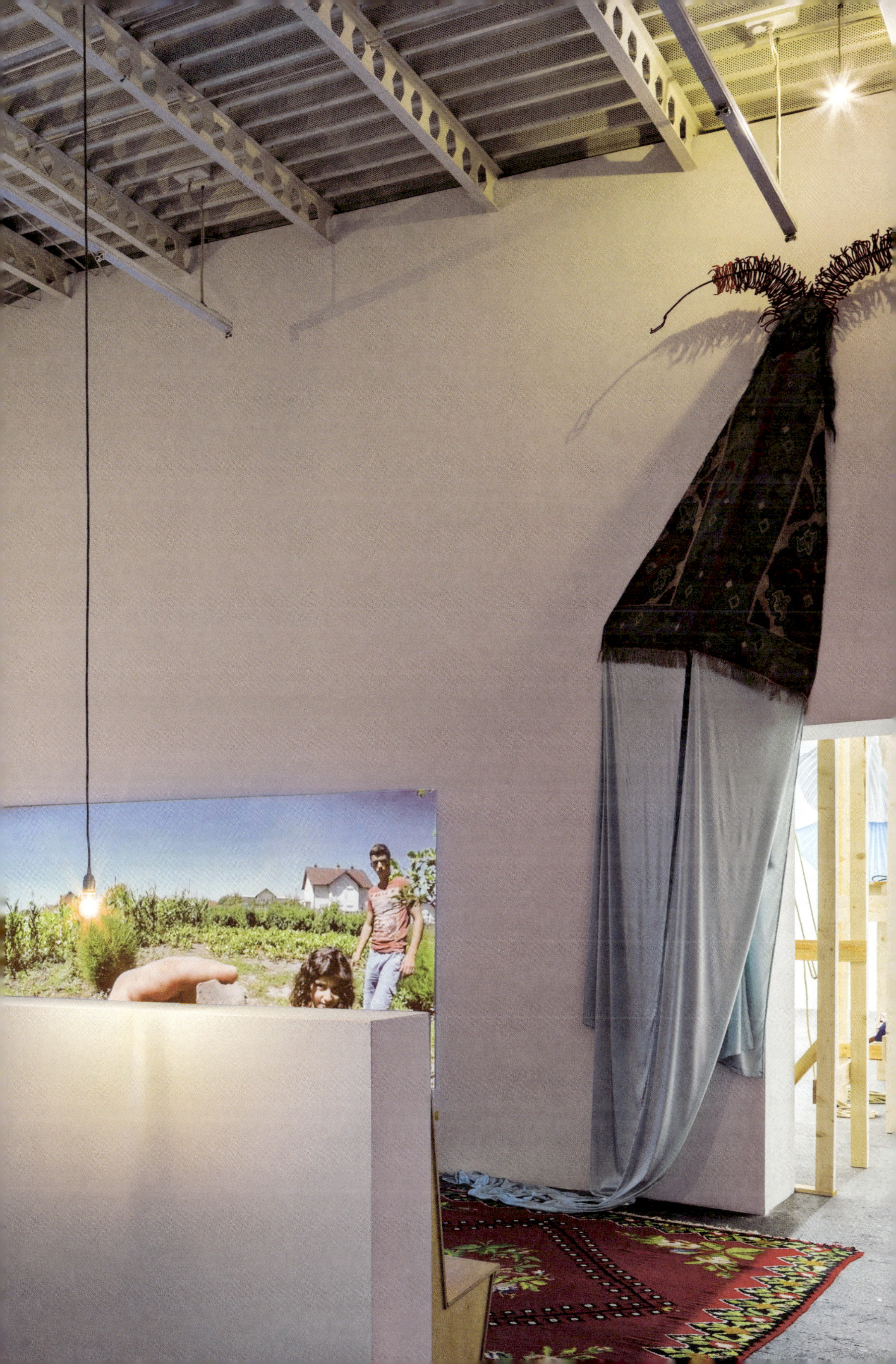

Petrit Halilaj. An Opera Out of Time

Catherine Nichols

Ich kann mich nicht konzentrieren. Ich gehe mit meiner Hündin spazieren. Im Park treffe ich meine Freundin Daniela. Ich bin gerade aus dem Kosovo zurück, sage ich. Mit Petrit Halilaj war ich dort – für seine Oper *Syrigana*. Ich erzähle ihr, dass die Oper – Petrits erste – von der Legende inspiriert ist, nach der Adam und Eva nach Syrigana, dem Dorf seiner Mutter, gekommen seien, um zu heiraten. Ich schildere, dass sie am Fuß eines sagenumwobenen Felsens aufgeführt wurde, der sich am Rand des Dorfes aus der Landschaft erhebt – an einem Ort, an dem ethnische Albaner*innen und ethnische Serb*innen ihre eigenen Gärten hüten und wo Bäuer*innen, Bergleute und Archäolog*innen um das Land ringen. Ich berichte, dass über tausend Menschen, die meisten aus der Region, bei Sonnenuntergang den Hügel von Syrigana hinaufgekommen sind, um mitzuerleben, wie sich seine queere, interspezifische Liebesgeschichte entfaltete; und dass die Oper – nun in eine immersive Installation übersetzt – das Herzstück von Petrits Einzelausstellung im Hamburger Bahnhof bildet. Dies im Dialog mit Werken, die ihr den Weg bereitet haben. Denk an den Garten Eden, sage ich. Denk an *Ein Sommernachtstraum*. Denk an

I can't think. I take the dog for a walk. I encounter my friend Daniela in the park. I'm just back from Kosovo, I say. I was there with Petrit Halilaj – for his opera, *Syrigana*. I tell her how the opera, Petrit's first, was inspired by the legend that Adam and Eve came to Syrigana, his mother's village, to get married. I tell her how it was performed at the foot of a fabled rock soaring up out of the landscape at the edge of the village, a place where ethnic Albanians and ethnic Serbs keep to their own gardens, and farmers, miners and archaeologists vie for the land. I tell her how over a thousand people, most of them local, gathered on the hill of Syrigana at sunset to witness his queer, interspecies love story unfold; and how the opera – now transposed into an immersive installation – lies at the heart of Petrit's solo show at Hamburger Bahnhof amid many of the works of art that

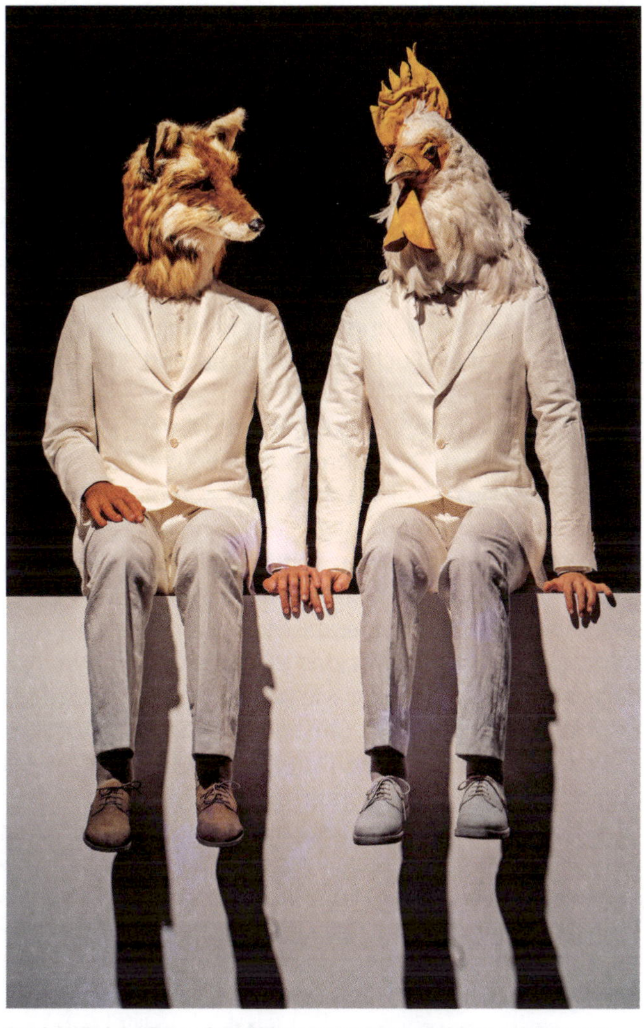

Petrit Halilaj. An Opera Out of Time, Ausstellungsansicht / exhibition view
Hamburger Bahnhof – Nationalgalerie der Gegenwart, Berlin, 2025

Romeo und Julia. Denk an eine ausgelassene kosovarische Hochzeit – und dann denk noch einmal neu.

Als ich Danielas Verwunderung spüre, hole ich mein Telefon hervor, um ihr das eindringliche Duett der Sopranistinnen Nina Guo und Urta Haziraj vorzuspielen:

They say, a garden out of time;
They say, a pear tree, so divine;
They say, a garden that was lost …

[Sie sagen, ein Garten außerhalb der Zeit;
Sie sagen, ein Birnenbaum, so himmlisch;
Sie sagen, ein Garten, der verloren wurde …]

foreshadowed it. Think *Garden of Eden*, I say. Think *A Midsummer Night's Dream*. Think *Romeo and Juliet*. Think exuberant Kosovar wedding – and then think again.

Sensing Daniela's bewilderment, I pull out my phone to play her the haunting duet sung by sopranos Nina Guo and Urta Haziraj:

They say, a garden out of time;
They say, a pear tree, so divine;
They say, a garden that was lost …

Daniela is visibly moved. Like everyone I've shown my recording to. When the video loops and starts again, she watches it a second time.

Daniela ist sichtlich bewegt. Wie jede Person, der ich meine Aufnahme gezeigt habe. Als das Video von vorn beginnt, schaut sie es sich ein zweites Mal an. Bei aller Unbeholfenheit meiner Aufnahme vermitteln Musik, Landschaft und Szenerie dennoch etwas, das sich für mich immer noch zu nah, zu frisch, zu überwältigend anfühlt, um es zu begreifen oder in Worte zu fassen.

Als ich noch erwähne, dass die Protagonisten der Oper ein Fuchs und ein Hahn sind, ihre Erzähler*innen und der Chor hingegen ein Vogelschwarm, fühlt sich Daniela an Olivier Messiaen erinnert. Kennst du seine Oper über Vögel?, fragt sie mich. Ich schüttele den Kopf. *Blah blah blah d'oiseaux*, sagt sie. So ähnlich heiße sie, glaubt sie. Wieder schüttle ich den Kopf. Ich weiß wirklich nicht viel über Messiaen, gebe ich zu. Ich meine, außer, dass er ein französischer Komponist des 20. Jahrhunderts war, weiß ich so gut wie nichts. Meine Hündin zieht an der Leine. Es ist doch *ihr* Spaziergang, erinnert sie mich. Damit ist das Gespräch zu Ende, und wir gehen unserer Wege.

Später am Abend ruft mich Daniela an, um mir Näheres zu erzählen. Also Messiaen, sagt sie, sei von Vögeln und ihrem Verhalten ebenso hingerissen gewesen wie Petrit, dessen Werk voller fantastischer vogelartiger Kreaturen steckt, die watscheln, stolzieren, sitzen, flattern, schweben. Messiaen, fährt sie fort, habe sich offenbar bei unzähligen Kompositionen vom Vogelgesang inspirieren lassen. *Catalogue d'oiseaux* – übrigens keine Oper – sei ja nur eines von vielen Stücken mit, über oder für Vögel. Dazu kämen *Réveil d'oiseaux, Oiseaux exotiques, Petites esquisses d'oiseaux…* Manche für Klavier solo, andere für Klavier und Orchester. Es heißt, er habe Gesänge von über 500 verschiedenen Arten einbezogen: aus Europa und Asien, aus Nord-, Mittel- und Südamerika – kurz, aus aller Welt.[1] Messiaen, so legen es seine Notizbücher nahe, habe Jahre damit verbracht, auf Märkten, in Straßen und Wäldern den Vögeln beim Sprechen und Singen, Flirten, Kämpfen, Nisten und beim Versorgen ihrer Jungen zu lauschen und ihre Laute dabei festzuhalten. Auch in seiner Oper *Saint François d'Assise*,

For all the clumsiness of my recording, the music, the landscape, the scenography convey what for me still feels too close, too fresh, too overwhelming to grasp, to express in words.

When I mention that the opera's protagonists are a fox and a rooster, its narrators and chorus a flock of birds, Daniela feels reminded of Olivier Messiaen. You know his opera about birds?, she asks me. I shake my head. *Blah blah blah d'oiseaux*, she continues. Something like that, she thinks it's called. I shake my head again. I really don't know much about Messiaen, I concede. I mean, beyond the fact that he was a 20th century French composer, I know next to nothing at all. The dog pulls on her lead. It is *her* walk, she reminds me. The conversation comes to an end. We go our separate ways.

Later that evening, Daniela calls to tell me more. As it turns out, she says, Messiaen was as entranced by birds and their behaviour as Petrit, whose oeuvre is full of fanciful bird-like creatures waddling, strutting, perching, fluttering, hovering. Messiaen, she continues, seems to have composed countless pieces inspired by birdsong. *Catalogue d'oiseaux* – which, by the way, isn't an opera – is just one among many works with, about, or for birds. There's *Réveil d'oiseaux, Oiseaux exotiques, Petites esquisses d'oiseaux…* Some were written for solo piano, some for piano and orchestra. People say he drew on the songs of over 500 different species: birds from Europe and Asia, birds from North, Central and South America, birds from all over the world.[1] Messiaen, his notebooks suggest, spent years wandering around marketplaces, along streets, through forests noting down the vocalisations of the birds he heard speaking and singing, flirting and fighting, nesting and nurturing their young. And in his opera – *Saint François d'Assise*, as it's actually called – birds feature prominently too. Take Saint Francis's "Sermon to the Birds", for example. That scene alone – at 45 minutes the longest in the opera – incorporates the songs of over 30 different species, among them blackbirds, nightingales, skylarks and robins, swallows, lyrebirds and wrens.

After the call, I head straight online to listen to the opera myself.[2] I'm curious to see where Daniela's association of *Syrigana* with *Saint*

wie sie tatsächlich heißt, spielen Vögel eine wichtige Rolle. Man denke nur an die „Predigt an die Vögel" des heiligen Franziskus. Allein diese Szene – mit 45 Minuten die längste der Oper – vereint die Gesänge von über 30 Arten, darunter Amseln, Nachtigallen, Feldlerchen und Rotkehlchen, Schwalben, Leierschwänze und Zaunkönige.

Nach dem Anruf gehe ich sofort online, um mir die Oper selbst anzuhören. Danielas Hinweis auf eine Verbindung zwischen *Syrigana* und *Saint François* lässt mich nicht los. Ungeduldig springe ich direkt zur „Predigt an die Vögel", ehe ich wieder an den Anfang zurückkehre und das Werk in seiner Gesamtheit höre.[2] Messiaen bezeichnete diese Szene als seinen „größten Erfolg im Vogelgesangsstil", als den Moment mit den „besten Vogel-Tuttis".[3] Doch gibt es jenseits des Motivs der Vögel tatsächlich eine Verbindung? Hat Messiaens zutiefst spirituelles, Multispezies-Opernwerk der 1980er-Jahre irgendetwas zu tun mit Petrits heutigem, dezidiert politischem *Trrrr-tschii tschii-witt-witt trrr-ka-ka*? Vielleicht eröffnet gerade die Gegenüberstellung eine neue Perspektive auf die Reichweite und Wirkung von Oper in Petrits künstlerischer Praxis – sei es als Denkform, als politische Imagination, als mehr-als-menschliches Werden, als queerende, weltbildende Kraft – trotz der unterschiedlichen Zeitrahmen, kulturellen Klimata und geografischen Kontexte ihrer Entstehung?

So sehr mich die Klänge von Messiaens Vögeln verzaubern, wie sie aus Geigen, Flöten, Piccolos, Klarinetten, Xylophonen, Marimbas, Glockenspielen und einem Ondes Martenot – einem frühen elektronischen Tasteninstrument – hervorsprudeln, so sehr wundert mich zugleich die Eigenwilligkeit der Gesamtkonstruktion: das Fehlen eines Antagonisten, der Mangel an politischer Intrige, die Abwesenheit einer Liebesgeschichte und die generelle Armut an Drama und Konflikt – also all das, was für mich bislang eine Oper ausgemacht hätte. Was genau ist eigentlich eine Oper?, frage ich mich. Was qualifiziert ein Werk als solche? Was bewog Messiaen, einen Auftrag der Pariser Oper anzunehmen, obwohl er noch

François might take me. Impatient, I skip ahead to the "Sermon to the Birds" scene – Messiaen considered it his 'greatest success in the birdsong style', the one with his 'best bird tuttis'[3] – before returning to the beginning and listening to the piece all the way through. Is there a link, I wonder... I mean, beyond the role of birds? Does Messiaen's profoundly spiritual multispecies operatic work from the 1980s have anything to do with Petrit's resolutely political *Trrrr-chii chii-whit-whit trrr-ka-ka* of today? Could the juxtaposition help probe the scope and impact of opera in Petrit's practice – as a mode of thinking, of political imagination, of more-than-human becoming, of queering, of worlding – despite the differing time frames, cultural climates and geographies of their creation?

As enchanted as I am by the sounds of Messiaen's birds springing forth from violins, flutes, piccolos, clarinets, xylophones, marimbas, glockenspiels and an Ondes Martenot, an early

---

1 Vgl. das Gespräch „My Birds" in: Olivier Messiaen, *Music and Color: Conversations with Claude Samuel*, Portland, OR: Amadeus Press, 1994, S. 85–97.
2 Die von mir gewählte Aufnahme wurde bei den Salzburger Festspielen 1999 vom Hallé Orchestra Manchester und dem Arnold Schoenberg Chor unter der Leitung von Kent Nagano eingespielt und von Deutsche Grammophon veröffentlicht. Vgl. https://www.youtube.com/watch?v=0TufQgNdfss&t=8221s, zuletzt abgerufen am 5. August 2025. Die „Predigt an die Vögel" beginnt bei 2:11:06.
3 Vgl. das Gespräch „Saint Francis of Assisi" in: Messiaen, *Music and Color*, S. 207–250, hier S. 239. (Alle Zitate aus dem Englischen übersetzt von Catherine Nichols.)

---

1 See the conversation entitled "My Birds" in: Olivier Messiaen, *Music and Color: Conversations with Claude Samuel,* Portland, OR: Amadeus Press, 1994, pp. 85–97.
2 The recording I selected was performed by Manchester's Hallé Orchestra and the Arnold Schoenberg Choir under the baton of Kent Nagano at the Salzburg Festival in 1999 and released by Deutsche Grammophon. See https://www.youtube.com/watch?v=0TufQgNdfss&t=8221s, last accessed on 5 August 2025. The "Sermon to the Birds" begins at 2:11:06.
3 See the conversation entitled "Saint Francis of Assisi" in: Messiaen, *Music and Color,* pp. 207–250; p. 239.

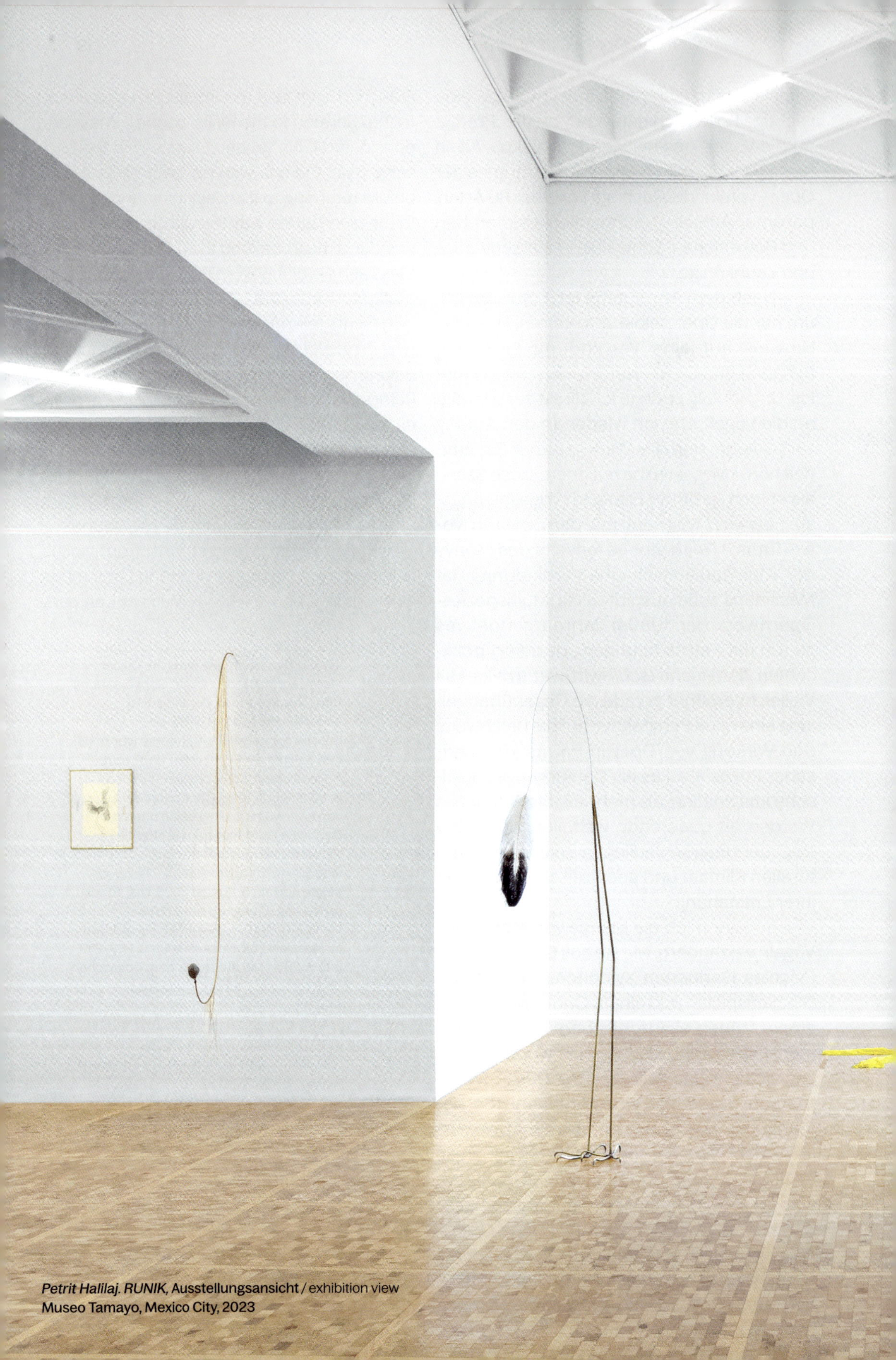

Petrit Halilaj. RUNIK, Ausstellungsansicht / exhibition view
Museo Tamayo, Mexico City, 2023

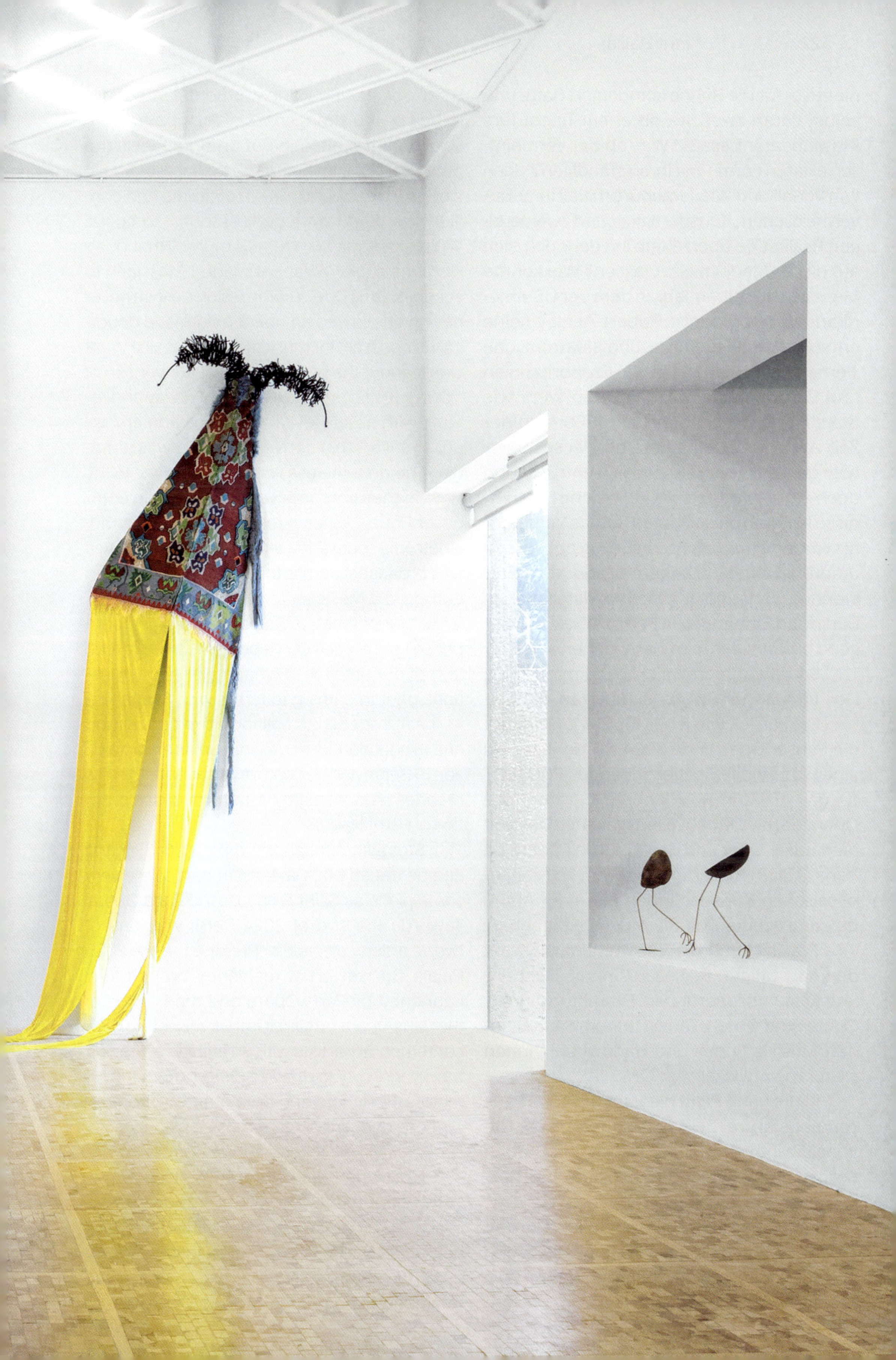

nie zuvor für die Bühne komponiert hatte und selbst daran zweifelte, ob er ein Talent fürs Musiktheater besaß?[4] Was an der vermeintlich elitären Form – mit ihren ständigen Zyklen von Verfall und Wiedergeburt, mit all ihrer unvermeidlichen „Kunstfertigkeit und zweideutigen Realität"[5] – überzeugte ihn dennoch, sich auf dieses Medium einzulassen? Wie konnte Messiaen im selben Jahr, in dem der US-amerikanische Komponist Robert Ashley seine entschieden zeitgenössische elektronische ‚Fernsehoper' *Perfect Lives* in Großbritannien und Europa ausstrahlen ließ, ein Werk wie *Saint François* schaffen, das ‚außerhalb der Zeit' zu stehen scheint? Ist Oper per se außerhalb der Zeit? Kann sie zugleich entrückt und doch gegenwärtig sein? Und welche Erkenntnisse könnten diese Fragen für das Verständnis von *Syrigana* liefern – in Bezug auf dessen ursprüngliche Motivation, kollaborative Entstehung, Verwandlung in eine Installation in Berlin und Einbettung in Petrit Halilajs vorwiegend bildkünstlerische Herangehensweise?

So unwahrscheinlich es klingen mag: Der Impuls für *Syrigana* führt an denselben Ort zurück wie jener für *Saint François*: die Pariser Oper. Ende 2024 wurde Petrit als einer von zwölf Künstler*innen für PROJECT 12, das Artist-in-Residence-Programm der Opéra Garnier für 2025, ausgewählt. Das von der Pariser Oper und den Amis de l'Opéra de Paris (AROP) initiierte Programm soll zeitgenössischen Künstler*innen mit einer Affinität zur Inszenierung die Möglichkeit geben, ihre Praxis durch die Zusammenarbeit mit den dort tätigen Regisseur*innen, Bühnen- und Kostümbildner*innen, Dramaturg*innen, Choreograf*innen, Tänzer*innen, Sänger*innen, Musiker*innen und Handwerker*innen weiter zu entwickeln.[6]

Kaum hatte Petrit die Nachricht aus Paris verdaut, stand er bei einem Konzert in der Nationalbibliothek von Prishtina neben Dardan Selimaj, dem Direktor der kosovarischen Philharmonie. Ein flüchtiger Blick hinauf zur markanten Kuppel des Gebäudes ließ Dardan an *Forget Me Not* denken – eine Installation aus überlebensgroßen Blütenskulpturen, die Petrit gemeinsam mit seinem Partner Álvaro

electronic keyboard instrument, I'm equally struck by the strangeness of the opera's construction: the absence of an antagonist, the paucity of political intrigue, the lack of a love story and the overall dearth of drama and conflict I would have thought essential to opera. What exactly is an opera?, I muse. What qualifies it as such? What persuaded Messiaen to accept a Paris Opera commission despite never having composed an opera before and doubting he had a gift for musical theatre at all?[4] What was it about the seemingly elitist convention of opera with its perpetual cycles of decay and rebirth, with all its inevitable 'artifice and ambiguous reality'[5] that convinced him it was a medium he nonetheless wanted to engage with? How, in the very same year as American composer Robert Ashley's resolutely contemporary electronic "opera for television" *Perfect Lives* was broadcast across the United Kingdom and Europe, did Messiaen create an opera as radically "out of time" as *Saint François*? Is opera per se out of time? Can it be at once out of time and of our time? And what might such questions offer in coming to terms with *Syrigana* – its initial impetus, its collaborative conception and production, its reimagination as an installation in Berlin and its contextualisation within the broader, predominantly visual arts-based practice of Petrit Halilaj?

Strangely enough, the impetus for *Syrigana* can be traced back, at least in part, to the very same place as *Saint François*: the Paris Opera. Towards the end of 2024 Petrit was one of twelve artists selected for PROJECT 12, the 2025 Palais Garnier artist residency programme. Launched by Paris Opera and the Friends of the Paris Opera (AROP), it is their mission to offer contemporary artists with an affinity for staging the opportunity to draw inspiration from the directors, designers and dramaturges, choreographers, dancers, singers, musicians and craftspeople working together under its roof.[6]

Not long after the news from Paris, Petrit found himself standing beside Kosovo Philharmonic director Dardan Selimaj at a recital held at the National Library in Prishtina. Looking up at the library's central cupola, Dardan felt reminded of *Forget Me Not*, an installation of

Urbano 2021 dort präsentiert hatte.[7] Die Blüten sind Teil einer stetig wachsenden Werkgruppe, die ursprünglich für die Hochzeit der beiden im *Palacio de Cristal* des Reina Sofía in Madrid entstand. Sie markieren besondere Momente ihrer Beziehung und sind zugleich ein ausgelassenes öffentliches Bekenntnis zu queerer Liebe. Angesichts der großen Resonanz dieser Arbeit lud Dardan Petrit spontan ein, ein Bühnenbild für die Philharmonie zu entwerfen. Das Orchester, gegründet im Jahr 2000 nach dem Kosovokrieg (1998/99), plante für 2025 eine Reihe besonderer Veranstaltungen anlässlich seines 25-jährigen Bestehens.

Aus einer Idee für ein Bühnenbild erwuchs in kurzer Zeit eine ganze Oper – *Syrigana* –, die bald von der kosovarischen Philharmonie offiziell in Auftrag gegeben wurde. Schon nach wenigen Tagen stand für Petrit fest, dass dieses Werk zugleich das Herz seiner Einzelausstellung im Hamburger Bahnhof bilden könnte. Doch vor seinem inneren Auge erschien weder die Bühne der Opéra Garnier noch der rote Saal des monumentalen Palasts der Jugend und des Sports, wo die Philharmonie ihren Sitz hat. Stattdessen sah er die Oper direkt in Syrigana entstehen – unter freiem Himmel, inmitten jener Landschaft, die ihre Geschichte hervorgebracht hatte. Dort sollte sie Gestalt annehmen: losgelöst von den sozialen, räumlichen und ästhetischen Zwängen eines herkömmlichen Opernhauses.

Im Gegensatz zu anderen bildenden Künstler*innen, die sich mit der Oper als Genre auseinandergesetzt haben – etwa William Kentridge, Shirin Neshat oder Jonathan Meese –, begegnete Petrit vielen ihrer traditionellen Merkmale mit Skepsis: der Pracht der Opernhäuser, der exklusiven Ticketvergabe, dem kanonischen Repertoire und dem hierarchischen Gefüge zwischen Komponist*in, Regisseur*in, Dirigent*in, Librettist*in, Darsteller*innen und Publikum. Er setzte stattdessen auf prozessorientierte, ortsspezifische Zusammenarbeit, die die Bräuche, Traditionen, Dringlichkeiten und Komplexitäten der Region berücksichtigt. Er schien intuitiv zu begreifen, was der Theoretiker und Regisseur Yuval Sharon als das inhärent „Ungezähmte"

way-larger-than-life-sized flower sculptures that Petrit and his partner Álvaro Urbano had presented there in 2021.[7] Part of an ongoing series originally conceived for their wedding at Palacio de Cristal, Reina Sofía in Madrid, the flowers signify special moments in their relationship – and an exuberant public declaration of queer love. Upon recalling their broad appeal, Dardan spontaneously invited Petrit to design a scenography for the Kosovo Philharmonic which, founded in 2000, in the aftermath of the Kosovo War (1998–99), was preparing a series of special events to mark its 25th anniversary.

What began in Petrit's mind as a scenography soon evolved into something far more ambitious – an opera set in Syrigana – which quickly became an official commission from the Kosovo Philharmonic. Within days, Petrit realised that the work he wanted to create for his solo exhibition at Hamburger Bahnhof would be the museum version of that very same opera. Not one destined for the stage of the Opéra Garnier, however, nor for the Red Hall of Prishtina's landmark Palace of Youth and Sports, home to the Kosovo Philharmonic. Instead, it would be an opera to be enacted outdoors, in the landscape of Syrigana – the very place its story was born – free from the social, spatial and aesthetic restraints of a conventional opera house. In contrast with many other visual artists engaging with the genre, among them William Kentridge,

---

4 Ebd., S. 208.
5 Yuval Sharon, *A New Philosophy of Opera*, New York: W. W. Norton, 2024, S. 90.
6 Vgl. https://www.operadeparis.fr/en/info/a-unique-artist-residency-in-the-heart-of-the-palais-garnier, zuletzt abgerufen am 5. August 2025.
7 Die Blumen, die 2020 im Palacio Cristal, Madrid, debütierten, wurden in Prishtina im Rahmen der 3. Autostrada Biennale gezeigt, kuratiert von Övül Ö. Durmuşoğlu und Joanna Warsza.

---

4 Ibid., p. 208
5 Yuval Sharon, *A New Philosophy of Opera*, New York: W. W. Norton, 2024, p. 90.
6 See https://www.operadeparis.fr/en/info/a-unique-artist-residency-in-the-heart-of-the-palais-garnier, last accessed on 5 August 2025.
7 The flowers, having debuted at Palacio Cristal, Madrid in 2020, were shown in Prishtina as part of the 3rd Autostrada Biennial, curated by Övül Ö. Durmuşoğlu and Joanna Warsza.

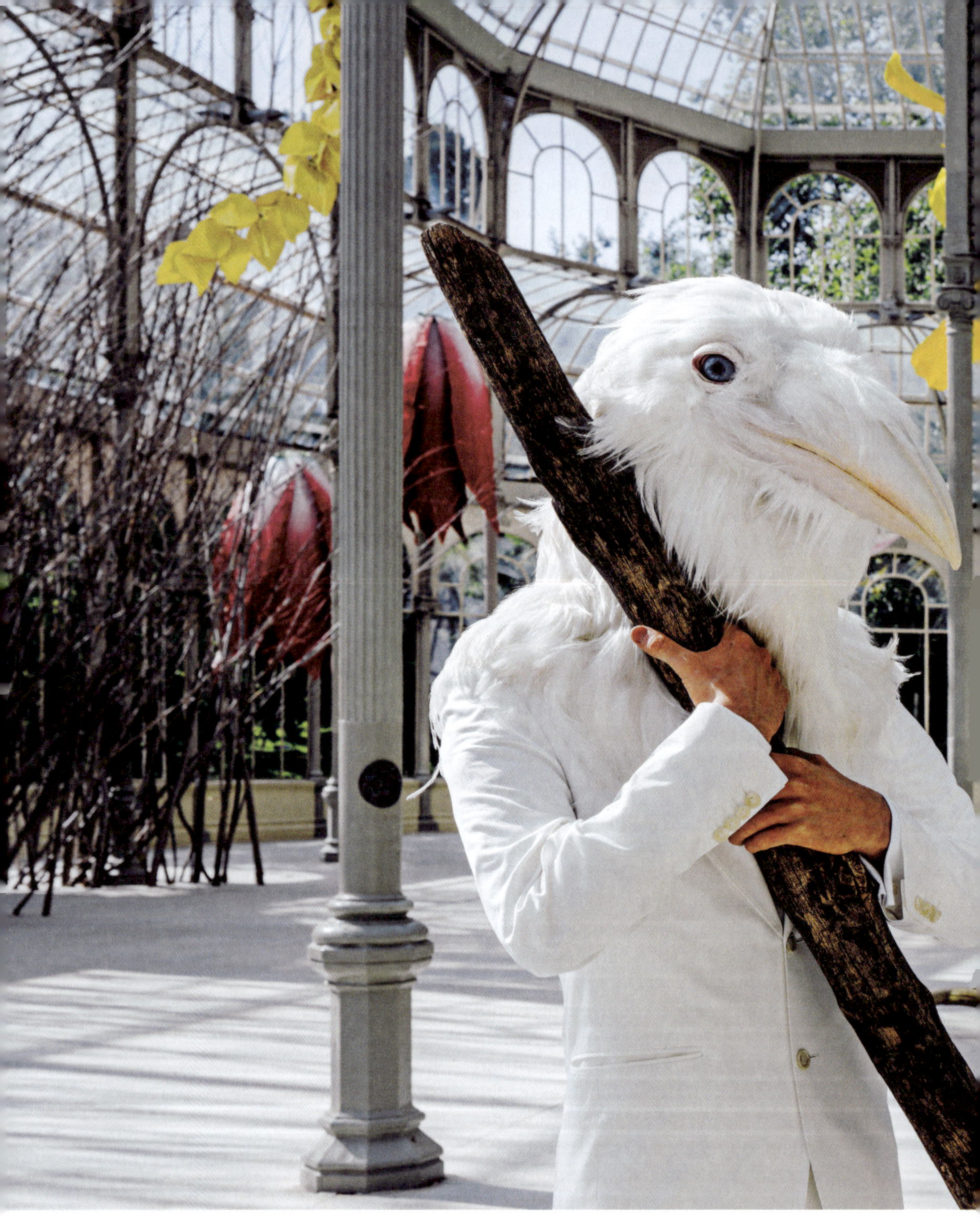

Petrit Halilaj, *The History of a Hug,* 2020, Stahl, Stoff, Federn,
Leder, Heupfahl aus dem Kosovo, Silikon, Farbe, Haare /
steel, fabric, feathers, leather, hay pole from Kosovo, silicon,
paint, hair, 200 × 60 × 60 cm

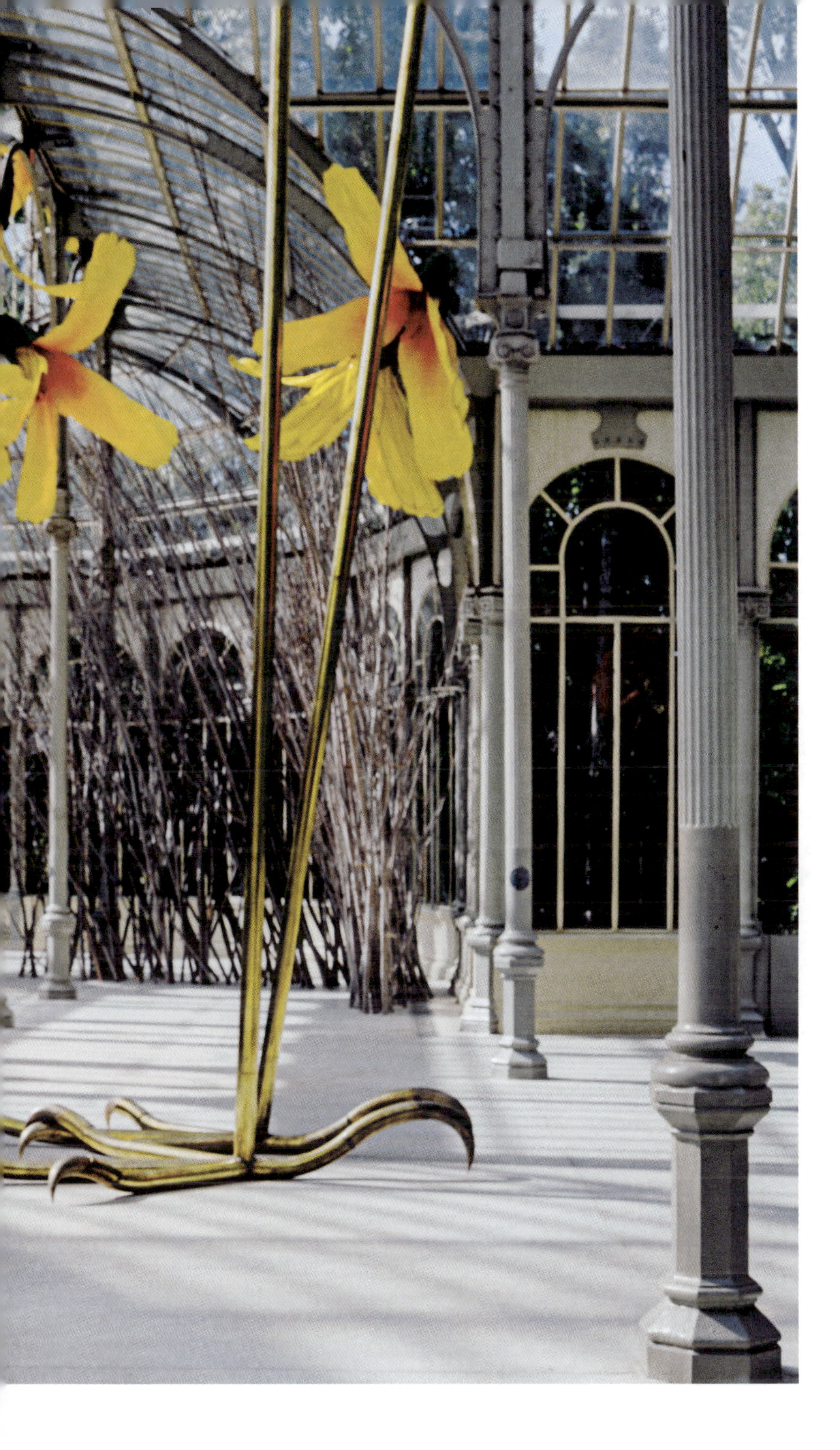

und die Instabilität der Oper beschreibt – ihre Fähigkeit, als „Mechanismus für ein Zusammentreffen von Gedanken, das jede Konvention sprengt" zu dienen, als experimenteller, offener, von Natur aus kollektiver Akt des Forschens, Gestaltens, Austauschens und Feierns, als „mehrdeutige Suche nach dem, was sich nicht klassifizieren und nicht aussprechen lässt".[8]

Die Einladungen aus Paris und Prishtina, die ihn in die Opernwelt führten, mögen Petrit überrascht haben. Und doch lässt sich eine klare Linie erkennen, wenn man seine künstlerische Praxis bis ins Jahr 2010 zurückverfolgt. Damals erregte er erstmals internationale Aufmerksamkeit mit *The places I'm looking for, my dear, are utopian places, they are boring and I don't know how to make them real* – seiner Installation für die Berlin Biennale, in der er die geisterhafte Hülle seines Elternhauses in Prishtina in der Haupthalle des KW Institute for Contemporary Art aufhängte und von gackernden Hühnern umgeben präsentierte. Die aktuelle Ausstellung folgt der allmählichen Ausbildung einer operatischen Sensibilität, einer Denk- und Arbeitsweise, die zwischen Zeichnung und Skulptur, Performance und Installation mäandert – vom Gackern und Fuchsen zum Singen, vom Skizzenbuch in die Galerie und von dort über die Bühne ins Dorf – und wieder zurück.

Wer durch die Ausstellung im Hamburger Bahnhof schlendert oder diesen wie auch jeden anderen Katalog von Petrit zur Hand nimmt, wird feststellen, dass seine Installationen häufig wie Bühnenbilder wirken – wie Environments, bevölkert von einem wachsenden Ensemble mehr-als-menschlicher Akteur*innen: Motten, Vögel und Füchse, aber auch Nester, Häuser, Raumschiffe und Sterne. Innerhalb dieser Szenarien, so bemerkt der Kunsthistoriker Mark Godfrey, werden die Betrachtenden selbst zu einer Art Protagonist*innen, die die Geschichte sowohl physisch als auch imaginativ erkunden. Diese immersive Qualität, die – so Godfrey – damit zu tun hat, dass viele von Petrits Arbeiten aus Situationen hervorgehen, die er selbst erlebt hat, ermöglicht es den Menschen, die

Shirin Neshat or Jonathan Meese, he rejected many of the conventional trappings of the genre of opera – sumptuous opera houses, exclusive ticketing, canonical repertory and hierarchical relationships between composer, director, conductor, librettist, performers and audience – in favour of process-based, site-specific collaboration attuned to the customs, traditions, urgencies and complexities of the region. He seemed to intuitively embrace what theorist and director Yuval Sharon views as opera's inherent unruliness and instability, its capacity to serve as a 'mechanism for a meeting of minds, spilling beyond every convention', as an experimental, open-ended innately collective act of research, creation, exchange and celebration, as 'an ambiguous search for what is unclassifiable and unspeakable'.[8]

The invitations from Paris and Prishtina luring him into the opera world may well have taken Petrit by surprise. And yet, if you consider his artistic practice from the moment he first found himself in the international spotlight at the 2010 Berlin Biennale with *The places I'm looking for, my dear, are utopian places, they are boring and I don't know how to make them real* – the ghostlike shell of his family home in Prishtina suspended in the main hall of KW Institute for Contemporary Art amid clucking chickens – through to the present, the arc becomes clear. As the current exhibition reflects, you can trace the evolution of an operatic sensibility: an operatic mode of thinking and making, a wandering line from drawing and sculpting to performance, from clucking and foxing to singing, from sketchbook to gallery to stage to village and back again.

Meander through the exhibition at Hamburger Bahnhof, flip through this or any other catalogue of Petrit's and you will observe that his installations more often than not resemble stage sets or environments populated with a growing ensemble of more-than-human characters: moths, birds and foxes but also nests, houses, spaceships and stars. Within these settings, as art historian Mark Godfrey observes, 'the viewer becomes a kind of protagonist', exploring 'the story physically and imaginatively'.[9] This immersive quality, which,

Resonanzen der von ihm aufgerufenen und untersuchten Geschichten unmittelbar zu spüren – ganz gleich, wie vertraut ihnen deren Realitäten sind.[9]

Man denke etwa an *Do you realise there is a rainbow even if it's night!?*, die fortlaufende Serie von Motten-Skulpturen, mit der die Ausstellung eröffnet und die sich durch sie hindurchzieht. Die über viele Monate hinweg von Hand gefertigten Motten nehmen die Form von Ganzkörperkostümen an, die vom Künstler selbst getragen werden können. Ihre gemusterten Flügel bestehen aus traditionellen kosovarischen Teppichen, die langen Schwänze aus bunt gefärbter Seide, die pelzigen Körper, Köpfe und Fühler aus weichen, synthetischen Stoffen, wie man sie üblicherweise für Spielzeug, Möbel oder Kleidung verwendet. Die Installation, geboren aus einer anhaltenden Faszination für diese fragilen nachtaktiven Wesen und ihre fatale Anziehung zum Licht, wurde erstmals für die schummrigen Hallen des Arsenale in Venedig während der Biennale 2017 entwickelt. Dort, im Flackern nackter Glühbirnen, verharrten die farbprächtigen geflügelten Wesen an den Wänden, in den Dachbalken und auf dem Boden – wie stumme Zeugen von Geschichten, die erst noch ans Licht gebracht werden müssten.

Für eine Lecture-Performance der Summer School 2016 am Stacion – Center for Contemporary Art Prishtina entstand die erste Motte der Serie – ein Werk, das Petrit in enger Zusammenarbeit mit seiner Mutter Shkurte Halilaj schuf. Unter dem Titel *But how to grow without being bored?* griff die Performance auf einen früheren subversiven Akt des Künstlers zurück: das Entfernen von Schmetterlings- und Mottenpräparaten aus der Lepidoptera-Sammlung des Naturhistorischen Museums des Kosovo, nachdem er entdeckt hatte, dass diese im Depot langsam vor sich hin rotteten. Wie der gesamte Bestand des Museums waren auch diese Exponate nach der politisch erzwungenen Schließung der Institution Anfang der 1990er-Jahre dem Verfall überlassen worden. Als das Gebäude 2003 – nach einem Jahrzehnt von Krieg und

Godfrey contends, has to do with the fact that much of Petrit's practice originates from situations he encounters, allows people to 'viscerally feel the resonances' of the histories he evokes and examines, regardless of how familiar they may be with their underlying realities.[10]

Consider, for instance, *Do you realise there is a rainbow even if it's night!?*, the ongoing series of moth sculptures which opens, and recurs throughout the exhibition. Made by hand over many months, the moths take the form of full-body costumes designed to be worn by the artist himself. Their patterned wings are crafted from traditional Kosovar carpets, their long tails from brightly coloured silk and their furry bodies, heads and antennae from soft synthetic fabrics typically used for toys, domestic furnishings and clothing. The installation, inspired by a sustained fascination with these fragile, nocturnal creatures and their fatal attraction to light, was first developed for the half-lit halls of the Arsenale in Venice during the 2017 Biennale. There, amid the flicker of bare lightbulbs, the vivid winged creatures lingered on the walls, in the rafters, on the floor like silent witnesses to histories yet to be brought to light.

The first moth in the series was conceived for a lecture performance presented at the 2016 Summer School at Stacion – Center for Contemporary Art Prishtina and made by Petrit in collaboration with his mother, Shkurte Halilaj. Entitled *But how to grow without being bored?*, the performance revisted the artist's earlier subversive act of removing butterfly and moth specimens from the Lepidoptera Collection of the Kosovo Natural History Museum after discovering they were rotting in storage. Like the

---

8 Sharon, *A New Philosophy*, S. 10
9 Mark Godfrey, „Flight Fantasies" in: *Artforum International* 60:3 (November 2021), https://www.artforum.com/features/mark-godfrey-on-the-art-of-petrit-halilaj-250832/, zuletzt abgerufen am 5. August 2025.

---

8 Sharon, *A New Philosophy*, p. 10
9 Mark Godfrey, "Flight Fantasies" in: *Artforum International* 60:3 (November 2021), https://www.artforum.com/features/mark-godfrey-on-the-art-of-petrit-halilaj-250832/, last accessed on 5 August 2025.
10 Ibid.

wechselnden Regimen – restauriert und wiedereröffnet wurde, präsentierte es sich nicht mehr als Naturkundemuseum, sondern als ethnografisches Museum, das sich ausschließlich der albanischen Kultur widmete. Aus einem Denkmal der Biodiversität und einer zentralen Wissensquelle über die Natur war so ein Symbol einer einzigen, eng gefassten kulturellen Identität geworden – einer Identität, die dem Nachkriegsprojekt nationaler Kohäsion und den langfristigen Zielen von Staatsbildung und Unabhängigkeit wohl dienlicher erschien.

Petrits Plündern der Sammlung war zugleich ein Akt des Begehrens und der Fürsorge. Für ihn bedeutete es ein Eingreifen gegen die strukturelle Vernachlässigung der Natur, gegen das systematische Auslöschen unbequemer Geschichte(n) und gegen die Weigerung, sich mit komplexen kollektiven Identitäten auseinanderzusetzen, die nicht in die gängigen Kategorien von Ethnie, Blut und Boden passen. Und doch blieb es Diebstahl. Die Aneignung von Kulturgut und Wissensbeständen, die nicht ihm gehörten, verlangte nach Bekenntnis und öffentlicher Diskussion. Um einen Weg zu finden, über dieses Überschreiten zu sprechen, verwandelte Petrit gemeinsam mit seiner Mutter einen Teppich der Familie in ein Mottenkostüm. Zum Falter zu werden – geflügelt, verborgen, randständig, anders – erlaubte es ihm, die Scham hinter sich zu lassen, eine nonverbale Sprache zu entwickeln und Zugang zu einer Weise des Wahrnehmens, Kommunizierens, Interagierens, ja des Denkens und Träumens zu finden, die ihm sonst verschlossen geblieben wäre.

Diese Erfahrung der Maskerade war Petrit nicht fremd. Schon seit 2014 trat er wiederholt als Kanarienvogel auf – eine Praxis, die an die erste gemeinsame Skulptur mit seinem Partner Álvaro anschloss: *She, fully turning around, became terrestrial (stolen canary)* aus dem Jahr 2013. Das winzige Kanarienpräparat, ebenfalls subversiv aus dem stillgelegten Naturhistorischen Museum des Kosovo ‚geborgen', trägt eine zarte blaue Papiermaske. Sie verbirgt eine Identität und bringt zugleich eine andere hervor, die sie projiziert

rest of the museum's holdings, these specimens had been left to decay in the basement after the institution's politically imposed closure in the early 1990s. When the building was restored and reopened to the public in 2003 – after a decade marked by war and shifting regimes – it emerged not as a natural history museum but as an ethnographic museum devoted exclusively to Albanian culture. Once a monument to biodiversity and a vital source of knowledge about the natural world, the institution was recast as a symbol of a singular, narrowly framed cultural identity – one deemed better suited to the postwar project of forging national cohesion and advancing the long-term aims of state-building and independence.

At once an act of desire and an act of care, Petrit's plundering of the collection was, in his view, an intervention against the intrinsic neglect of nature, the systemic erasure of inconvenient histories and the reluctance to engage with complex collective identities beyond received categories of ethnicity, blood and soil. And yet, it was theft all the same. The appropriation of cultural property and learning resources not his own called for acknowledgement and public discourse. To find a way to speak about his transgression, Petrit and his mother transformed one of the family carpets into a moth costume. Becoming moth – becoming winged, hidden, peripheral, other – enabled him to move beyond shame, to develop a non-verbal language, to access a modality of perceiving, communicating, interacting and ultimately thinking and dreaming that would otherwise have remained unavailable to him.

It was an experience of masquerade already familiar to Petrit from his recurrent performances as a canary, begun in 2014. These followed his first collaborative sculpture with his partner, Álvaro: *She, fully turning around, became terrestrial (stolen canary)* from 2013. The tiny canary specimen – also subversively salvaged from Kosovo's defunct Natural History Museum – wears a delicate, blue paper mask, hiding one identity while adopting, projecting, embodying another. Perched at eye level, the masked bird meets the viewer's gaze, drawing

und verkörpert. Der maskierte, auf Augenhöhe platzierte Vogel erwidert den Blick der Betrachtenden, zieht sie in seine Maskerade hinein und lädt dazu ein, sich vorzustellen, wer – oder was – sich hinter seiner fragilen Verkleidung verbirgt. Die Maske öffnet einen Raum, in dem Wünsche, Verkörperungen und Ausdrucksformen sichtbar werden können, die in normativen Kontexten unterdrückt bleiben. So wird der Kanarienvogel mehr als ein totes Präparat und mehr als eine Metapher: Er wird zu einer Figur, zu einem Charakter der Liebe, des queeren Begehrens und des Werdens, durch den Petrit und Álvaro – als Partner in Leben und Kunst – die Fluidität von Identität, die Intimität gemeinsamer Schöpfung und das befreiende Potenzial der Selbsterschaffung jenseits heteronormativer Rahmen erkunden.

Während die Motten und der Kanarienvogel ihre eigenen Umgebungen schaffen, wo immer sie gezeigt werden, erscheinen andere Figuren innerhalb fein gearbeiteter Environments, die der Künstler selbst erschafft. Viele dieser inszenierten Situationen bestehen aus Ästen, Zweigen, Schlamm und Dung, manchmal ergänzt um winzige Fragmente gefundener Objekte. Zwei solcher Environments – *RU (Aves Migrantis)* (2017/25) und *Yes but the sea is attached to the Earth and it never floats around in space. The stars would turn off and what about my planet?* (2014) – sind im ⊢⌐amburger Bahnhof zu sehen.

RU (Aves Migrantis) knüpft an zwei frühere Werkgruppen an: *I'm hungry to keep you close. I want to find the words to resist but in the end there is a locked sphere. The funny thing is that you're not here, nothing is,* Petrits Installation für den Kosovo-Pavillon der Biennale in Venedig 2013, sowie *RU,* das erstmals 2017 für das New Museum in New York entwickelt wurde. In Berlin zieht dieser dunkle, nestartige Tunnel die Besucher*innen bereits beim Betreten der Ausstellung in seinen Bann. Er schwebt leicht über dem Boden, als hinge er zwischen zwei Welten. Auf den verschlungenen Ästen, die sich zum Tunnel wölben, hocken Dutzende kleiner vogelähnlicher Skulpturen. Diese freundlichen, flügellosen

them into its masquerade and inviting them to imagine who – or what – might be concealed behind its fragile disguise. The mask tentatively opens a space for the emergence of desires, embodiments and expressions suppressed in normative contexts. In this way, the canary becomes more than a dead specimen and more than metaphor: it is a character, a figure of love, of queer desire and becoming, through which Petrit and Álvaro, as partners in life and art, explore the fluidity of identity, the intimacy of shared creation and the liberatory potential of self-invention beyond heteronormative frames.

Whereas the moths and canary establish their own environments wherever they are displayed, other characters appear within intricately constructed environments of the artist's own making. Many of these staged situations are composed of branches, twigs, mud and dung, sometimes incorporating tiny fragments of found objects. Two such environments, *RU (Aves Migrantis)* (2017/25) and *Yes but the sea is attached to the Earth and it never floats around in space. The stars would turn off and what about my planet?* (2014), are on display at ⊢⌐amburger Bahnhof.

RU (Aves Migrantis) extends from two earlier bodies of work: *I'm hungry to keep you close. I want to find the words to resist but in the end there is a locked sphere. The funny thing is that you're not here, nothing is,* Petrit's installation for the Kosovo Pavilion at the 2013 Venice Biennale, and *RU,* first developed for the New Museum in New York in 2017. In Berlin, visitors are drawn towards this dark nest-like tunnel from the moment they enter the exhibition. It hovers slightly above the ground, as if suspended between two worlds. Perched upon the tangled branches arching into a tunnel are dozens of diminutive bird-like sculptures. These affable, wingless figures, teetering endearingly on spindly brass legs, are part of a vast migratory flock. Each "bird" stands in for one of more than five hundred neolithic artefacts unearthed in Runik, the most valuable of which were "borrowed" by the Gallery of the Academy of Arts and Sciences of Serbia in 1999 for the *Archaeological Treasures from Kosovo* exhibition and never returned, whereas

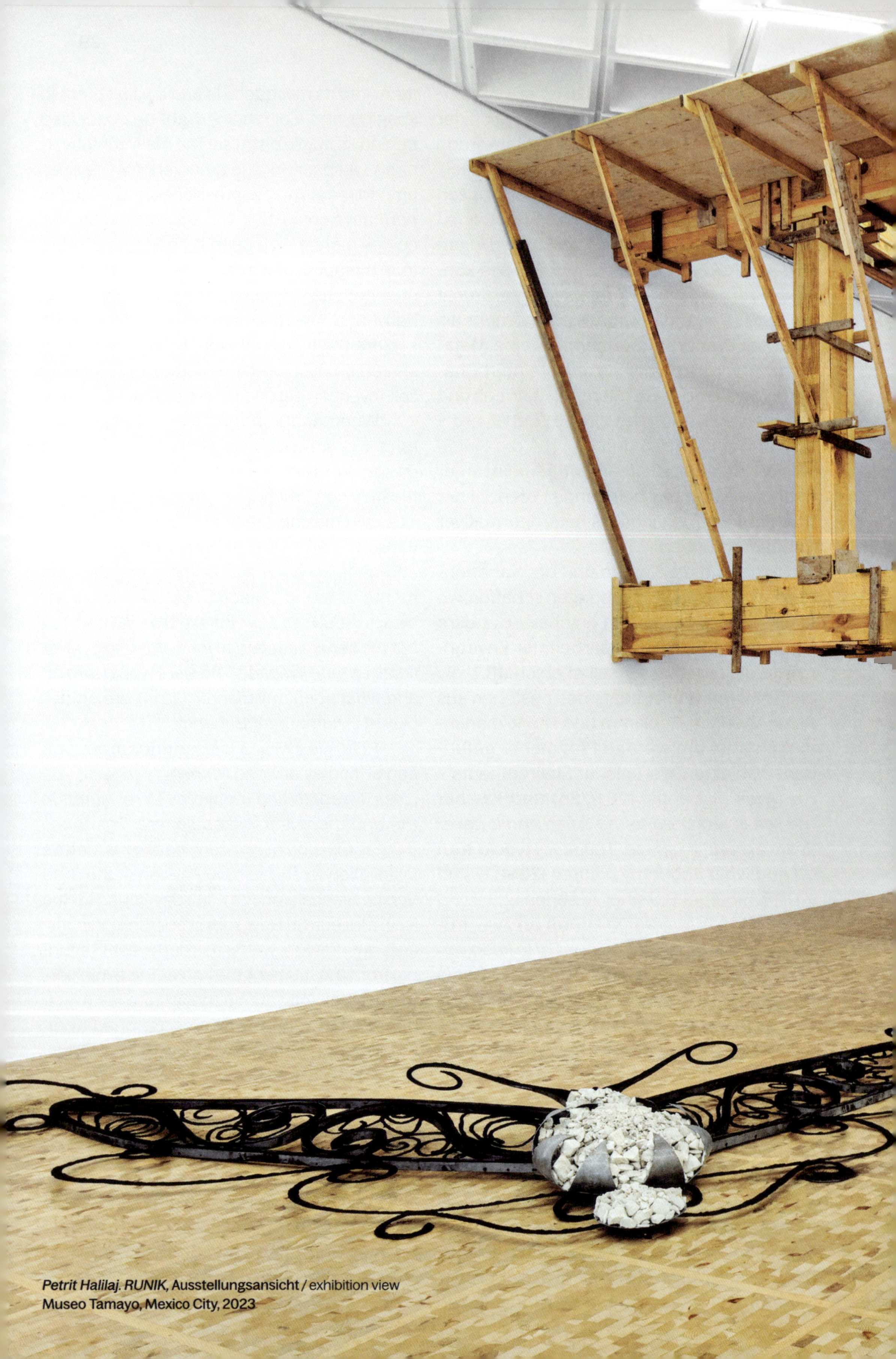

Petrit Halilaj. RUNIK, Ausstellungsansicht / exhibition view
Museo Tamayo, Mexico City, 2023

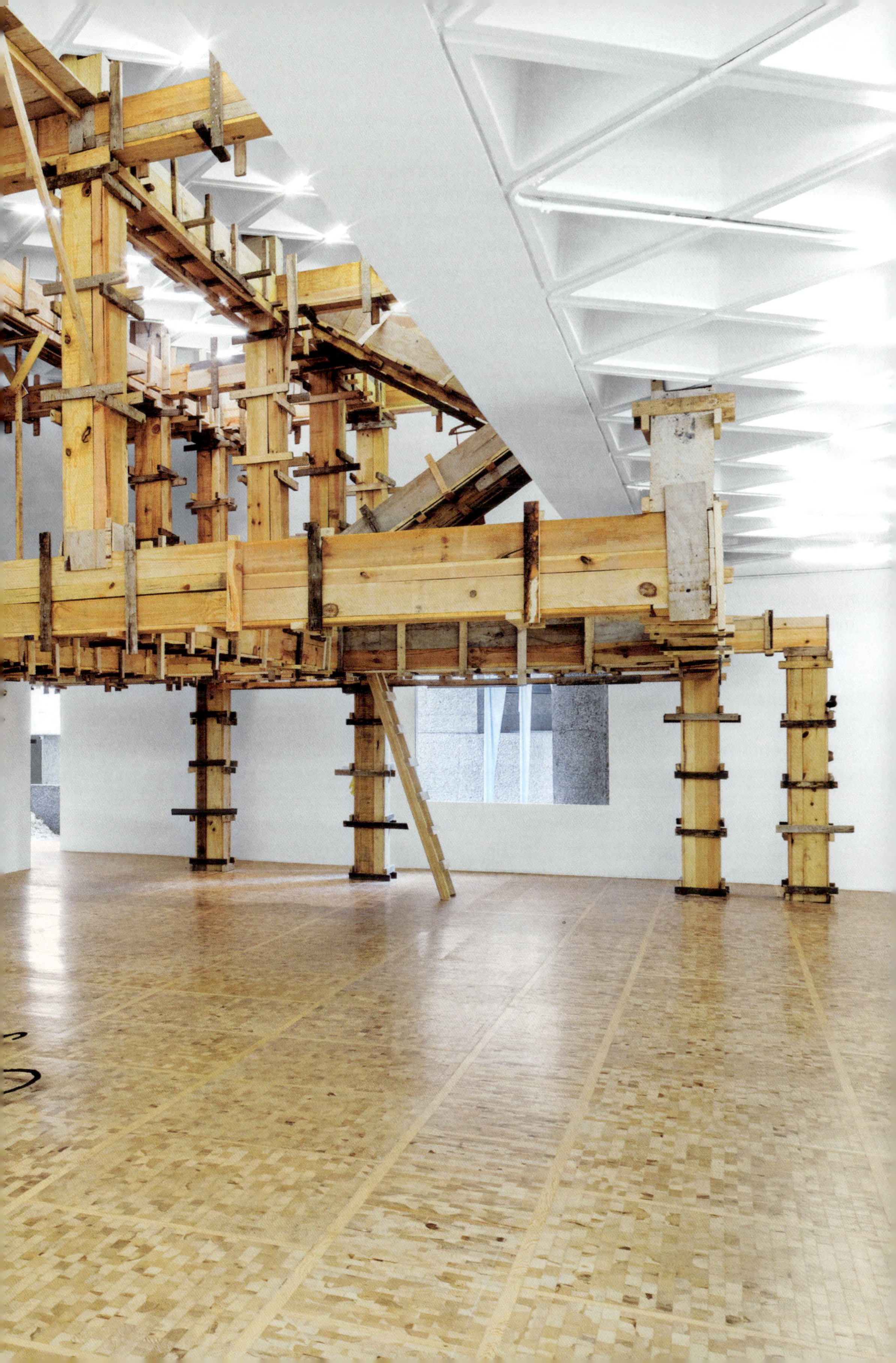

Gestalten, die auf dünnen Messingbeinen wackelig balancieren, gehören zu einem riesigen Zugvogel-Schwarm. Jeder ,Vogel' steht stellvertretend für eines von mehr als fünfhundert neolithischen Artefakten, die in Runik ausgegraben wurden. Die wertvollsten wurden 1999 von der Galerie der Akademie der Wissenschaften und Künste Serbiens für die Ausstellung *Archaeological Treasures from Kosovo* ,ausgeliehen' und nie zurückgegeben, während andere während des Kosovokrieges geplündert wurden.[10] Trotz jahrelanger diplomatischer Bemühungen befindet sich die Mehrheit bis heute im Nationalmuseum und im Ethnologischen Museum in Belgrad. Unter den 1.247 entwendeten Objekten befindet sich auch die Okarina, ein uraltes Blasinstrument, das vermutlich in Runik entstand. Weitere Artefakte sind über verschiedene Institutionen des Kosovo verstreut, wohin sie während des Krieges in Sicherheit gebracht wurden. Die meisten jedoch liegen noch immer in Depots, der Öffentlichkeit entzogen. Um Nachbildungen der verschwundenen Schätze zu schaffen, arbeitete Petrit mit Katalogfotografien und Archivunterlagen, in denen jedes Objekt unter Inventarnummern mit dem Präfix „RU" verzeichnet war.

Von oben und unten sickert warmes, gelbes Licht aus den Wänden des Tunnels und deutet auf ein geheimes Reich dahinter. Betreten lässt sich dieser Raum zwar nicht, doch zwei Öffnungen auf einer Seite – eine hoch, eine niedrig – erlauben einen Blick ins Innere. Durch die obere Öffnung ist ein kanariengelbes Damenkostüm zu sehen, das für die Installation in Venedig eigens für den Künstler angefertigt und von einem Ast gehängt wurde. Es gehört zu den Kleidern und Nachthemden, die Petrit sich im Vorfeld von Venedig in Kosovo maßschneidern ließ. Das Schneidernlassen war für ihn ebenso sehr Ausdruck des Wunsches, die Stücke zu besitzen und zu tragen, wie ein Anlass, mit den Schneider*innen über seine Sexualität ins Gespräch zu kommen – Unterhaltungen, von denen er wusste, dass sie sich bei den Anproben unweigerlich ergeben würden. Diese Begegnungen erinnerten ihn an die sozialen Interaktionen

others were looted during the Kosovo War.[11] Despite years of diplomatic appeals, the majority still remain at the National Museum and the Ethnological Museum in Belgrade today. Among the 1,247 stolen objects is the ocarina, an ancient wind instrument thought to have originated in Runik. Other artefacts are dispersed across Kosovo in various institutions where they were moved for safekeeping during the Kosovo War. The majority are still locked away in storage, out of public view. To create replicas of the missing treasures, Petrit worked from catalogue photographs and archival records, where each object appeared under inventory numbers prefixed with 'RU'.

From above and below the tunnel's walls a warm yellow light seeps out, hinting at a secret realm behind them. Though this space cannot be entered, two openings on one side – one high, one low – allow the viewer to look inside. Through the upper opening a canary-like yellow women's suit, custom-made for the artist for the Venice installation, can be seen hanging from a branch. The suit was among the pieces of women's clothing Petrit had tailored for himself in Kosovo in the leadup to Venice. Having them made was as much about the desire to own and to wear the dresses and nightgowns as it was about initiating conversations with the tailors about his sexuality, exchanges he knew would inevitably arise during fittings. These encounters recalled the social interactions between his mother, herself a seamstress, and her clients, which he had witnessed as a child in the living room that doubled as her atelier. They were the kinds of conversations he longed to have with his mother at the time, though neither of them was fully ready. In 2013, the suit shared its "nest" with two live canaries. Here, it keeps company instead with three "migratory birds" from *RU (Aves Migrantis)*, huddled together on the ground and visible through the lower opening.

The interlaced branches of *RU* form a kind of sanctuary – a sheltering space in which to explore, gently and tentatively, what it might mean to freely live out one's cultural and sexual identity when that freedom has never been known. By contrast, in *Yes but the sea is attached to the earth and it never floats around in space. The*

seiner Mutter, selbst Schneiderin, mit ihren Kund*innen, die er als Kind im Wohnzimmer miterlebt hatte, das zugleich ihr Atelier war. Es waren jene Gespräche, die er sich damals auch mit seiner Mutter gewünscht hätte, für die jedoch keiner von beiden wirklich bereit war. 2013 teilte das Kostüm sein ‚Nest' noch mit zwei lebenden Kanarienvögeln. Hier hingegen wird es von drei ‚Zugvögeln' aus *RU (Aves Migrantis)* begleitet, die am Boden zusammengedrängt und durch die untere Öffnung sichtbar sind.

Die ineinander verschränkten Äste von *RU* bilden eine Art Schutzraum – einen Ort der Geborgenheit, an dem sich vorsichtig erproben lässt, was es bedeuten könnte, die eigene kulturelle und sexuelle Identität frei zu leben, wenn eine solche Freiheit bislang nie gekannt war. Ganz anders hingegen in *Yes but the sea is attached to the earth and it never floats around in space. The stars would turn off and what about my planet?:* Hier schaffen die Äste eine Umgebung, die von Abwesenheit und Tod gezeichnet ist. Sie vermischen sich mit Erde, Steinen, Blättern und kleinen, grob geformten Tonfiguren – Artefakten ohne klar erkennbare Funktion oder Wert – und formen so das Ufer eines großen rosafarbenen Sees. Dessen leuchtender Farbton taucht den Raum in ein unheimliches, übernatürliches Licht. Aus der Mitte des Sees – dessen Oberfläche den scharfen, künstlichen Geruch des billigen Waschmittels verströmt, aus dem er besteht – erhebt sich ein gespenstisches, überlebensgroßes Pferd. Über seine Schnauze gelegt hängt ein langes, traditionelles albanisches Gürtelband, eine *shoka,* deren eines Ende in der undurchsichtigen Oberfläche des Sees verschwindet. Es wirkt, als sei die gestickte Inschrift, die den Titel der Arbeit trägt, im Begriff, gemeinsam mit dem Gürtel in den See hinabzusinken.

Die *shoka* erinnert an den Gürtel, den Petrits Ururgroßvater Baba Gan getragen haben soll, der, so heißt es, ein großes weißes Pferd ritt. Als geachteter Intellektueller und Vermittler innerhalb der Gemeinschaft wurde er während der serbischen Invasion in den Kosovo 1912 wegen seiner Rolle im albanischen

stars would turn off and what about my planet?, the branches create an environment marked by absence and death. Here, the branches mingle with soil, stones, leaves and small, roughly modelled clay sculptures – artefacts of unidentifiable use and value – to form the banks of a large pink lake. The vivid hue of the lake washes the room in an eerie, otherworldly glow. From the lake's centre – its surface releasing the acrid, artificial scent of the cheap washing detergent it is made of – emerges a ghostly, larger-than-life-sized horse. Draped across the horse's muzzle is a long traditional Albanian belt, or *shoka,* one end disappearing into the opaque surface of the lake. It is as though the embroidered inscription, which bears the words of the title, were on the

---

10　Wie Nora Weller, Gründungsdirektorin der Cambridge Academy of Global Affairs und Rechtsexpertin für den Schutz von Kulturerbe, schreibt, wurden zusätzlich zu den 677 gestohlenen archäologischen Objekten rund 571 ethnologische Schatzstücke angeblich für die Ausstellung *Decorations and Gilding of Gold Works in Kosovo* ausgeliehen, die 1998 in den Museen von Novi Sad, Belgrad und Subotica gezeigt wurde. Auch diese wurden nach der Ausstellung in Belgrad zurückbehalten – ein Akt der Enteignung, der, so Weller, darauf abzielte, dem Volk des Kosovo seine Kultur zu entziehen und seine nationale Identität weiter zu schwächen. Vgl. Nora Weller, „Serbia Must Return Kosovo's Cultural Treasures" in: *Balkan Insight,* 21. Dezember 2017, https://balkaninsight.com/ 2017/12/21/serbia-must-return-kosovo- s-cultural-treasures-12-19-2017/, zuletzt abgerufen am 5. August 2025.

11　As Nora Weller, Founding Director of the Cambridge Academy of Global Affairs, and a legal expert in cultural heritage protection, writes, in addition to the 677 stolen archaeological artefacts, some 571 ethnological treasures were ostensibly borrowed for the *Decorations and Gilding of Gold Works in Kosovo* exhibition which in 1998 travelled to the museums of Novi Sad, Belgrade and Subotica. These were also kept in Belgrade after the exhibition, an act of dispossession intended, she argues, to strip the people of Kosovo of their culture with the intent of depriving them of it and damaging their national identity further. See Nora Weller, "Serbia Must Return Kosovo's Cultural Treasures" in: *Balkan Insight,* 21 December 2017, https://balkaninsight.com/ 2017/12/21/serbia-must-return-kosovo- s-cultural-treasures-12-19-2017/, last accessed on 5 August 2025.

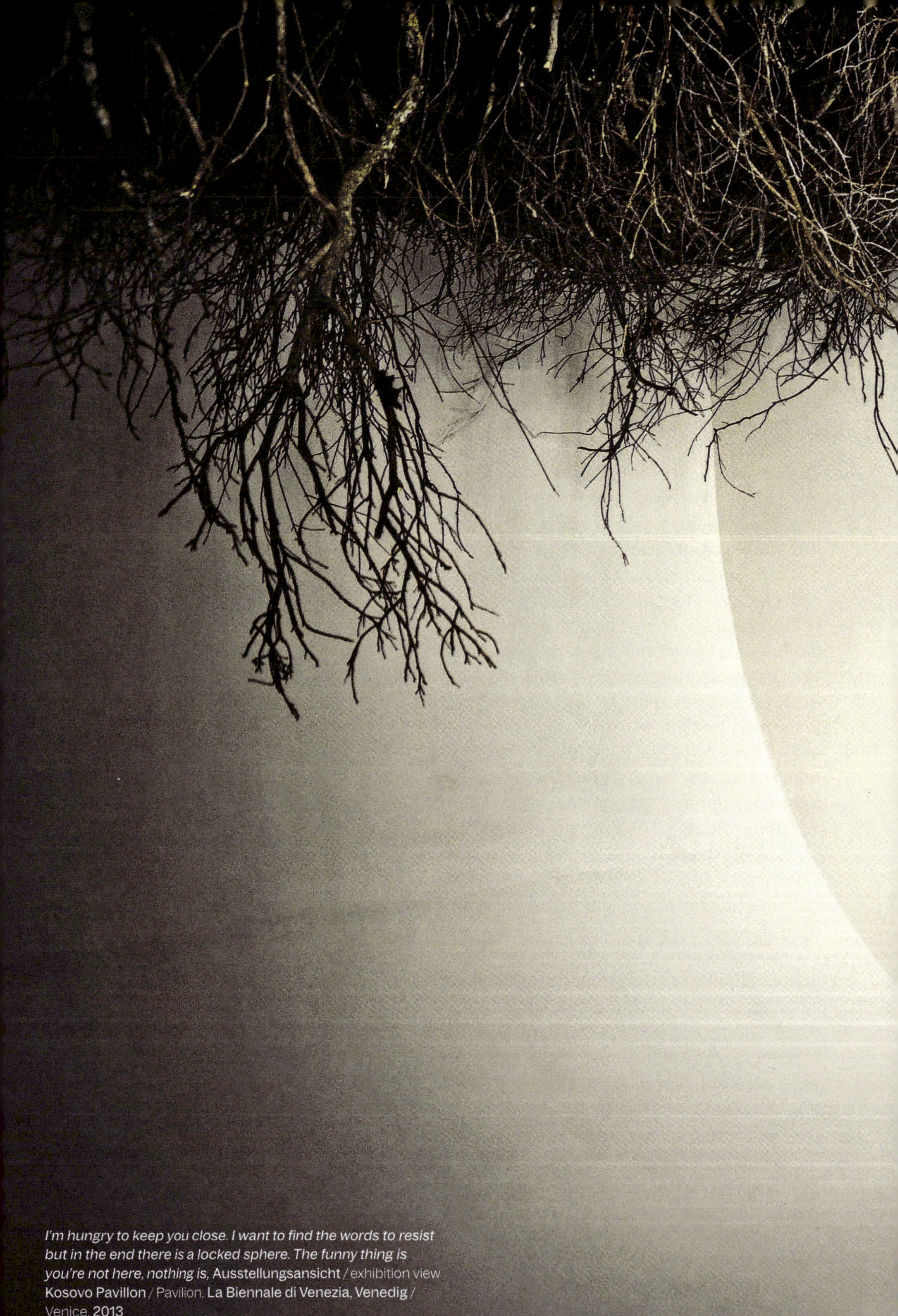

I'm hungry to keep you close. I want to find the words to resist but in the end there is a locked sphere. The funny thing is you're not here, nothing is, Ausstellungsansicht / exhibition view
Kosovo Pavillon / Pavilion, La Biennale di Venezia, Venedig / Venice, 2013

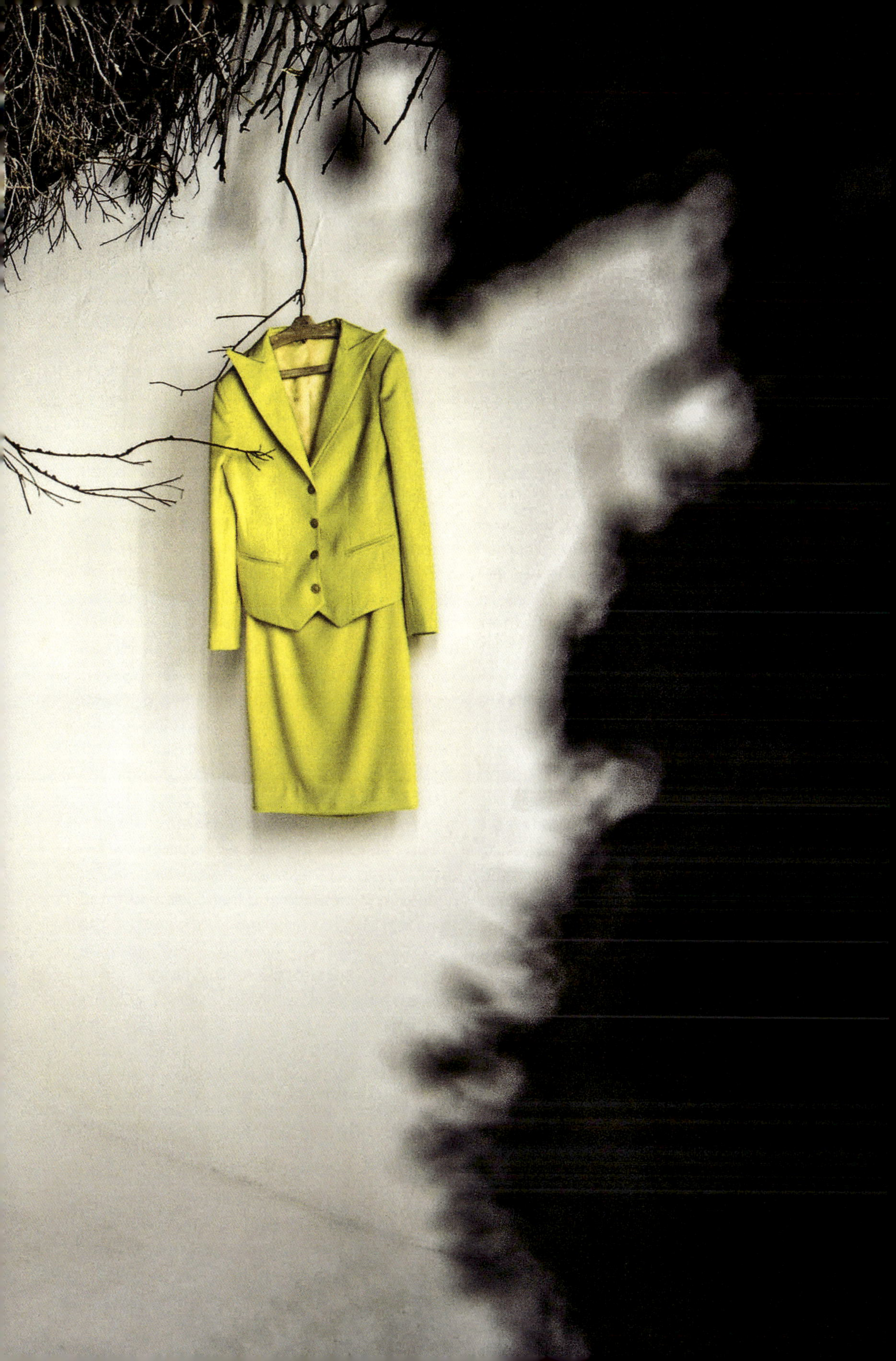

Widerstand ermordet. Man ließ ihn in einer Grube verdursten – einer Grube, die eigens ausgehoben worden war, um albanische Lehrer, Imame und Gemeindevorsteher zu beseitigen, als Teil einer sich verschärfenden ethnischen Repression, die sich über das gesamte 20. Jahrhundert hinweg wiederholte. Sie kündigte die genozidale Kampagne an, die Slobodan Milošević in den 1990er-Jahren entfesseln sollte. Diese unablässige Brutalität und gewaltsame Enteignung kappte zahlreiche Linien kultureller Überlieferung und brachte Stimmen zum Schweigen, die fähig gewesen wären, kulturelle Identität zu bewahren.[11] Das postapokalyptische Environment mit seinem toxischen See und der kargen Landschaft stellt ‚Säuberung' – sei sie ethnisch, intellektuell oder kulturell – als eine Verarmung dar, die nicht nur Gemeinschaften und Gesellschaften bedroht, sondern die Lebenskraft des gesamten Planeten. Die Warnung, die diesem Werk innewohnt, hat bis heute nichts von ihrer Dringlichkeit verloren.

Aus solchen Inszenierungen erwuchs schließlich jenes Werk, das am deutlichsten den Weg für Petrits operatische Praxis bereitete: *Shkrepëtima*. Diese einmalige Aufführung inszenierte er 2018 in den Ruinen des Kulturhauses von Runik. Darin sah er die Chance, „eine neue Erzählung zu schaffen, die aus Erinnerung und Geschichte hervorgeht".[12] Das Kulturhaus war in den 1950er-Jahren errichtet worden, um eine Bibliothek, ein Theater, ein Kino, eine landwirtschaftliche Genossenschaft und ein Teehaus zu beherbergen. 1989 wurde es gewaltsam geschlossen und 1999 im Krieg weitgehend zerstört. Der Titel – *Shkrepëtima* – bedeutet „Blitz", „Lichtstrahl" oder auch „ein plötzliches intensives Gefühl" und geht auf eine Kulturzeitschrift zurück, die in den 1970er- und 1980er-Jahren von Lehrer*innen und Schüler*innen der örtlichen Schule herausgegeben wurde. Zu ihren Gründer*innen gehörte eine von Petrits wichtigsten Mentorinnen: Sala Ahmetaj – die erste Frau, die in ihrem Dorf unterrichtete, die erste Frau aus der Region Drenica, die Professorin an einer Universität wurde, und eine entschiedene Verfechterin der Bildung für Mädchen.

verge of sinking beneath the surface along with the belt itself.

The *shoka* recalls the belt worn by Petrit's great-great-grandfather, Baba Gan, who is said to have ridden a tall white horse. A respected intellectual and community mediator, he was assassinated during the Serbian invasion of Kosovo in 1912 for his role in the Albanian resistance. He was left to die of dehydration in a pit dug to eradicate Albanian teachers, imams and community leaders as part of an intensifying ethnic repression that recurred throughout the 20th century. Foreshadowing the genocidal campaign waged by Slobodan Milošević in the 1990s, this relentless brutality and forced dispossession severed many lines of cultural transmission and silenced voices capable of preserving cultural identity.[12] The post-apocalyptic environment with its toxic lake and barren landscape portrays "cleansing", whether ethnic, intellectual or cultural, as an impoverishment threatening not only communities and societies but also the vitality of the planet as a whole. The warning inherent in the work has lost none of its pertinence.

From stagings such as these emerged the work that most evidently paved the way for Petrit's operatic work: *Shkrepëtima*. In this one-night performance, staged in 2018 in the ruins of Runik's House of Culture, Petrit saw a chance 'to write a new story that grows from memory and history'.[13] The House of Culture, built in the 1950s to host a library, theatre, cinema, agricultural cooperative and teahouse, was forcibly closed in 1989 and largely destroyed in the war in 1999. The title, meaning 'flash', 'lightning bolt', or 'a sudden intense feeling', comes from a cultural magazine published during the 1970s and 1980s by teachers and students at the local school. Among the magazine's founders was one of Petrit's key mentors, Sala Ahmetaj – the first woman to teach in her village, the first woman from the Drenica region to become a university professor and a staunch advocate of girls' education.

Shkrepëtima was operatic in scope, though not yet consciously engaging with the operatic medium as such. Combining sculpture, installation, live performance, music, archival research and engagement with both the arts community

Shkrepëtima war in seinem Ausmaß opernhaft, ohne jedoch bereits bewusst mit dem Medium Oper zu arbeiten. Die Aufführung verband Skulptur, Installation, Live-Performance, Musik, Archivrecherche sowie die Zusammenarbeit mit der Kunstszene und den Bürger*innen von Runik. Ziel war es, die Erinnerung an einen einst lebendigen Ort der Kultur und Bildung wachzurufen und die Hoffnung auf seine Wiederbelebung neu zu entfachen. Im Mittelpunkt stand ein schlafender Junge – halb Mensch, halb Vogel –, der in seinen Träumen klassische Dramen wiedererlebt, die in der Vergangenheit im Kulturhaus aufgeführt worden waren, etwa *Toka Jonë* [Unser Land], *Cuca e Maleve* [Das Mädchen aus den Bergen], *Nita* und *Hakmarrja* [Die Rache], und sie sich zugleich als Teil einer zukünftigen kulturellen Erneuerung vorstellt.

Unterdessen nimmt die Vision einer Restaurierung des Gebäudes Gestalt an – geboren aus einem beharrlichen kollektiven Träumen und unermüdlicher Arbeit. Petrit und ein Team unter Leitung der von ihm gegründeten Hajde!-Stiftung arbeiten Hand in Hand mit dem Kulturministerium des Kosovo, der Gemeinde Skënderaj und den Bürger*innen von Runik. Gemeinsam schaffen sie die Voraussetzungen dafür, dass Ende 2025 mit dem Wiederaufbau begonnen werden kann.

Die Bühne, der Vorhang, die Kulissen, das Bühnenbild und die Kostüme von *Shkrepëtima* wurden später in eine Installation überführt, die seither in unterschiedlichen ortsspezifischen Konstellationen gezeigt wurde. In ihrer jüngsten Form bildet sie einen integralen Bestandteil der aktuellen Ausstellung. Erstmals umfasst sie auch Ziegel und Kacheln, die aus den Ruinen geborgen wurden und auf ihre künftige Eingliederung in das restaurierte Kulturhaus von Runik warten. Ordentlich auf Paletten gestapelt erinnern sie an die Basaltsteine in Joseph Beuys' *Das Ende des 20. Jahrhunderts (erste Fassung)*, 1982/83, das in der Dauerausstellung des Hamburger Bahnhof zu sehen ist.

Wie *Shkrepëtima* ist auch die Oper *Syrigana* ein kollaboratives Werk, das auf Forschung und Prozess beruht. Regie führte

and the citizens of Runik, it sought to revive the memory of a once-vibrant cultural and educational site and rekindle aspirations for its renewal. The performance centred around a sleeping boy – half human, half bird – who, in his dreams revisits classical dramas performed in the past at the House of Culture, such as *Toka Jonë* [Our Land], *Cuca e Maleve* [Mountain Lass], *Nita* and *Hakmarrja* [The Revenge], and imagines them as part of a future cultural revival.

Meanwhile, the vision for the building's restoration is taking shape, born of sustained collective dreaming and steadfast effort. Petrit and a team led by the Hajde! Foundation he founded are working hand in hand with Kosovo's Ministry of Culture, the Municipality of Skënderaj and the citizens of Runik. Together, they are laying the groundwork for construction to begin towards the end of 2025.

The stage, curtains, backdrop, set and costumes used in *Shkrepëtima* were later transformed into an installation that has since been shown in a range of site-specific constellations. The most recent iteration forms an integral part of the present exhibition. For the first time, it includes bricks and tiles salvaged from the ruins which await their future incorporation into the restored House of Culture in Runik. They are stacked neatly upon pallets in a manner reminiscent of the basalt stones in Joseph Beuys's

---

11 Für eine umfassende Untersuchung dieser langwierigen Geschichte von Unterdrückung und Gewalt vgl. Noel Malcolm, *Kosovo: A Short History*, 2. Aufl., London / Basingstoke / Oxford: Pan Macmillan, 2022.

12 Vgl. Cristina Mari, „The Little Revolution of Runik: Town's House of Culture to host first show in 30 years on Saturday" in: *Kosovo 2.0*, https://new.kosovotwopointzero.com/en/the-little-revolution-of-runik, zuletzt abgerufen am 5. August 2025.

---

12 For a comprehensive study of this protracted history of oppression and violence, see Noel Malcolm, *Kosovo: A Short History*, 2nd edition, London / Basingstoke / Oxford: Pan Macmillan, 2022.

13 See Cristina Mari, "The Little Revolution of Runik: Town's House of Culture to host first show in 30 years on Saturday" in: *Kosovo 2.0*, https://new.kosovotwopointzero.com/en/the-little-revolution-of-runik, last accessed on 5 August 2025.

Petrit, komponiert wurde die Oper von Lugh O'Neill, mit dem Petrit und Álvaro bereits für die Performances rund um ihre Installation *Lunar Ensemble for Uprising Seas* (2023) im Ocean Space in Venedig zusammengearbeitet hatten – ebenfalls ein wichtiger Meilenstein auf dem Weg zu *Syrigana*. Für das Libretto tat sich Petrit mit der Dramaturgin und Autorin Doruntina Basha, der Kuratorin und Autorin Amy Zion sowie dem Choreografen und Tänzer Robert Schulz zusammen, der auch die Choreografie entwickelte. Das Bühnenbild entwarf Petrit selbst, wobei einzelne Werke – etwa die Birne und die Blumen – aus seiner gemeinsamen künstlerischen Praxis mit Álvaro hervorgehen.

Die Oper greift Geschichten aus Petrits eigenem Leben und dem seiner Weggefährt*innen auf. Viele seiner vertrauten Figuren – Vögel und Blumen, ein Fuchs, ein Hahn, eine Okarina und eine Motte – treten in Dialog mit neuen Charakteren und verweben sich zu einem anderen Geflecht von Erzählungen. Während sie klassische Opernstoffe wie verbotene Liebe, Eifersucht, Verwechslung und übernatürliche Kräfte aufnimmt, macht *Syrigana* den Ort selbst zur Hauptfigur. Syrigana ist ein über 3.000 Jahre altes Dorf in der nordwestlichen Gemeinde Skënderaj. Es liegt in der Region Drenica, die als historisches und symbolisches Herz des kosovarisch-albanischen Widerstands gilt und zugleich für ihr neolithisches archäologisches Erbe geschätzt wird – auch wenn, wie in Runik, kaum etwas zu dessen Bewahrung unternommen wurde. Fragmente des alten Lebens liegen noch im Boden begraben, vermischt mit den verkohlten Resten der Häuser, die während des Kosovokrieges niedergebrannt wurden.

Die stille Schönheit der sanft geschwungenen Hügel und der fruchtbaren Agrarlandschaft erzählt eine Geschichte. Die starke Kultur der Gemeinschaft und des Feierns erzählt eine andere. Doch beide überdecken die fortdauernde Erinnerung – und die gegenwärtige Realität von – ethnischer Spaltung in der Region. Nirgendwo tritt dieser Kontrast schärfer hervor als an der Kreuzung des Dorfes, wo eine Polizeistation und ein Teehaus Seite

Das Ende des 20. Jahrhunderts [The End of the 20th Century; 1st version], 1982–83, on view in the permanent exhibition at Hamburger Bahnhof.

Like *Shkrepëtima*, the opera *Syrigana* is a research- and process-based collaborative work. Directed by Petrit, the opera was composed by Lugh O'Neill, with whom Petrit and Álvaro had previously collaborated for the performances surrounding their 2023 installation *Lunar Ensemble for Uprising Seas* at Ocean Space in Venice – also a vital stepping stone on the path to *Syrigana*. For the libretto, Petrit joined forces with dramaturge and scriptwriter Doruntina Basha, curator and writer Amy Zion and choreographer and dancer Robert Schulz, who also developed the choreography. The scenography was developed by Petrit, although some of the works – the pear and flowers – draw on his shared artistic practice with Álvaro.

The opera explores stories from Petrit's own life and those of the people he grew up with. It brings many familiar members of his cast of characters – birds and flowers, a fox, a rooster, an ocarina and a moth – into conversation with new characters, weaving them into a different complex of narratives. While playing on classic operatic tropes, such as illicit love, jealousy, mistaken identity and supernatural forces, *Syrigana* casts the place itself as its main protagonist. Syrigana is a village over 3,000 years old located in the north-western municipality of Skënderaj. It is nestled within the Drenica region, celebrated as the historical and symbolic heart of Kosovar-Albanian resistance and cherished for its neolithic archaeological heritage, though, as with Runik, little has been undertaken to preserve it. Fragments of ancient life lie buried in the soil where they mingle with the charred remains of homes burned during the Kosovo War.

The tranquillity of Syrigana's gently rolling hills and fertile agrarian terrain tells one story. Its strong culture of community and celebration tells another. But both belie the persistent memory and ongoing reality of ethnic division in the region. Nowhere is this contrast starker than at the village junction, where a police station and a teahouse stand side by side: one road leads up to the Albanian community, the other down

an Seite stehen: Die eine Straße führt hinauf zur albanischen Gemeinde, die andere hinab zur serbischen. Eine unsichtbare Grenze – allen bewusst, außer den Füchsen, Hühnern und anderen ahnungslosen Streunern – markiert die Trennung. Hier sind Gewalt und Trauma stets knapp unter der Oberfläche, wie ein Brandanschlag auf Petrits Requisiten für *Syrigana* kurz vor der Aufführung zeigte.[13] Ein Vierteljahrhundert nach dem Krieg sind die Folgen der Zerschlagung kultureller und bildungspolitischer Institutionen sowie der Unterdrückung von politischer Teilhabe, öffentlichem Engagement und Pluralität noch immer schmerzhaft spürbar.

Mündliche Überlieferungen, weitergegeben in Liedern und Gedichten, spielen im Dorf eine zentrale Rolle. Ein Großteil des kulturellen Lebens kreist um die Vorbereitung und Feier von Hochzeiten. Woche für Woche kommen die Dorfbewohner*innen im Teehaus neben der Polizeistation zusammen, um zu singen, Geschichten zu erzählen und zu tanzen. Unter den vielen Mythen und Legenden, die von Generation zu Generation weitergegeben wurden, findet sich auch die Behauptung, dass Adam und Eva nach Syrigana gekommen seien, um dort zu heiraten. *Syrigana: An Opera in Five Acts* erzählt die Geschichte ihrer Ankunft im Dorf.

Vorgetragen wird sie von zwei Sopranistinnen: Vogeline und Vogelotte. Mal singend, mal zwitschernd, verweben die beiden Vögel Vogelklänge mit menschlicher Sprache, während sie das Publikum durch die fünf Akte der Oper führen. Der Plot verläuft in etwa so:

Im Dorf Syrigana entfaltet sich eine magische Geschichte – eine epische Liebeserzählung, in der Adam und Eva als Fuchs und Hahn wiederkehren, zwei Fremde aus einem fernen Land. Bei Sonnenuntergang versammeln sich Darsteller*innen und Gäste im Teehaus, von wo aus ein farbenprächtiger Zug in Richtung des heiligen Felsens, Gjyteti, aufbricht. Fuchs und Hahn, aus dem Paradies verstoßen, erreichen den Ort mit einem Helikopter der KFOR, der NATO-geführten Friedensmission im Kosovo. Auf dem felsigen Plateau abgesetzt, betreten sie eine surreale Welt, die Neugier und

to the Serbian. An invisible border, noticed by all but the foxes, chickens and other unsuspecting wanderers, marks the divide. Here, violence and trauma are never far beneath the surface, as an arson attack on Petrit's props for *Syrigana* shortly before the performance attests.[14] Here, a quarter of a century after the war, the consequences of dismantling cultural and educational institutions, and discouraging political participation, public engagement and plurality remain painfully present.

Oral history, transmitted through songs and poetry, plays an important role in the village. Much of cultural life revolves around preparing and celebrating weddings. Each week members of the village gather at the teahouse next to the police station to sing, tell stories and dance. Among the many myths and legends passed down through the generations is one that claims that Adam and Eve came to Syrigana to get married. *Syrigana: An Opera in Five Acts* tells the story of their arrival at the village.

The story is narrated by two sopranos: Birda and Birdy. At times singing, at times twittering, the two birds blend birdy sounds with human speech as they guide the audience through the opera's five acts. The plot goes something like this:

In the village of Syrigana, a magical tale unfolds – an epic love story between Adam and Eve recast as Fox and Rooster, two strangers from a faraway land. At sunset, performers and guests gather at the teahouse for a vibrant procession up towards the sacred rock, Gjyteti. Fox and Rooster, having been expelled from paradise, arrive here by a helicopter belonging to KFOR, the NATO-led peacekeeping mission in Kosovo. Set down on the rocky plateau, they descend into a surreal world, stirring curiosity and mythic storytelling among the village's bird-like inhabitants.

---

13 Für eine ausführliche Diskussion des Angriffs, seiner möglichen Beweggründe und Implikationen vgl. das Gespräch zwischen Petrit und Amy Zion im vorliegenden Katalog, S. 48–67.

---

14 For a detailed discussion of the attack, its possible motivations and implications, see the conversation between Petrit and Amy Zion in the present catalogue, pp. 48–67.

mythisches Erzählen unter den vogelähnlichen Dorfbewohner*innen entfacht.

Unter einem Birnbaum beginnt die Liebe zwischen Fuchs und Hahn zur Melodie einer Okarina aufzublühen. Doch bald tritt die Versuchung in Gestalt einer Schlange auf und stört ihr neu gewonnenes Paradies. In Anklang an den Sündenfall von Adam und Eva – die Urszene, die drei der großen monotheistischen Religionen prägt: Judentum, Christentum und Islam – kosten sie von der verbotenen Frucht, einer reifen, saftigen Birne des Baumes. Sie verlieren ihre Unschuld und werden erneut verstoßen. Doch als der Helikopter sie zurück nach Syrigana bringt, empfangen die Dorfbewohner*innen sie mit offenen Armen. Verzaubert von ihrer Liebe beschließen sie, die beiden zu verheiraten.

Als die Hochzeitsvorbereitungen beginnen, kommt es zum Verrat. Ein böswilliger Schneider, getrieben von Begierde und Lust, verkleidet sich als Hahn, um in einem trügerischen Versuch den Fuchs zu heiraten. Doch die Wahrheit kommt schließlich ans Licht, und die Liebe siegt: Fuchs und Hahn finden wieder zueinander, werden verheiratet und entscheiden sich – anstatt ihrer ersten Impulse zu folgen und zu fliehen – in Syrigana zu bleiben und das Dorf als ihre Heimat anzunehmen.

So wie *Shkrepëtima* die Ruinen des Kulturhauses von Runik neu belebte, nutzt *Syrigana* Allegorie, Fantasie und Mythos, um die Landschaft – den verlorenen Garten – von Syrigana als Ort kultureller Imagination und Neuerfindung zurückzugewinnen. Indem die Oper im Freien, in einem nicht-institutionellen, ländlichen Umfeld aufgeführt wird, unterläuft das kollaborative Werk nicht nur den oft mit der Oper verbundenen Elitismus, sondern bringt auch kulturelle Produktion an einen Ort zurück, der aufgrund politischer Repression und infrastruktureller Vernachlässigung lange davon ausgeschlossen war.

Mit seinen anders-als-menschlichen Figuren und seinem surrealen Setting gelingt es dem Werk, die starren Kategorien nationaler, ethnischer, sexueller und geschlechtlicher Identität zu umgehen. Stattdessen eröffnet es eine universellere emotionale und

Under a pear tree, Fox and Rooster's love begins to blossom to the sound of an ocarina. But temptation in the guise of a serpent soon disrupts their newfound paradise. Echoing the fall of Adam and Eve, the origin story common to three of the world's monotheistic religions – Judaism, Christianity and Islam – they taste the forbidden fruit, a ripe, juicy pear, from the tree. They lose their innocence and are cast out once more. Later returned by helicopter to Syrigana, they are welcomed by the villagers, who, enchanted by their love, decide to marry them.

As preparations for the wedding begin, betrayal strikes. A malicious Tailor, driven by desire and lust, disguises himself as Rooster in a deceitful attempt to marry Fox. The truth eventually comes to light, and love triumphs. Fox and Rooster are reunited, married, and, overcoming their initial urge to flee, choose instead to remain in Syrigana, embracing the village as their home.

Just as *Shkrepëtima* revived the ruins of Runik's House of Culture, *Syrigana* uses allegory, fantasy and myth to reclaim the landscape – the lost garden – of Syrigana as a site of cultural imagination and reinvention. By staging an opera outdoors, in a non-institutional, rural setting, the collaborative work not only subverts the elitism often associated with opera but also reinserts cultural production into a place historically excluded from it due to political repression and infrastructural neglect.

Its non-human protagonists and surreal setting allow the opera to bypass rigid categories of national, ethnic, sexual and gender identity, creating a more universal emotional and political landscape where questions of desire, betrayal, exile and belonging can be explored. For all its vicissitudes, the queer love story at the heart of *Syrigana* – Fox and Rooster's journey from exile to belonging, from confusion to affirmation – is portrayed not as tragic but as redemptive. Insofar as their love is embraced by the community, the opera posits a hopeful vision of social acceptance, interweaving queerness into collective myth in a manner that playfully challenges normative structures.

In contrast to *Shkrepëtima*, whose transposition into an installation dispenses with sound, movement and theatrical lighting, the museum

politische Landschaft, in der Fragen nach Begehren, Verrat, Exil und Zugehörigkeit verhandelt werden können. Trotz aller Widerstände wird die queere Liebesgeschichte im Zentrum von *Syrigana* – der Weg von Fuchs und Hahn vom Exil zur Zugehörigkeit, von Verwirrung zur Bestätigung – nicht als tragisch, sondern als erlösend erzählt. Indem ihre Liebe von der Gemeinschaft angenommen wird, entwirft die Oper eine hoffnungsvolle Vision sozialer Akzeptanz, in der Queerness spielerisch in kollektiven Mythos eingewebt wird – und so normative Strukturen herausfordert.

Im Gegensatz zu *Shkrepëtima,* dessen Überführung in eine Installation auf Klang, Bewegung und theatralisches Licht verzichtet, bringt die Museumsfassung von *Syrigana* alle Elemente der Oper ins Spiel. Die einzige Ausnahme sind die Darsteller*innen: Ihre Kostüme, nun als skulpturale Präsenz neu gedacht, werden durch die vollständige Partitur und das als Übertitel projizierte Libretto belebt. Eine fein abgestimmte Dramaturgie und Lichtchoreografie treibt in Abwesenheit menschlicher Akteur*innen die Handlung voran.

Unter freiem Himmel bestand das Bühnenbild der Oper aus zwei Traktoren mit Anhängern, die Rücken an Rücken gestellt eine Bühne bildeten, während ein dritter Traktor auf seinem Anhänger ein kleines Wandertheater trug. In der Museumsinstallation fehlen die Traktoren; hier steht das mobile Theater im Zentrum, das zugleich als Werkstatt des Schneiders dient. In beiden Fassungen bildet eine rückseitig beleuchtete Skulptur der untergehenden Sonne zusammen mit zahlreichen leuchtenden Sternen den Bühnenhintergrund, während der Zuschauerbereich mit traditionellen kosovarischen Teppichen ausgelegt ist, von denen viele Gärten darstellen. Zu den Requisiten gehören weitere skulpturale Elemente: ein Birnbaum, eine Birne, Birnbaumblüten und eine Okarina, eine Motte, ein schlangenförmiges Maßband sowie eine polygonale Skulptur aus zahlreichen Rahmentrommeln, den sogenannten *defas.* Für die Museumsfassung wurde die polygonale Skulptur zerlegt; die einzelnen *defas* erhielten

version of *Syrigana* brings all of the elements of the opera into play. The only exception is the performers, whose costumes, now reimagined as sculptural presences, are animated by the complete score and the libretto projected as surtitles. A finely calibrated dramaturgy and choreography of lights, in the absence of human actors, advances the narrative.

In the open landscape the opera set consisted of two tractors with trailers aligned back-to-back to form a stage, with a third tractor carrying a small travelling theatre on its trailer. The museum installation does without the tractors, relying on the mobile theatre which serves as the Tailor's workshop. In both versions the backdrop is formed by a rear-lit sculpture of the setting sun and multiple luminous stars, while the seating area is covered by traditional Kosovar carpets, many of them depicting gardens. The props include various other sculptural elements such as a pear tree, a pear, pear-tree blossoms and an ocarina, a moth, a serpentine tape measure and a polygonal sculpture composed of multiple frame drums known as *defas*. For the museum installation, the polygonal sculpture has been dismantled. The individual *defas* have been given bird legs, enabling them to gather like the members of the wedding band and guests in the outdoor performance. Neither in Syrigana nor in the museum is there a rigid separation between stage and audience, performers and viewers. Visitors are free to wander, interact and become participants in the story.

Like the "lost garden" of pre-war Syrigana, which, owing to displacement and transition, can be accessed only through the faculties of memory and imagination, the landscape evoked in the museum emerges not as a static backdrop but as the principal protagonist. Modulated by shifting light and sound, it becomes a mutable topography in which absence and presence, ruin and regeneration are held in a state of dramatic tension. In its resistance of narrative closure, *Syrigana* invites viewers not only to inhabit another world but also to navigate its ambiguities, ruptures and emotional undercurrents, its poetic and political dimensions.

Messiaen's birds sing of divine grace. Petrit's birds sing of love and resilience, questioning the

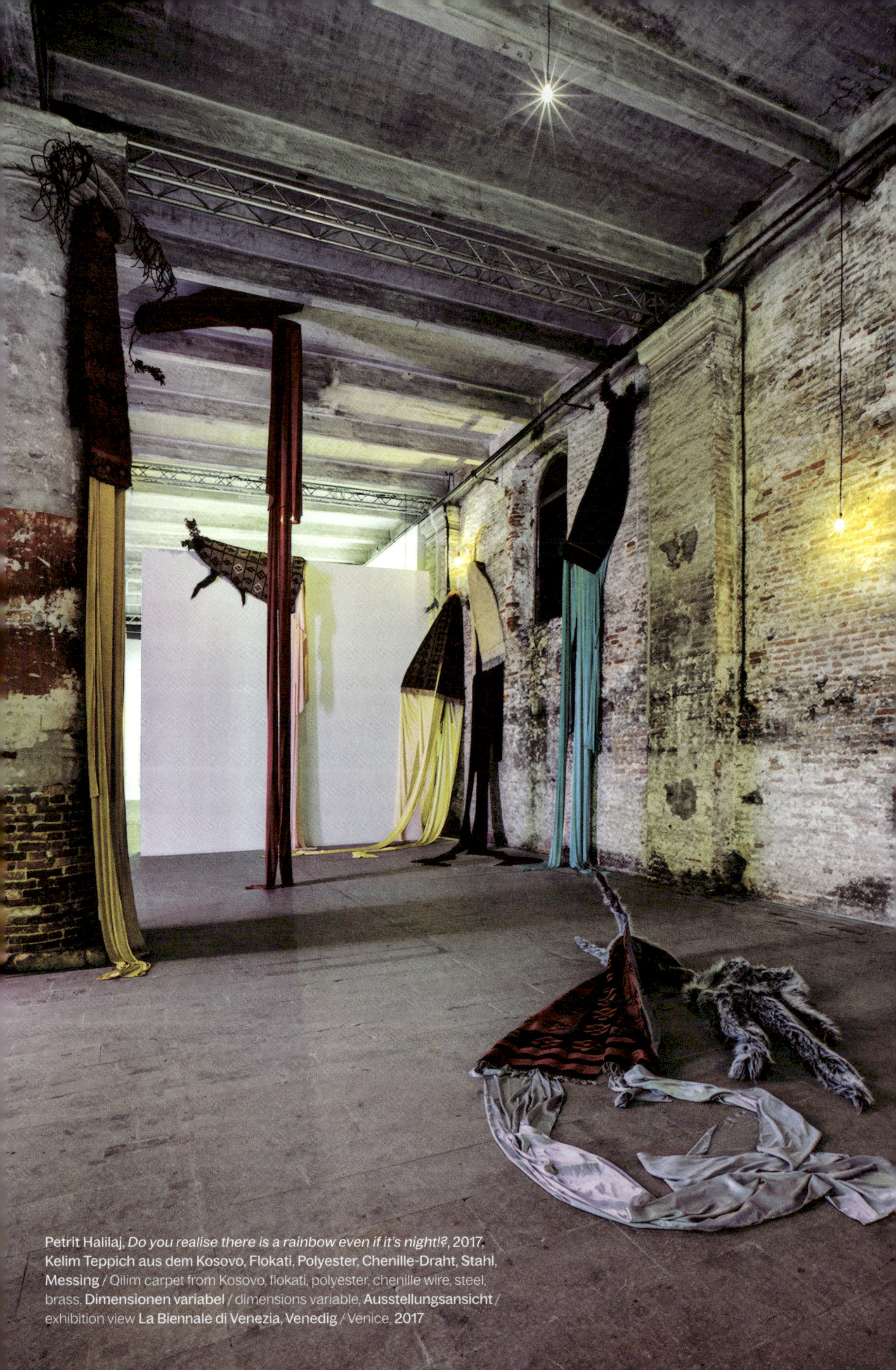

Petrit Halilaj, *Do you realise there is a rainbow even if it's night!?*, 2017,
Kelim Teppich aus dem Kosovo, Flokati, Polyester, Chenille-Draht, Stahl,
Messing / Qilim carpet from Kosovo, flokati, polyester, chenille wire, steel,
brass, Dimensionen variabel / dimensions variable, Ausstellungsansicht /
exhibition view La Biennale di Venezia, Venedig / Venice, 2017

Vogelbeine und können so wie Mitglieder der Hochzeitskapelle oder Gäste der Freiluftaufführung zusammenkommen. Weder in Syrigana noch im Museum gibt es eine starre Trennung zwischen Bühne und Publikum, Darsteller*innen und Zuschauer*innen. Besucher*innen können frei umhergehen, interagieren und selbst Teil der Geschichte werden.

Wie der ‚verlorene Garten' des vorkriegszeitlichen Syrigana, der aufgrund von Vertreibung und Umbrüchen nur noch über Erinnerung und Imagination zugänglich ist, erscheint auch die im Museum evozierte Landschaft nicht als statische Kulisse, sondern als eigentliche Hauptfigur. Durch wechselndes Licht und Klang moduliert, wird sie zu einer veränderlichen Topografie, in der Abwesenheit und Präsenz, Zerstörung und Erneuerung in dramatischer Spannung gehalten sind. Indem *Syrigana* einen narrativen Abschluss verweigert, lädt es die Besucher*innen ein, nicht nur eine andere Welt zu betreten, sondern auch ihre Ambivalenzen, Brüche und emotionalen Unterströmungen, ihre poetischen wie politischen Dimensionen zu erkunden.

Messiaens Vögel singen von göttlicher Gnade. Petrits Vögel singen von Liebe und Widerstandskraft. Sie stellen den Absolutheitsanspruch von Ursprungserzählungen in Frage und queeren die Konventionen der Oper, um einen Raum hervorzubringen, in dem politische Geschichte und mehr-als-menschliche Verwandtschaft zugleich aufeinanderprallen und ineinander übergehen. Für beide Künstler ist das geduldige Beobachten und Lauschen der Vögel – das Achten auf ihre Rufe, ihre Farben, ihre Bewegungen, ihr komplexes Sozialleben – ebenso sehr ein schöpferischer Akt wie eine Übung der Einstimmung in die Welt. Fand *Saint François* seine Radikalität darin, ‚außerhalb der Zeit' zu stehen, so liegt die Kraft von *Syrigana* darin, zugleich ‚zeitenthoben' und ‚zeitgenössisch' zu sein – eine Oper, deren Protagonistin eine Landschaft ist, die durch den Krieg unzugänglich geworden ist und nur noch über Erinnerung und Imagination erreicht werden kann; ein sorgsam inszeniertes Zusammenspiel von Skulptur und Musik, das vorschlägt, dass die Vitalität der Oper als eine

absolutism of origin stories and queering the conventions of opera to bring forth a space in which political history and more-than-human kinship both collide and converge. For both artists, the act of patiently observing and listening to birds – attending to their calls, their colours, their movements, their intricate social lives – is as much a form of creation as it is a practice of attunement to the world. If *Saint François* found its radicalism in being "out of time", *Syrigana* finds its potency in being both "out of time" and "of our time" – an opera whose protagonist is a landscape that war has rendered inaccessible except through memory and imagination, a carefully orchestrated interplay of sculpture and music proposing that opera's vitality as a mode of being and thinking otherwise lies not in fixed conventions but in its capacity for reinvention.

As I write the final lines of this essay, six weeks have gone by since the opera premiered in Syrigana, and its installation in Berlin is nearing completion. Many of Petrit's collaborators – most notably composer Lugh O'Neill and lighting designer Josep Maria Comas Jorda – have shaped its adaptation for the museum setting. In the months ahead, we will work to bring the Kosovo Philharmonic and the sopranos Nina Guo and Urta Haziraj to Berlin to perform the opera live in the space. We are only beginning to grasp the scope of this work and its position at the intersection of art and politics. Will it awaken a broader appetite for the performing arts? Will it travel again, and if so, what new forms might its restaging and reimagining take? Will it succeed in drawing attention to a cultural heritage under imminent threat from mining and other extractive practices? Might it help imagine a politics beyond ethnic identity and the territorial claims that so often accompany it? Will it, like *Shkrepëtima*, set a political process in motion? Could it contribute to reestablishing a shared connection to the land and its histories? Will it raise awareness of the tensions embedded in origin myths? Loosen inhibitions around love across constructed divides? Open new lines of thought? And if so, what will they be? I wonder. So does Petrit. So, I suspect, do all of us.

I whistle to the dog. We head out to the park. Our garden down the road, not yet lost.

andere Form des Seins und Denkens nicht in festgeschriebenen Konventionen liegt, sondern in ihrer Fähigkeit zur Neuerfindung.

Während ich die letzten Zeilen dieses Essays schreibe, sind sechs Wochen seit der Uraufführung in Syrigana vergangen, und in Berlin nähert sich die Installation ihrer Vollendung. Viele von Petrits Mitwirkenden – allen voran der Komponist Lugh O'Neill und der Lichtdesigner Josep Maria Comas Jorda – haben ihre Anpassung an den Museumsraum geprägt. In den kommenden Monaten werden wir daran arbeiten, die Philharmonie des Kosovo sowie die Sopranistinnen Nina Guo und Urta Haziraj nach Berlin zu holen, um die Oper live im Ausstellungsraum zur Aufführung zu bringen. Erst allmählich beginnen wir, das Ausmaß dieses Werks und seine Position im Spannungsfeld von Kunst und Politik zu erfassen. Wird es ein größeres Interesse an den darstellenden Künsten wecken? Wird es erneut reisen – und wenn ja, in welchen neuen Formen könnte eine Wiederaufführung, eine Neuinszenierung Gestalt annehmen? Wird es gelingen, die Aufmerksamkeit auf ein kulturelles Erbe zu lenken, das durch Bergbau und andere extraktive Praktiken unmittelbar bedroht ist? Könnte es helfen, eine Politik jenseits ethnischer Identität und der damit so oft verknüpften territorialen Ansprüche zu imaginieren? Wird es, wie *Shkrepëtima,* einen politischen Prozess anstoßen? Könnte es dazu beitragen, eine gemeinsame Beziehung zum Land und dessen Geschichte(n) wiederherzustellen? Wird es das Bewusstsein für die Spannungen, die in Ursprungserzählungen eingeschrieben sind, schärfen? Hemmungen gegenüber der Liebe über konstruierte Grenzen hinweg lösen? Neue Denkrichtungen eröffnen? Und wenn ja – welche? Ich frage mich das. Petrit auch. Und, so vermute ich, wir alle.

Ich pfeife nach dem Hund. Wir gehen hinaus in den Park. In unseren – noch nicht verlorenen – Garten am Ende der Straße.

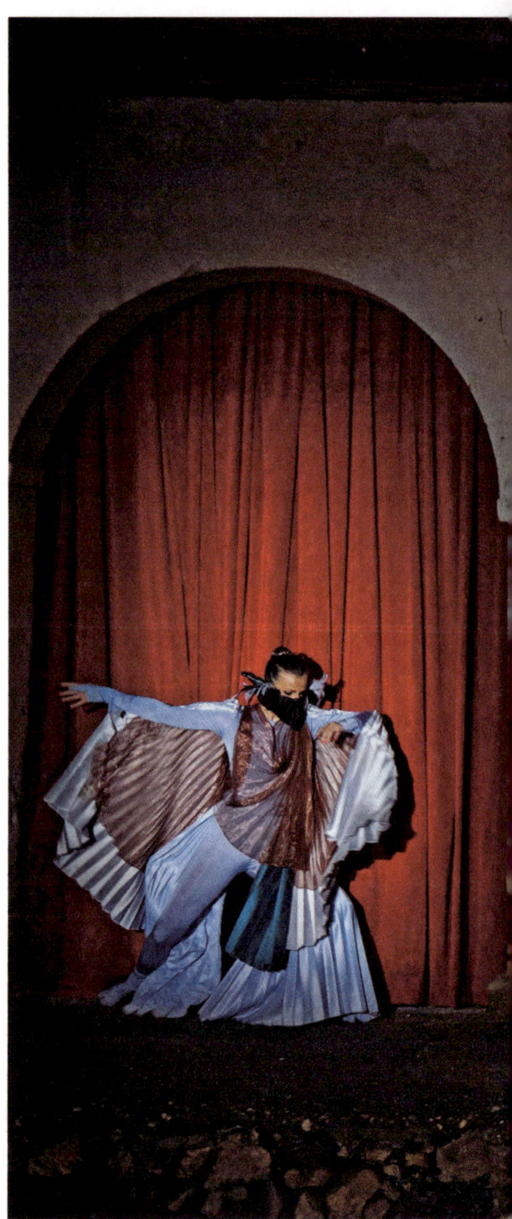

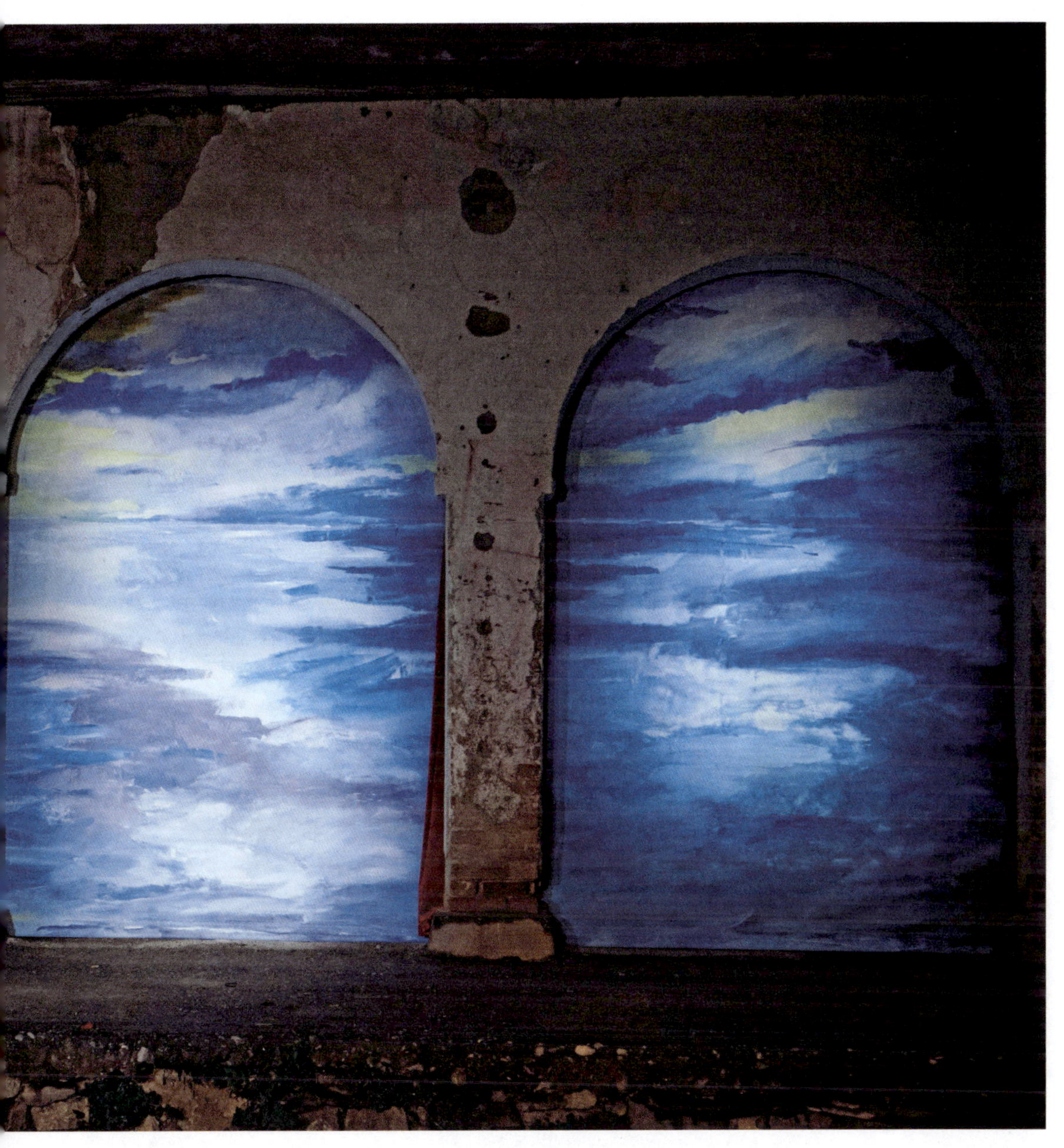

Shkrepëtima, Performance-Ansicht / performance view,
House of Culture, Runik, 2018

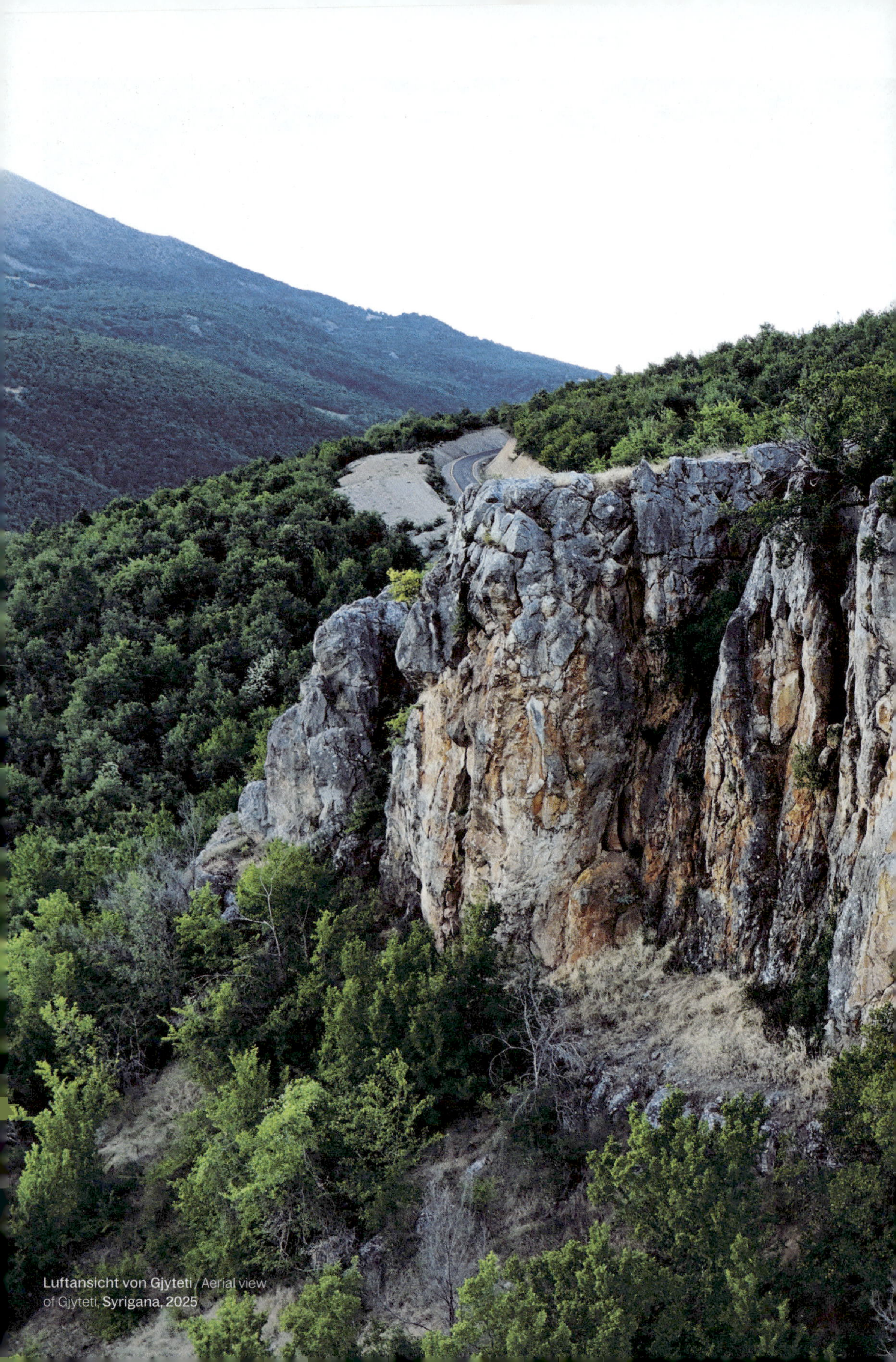

Luftansicht von Gjyteti / Aerial view of Gjyteti, Syrigana, 2025

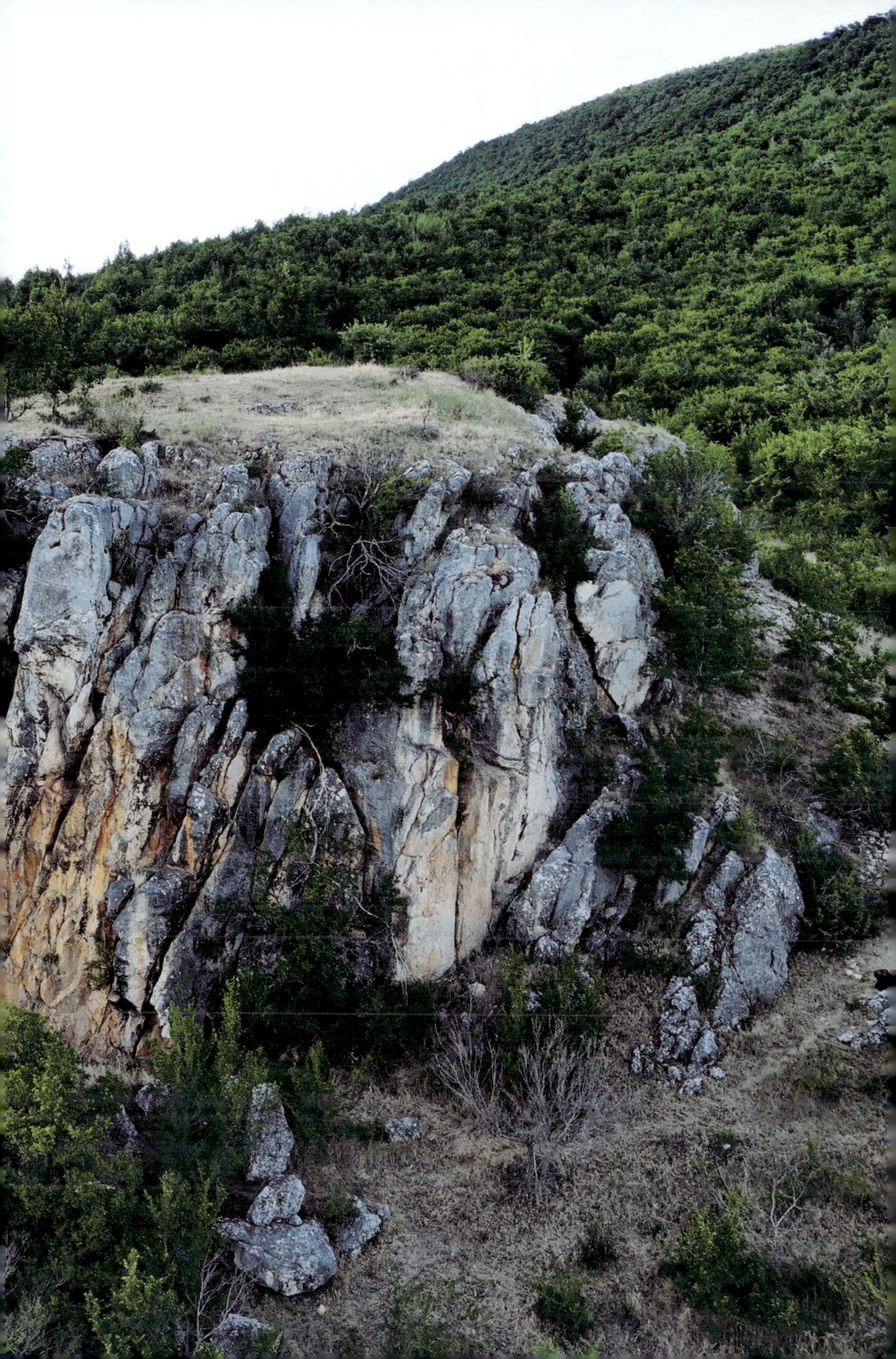

Ein Garten, der verloren wurde ...
A garden that was lost ...

Amy Zion im Gespräch mit /
in Conversation with
Petrit Halilaj

Der Künstler Petrit Halilaj sprach mit der Kuratorin und Autorin Amy Zion – einer langjährigen Wegbegleiterin und Mitstreiterin, mit der er gemeinsam mit Doruntina Basha und Robert Schulz das Libretto für *Syrigana* verfasste. Gemeinsam blicken Halilaj und Zion auf die Entstehung der Oper zurück, die im Hamburger Bahnhof präsentiert wurde – und auf die lokalen Spannungen im Kosovo, die das Projekt buchstäblich entfacht hat.

Amy Zion: Ich möchte mit einer ganz grundlegenden Frage beginnen: Wie kam es überhaupt zu der Idee, eine Oper zu produzieren? Ich würden gerne den Entstehungsprozess chronologisch nachzeichnen. Schließlich wurde das gesamte Werk innerhalb von nur sechs Monaten

Petrit Halilaj spoke to curator and writer Amy Zion, a longtime collaborator and interlocutor with whom he co-wrote the libretto for *Syrigana*, along with Doruntina Basha and Robert Schulz. Halilaj and Zion reflect on the genesis of the project and how it came to be presented at Hamburger Bahnhof as well as the local tensions that it quite literally inflamed in Kosovo.

Amy Zion: I want to start by asking a very basic question: where did the idea to make an opera come from? Can we plot out how it came about within a timeline? Because there were really only about six months

geschrieben, produziert und inszeniert – inklusive Libretto, Partitur, musikalischer Arrangements, Choreografie, Kostümdesign, Requisitenbau, Bühnenbild, Casting, Proben… die Liste ist lang. Und das alles war, gelinde gesagt, ein enormes Unterfangen.

Petrit Halilaj: Ja, das stimmt. Die Produktion begann zwar im Januar, aber die Idee selbst hatte ich bereits im November – bei einem Besuch meiner Familie im Kosovo. Damals arbeitete ich schon an einer Ausstellung für den Hamburger Bahnhof, war aber mit dem Konzept nicht zufrieden. Während dieses Aufenthalts im Kosovo sprach ich mit Dardan Selimaj, dem Direktor der Kosovo Philharmonic, über die Gestaltung eines Bühnenbilds für das Orchester. Etwa zur gleichen Zeit wurde ich von der Pariser Oper bezüglich einer möglichen Residency angefragt – das Thema Oper war also ohnehin präsent.

Als ich dich im Dezember traf, dachte ich plötzlich: Ich will eine Oper machen – über diesen Felsen, ein Wahrzeichen meiner Kindheit im Kosovo. Ich hatte dich 2018 dorthin mitgenommen, direkt nach der Aufführung von *Shkrepëtima*, zusammen mit anderen Freund*innen aus dem Projekt; wir wollten den Sonnenuntergang anschauen. Du erinnertest dich daran, weil die Aussicht so schön war. Damals war es nur ein vager Gedanke. Aber rückblickend wurde aus dieser simplen Idee etwas sehr Konkretes: Fast alles, was wir bei meinem ersten Vorschlag besprochen hatten, wurde umgesetzt. Die Oper fand zwar nicht auf dem Felsen statt, aber neben ihm – und der Felsen wurde selbst zu einer Figur darin.

Eine Oper zu machen bedeutete für mich, eine neue Richtung einzuschlagen – und war zugleich ein Mittel, den politischen Kontext im Kosovo auf andere Weise zu begreifen. Der Ort war perfekt: ein abgelegener Felsen zwischen dem serbischen und dem albanischen Teil desselben Dorfes – zwei Communities, die sich zwar dieselbe Infrastruktur teilen, dieselbe Schule, dieselbe Polizei, aber dennoch durch tiefgreifende Unterschiede geprägt sind. Nach dem Krieg standen sie eine

during which the entire opera was created, produced and staged. That included: a script, a score, musical arrangements, choreography, design and production of costumes, props and scenography, casting, rehearsals, the list goes on… And that's quite a task, to put it mildly.

Petrit Halilaj: Right. Production began in January, but the idea came in November, during a visit with my family in Kosovo. I was in the process of conceiving the exhibition for Hamburger Bahnhof in Berlin and I was stuck. But in Kosovo I had a conversation with Dardan Selimaj, director of the Kosovo Philharmonic, about developing a scenography for the orchestra. By chance, I'd been approached by the Paris Opera about a possible residency around the same time. So I had opera on my mind.

I saw you in December and I was like, oh my God, I want to do an opera on this Kosovar landmark of my childhood. It is a rock I took you to in 2018, the day after the performance of *Shkrepëtima*, along with other friends and people involved in the project to watch the sunset. You remembered it because the view is so beautiful. It was such an unrefined idea. But at the same time, if you think about how this came together, that basic story survived and mainly everything that we discussed the first time I brought up the idea happened. The opera didn't take place on the rock, but beside the rock. The rock became a character.

To do an opera was a fresh direction, and another way to understand the political context.

I thought it was perfect because it was in a very rural location, basically a rock in-between Serbian and Albanian parts of the same village, which are very different communities. They share the same infrastructure, the same school, albeit with different entrances, the same police.

---

1 KFOR is the name of NATO's peacekeeping forces that have remained in Kosovo since the intervention of 1999 and become part of their military; KFOR is shorthand for Kosovo Force.

Zeit lang unter KFOR-Schutz,[1] heute übernimmt das die kosovarische Polizei. Dieser komplexe, aber zugleich produktive Kontext war ideal für eine Oper über eine im Grunde unmögliche Liebesgeschichte.

AZ: Im Dezember sprachst du über die Oper und darüber, wie stark dich dein letzter Besuch im Kosovo inspiriert hatte. Gleichzeitig erzähltest du von deiner Einladung durch den Hamburger Bahnhof und davon, wie unklar dir war, wie du dich in die aktuelle Situation in Deutschland einbringen solltest. Ich hatte den Eindruck, dass die politischen Entwicklungen dort etwas in dir berührt haben – eine Erinnerung an deine Kindheit, an staatliche Kontrolle von Kultur und Meinungsfreiheit, und wohin das führen kann.

Später, im Januar, hast du bei einem Workshop mitgemacht, den ich im Rahmen der *Transmediale* in Berlin mitorganisiert habe.[2] Dort erzähltest du die Geschichte deines Vaters – und seiner Angst davor, was du in dein Schulheft – gezeichnet hattest…

PH: Das war 1998, vielleicht sogar schon 1997. Damals war der Kosovo von sogenannten paramilitärischen Polizeieinheiten überzogen – offiziell zur ,Erhöhung der Sicherheit für Serb*innen', tatsächlich ein Teil von Miloševićs Plan. Es begann damit, dass Albaner*innen als Bedrohung dargestellt wurden. Die Polizei führte willkürliche Straßenkontrollen durch. Gleichzeitig gab es Studierendenproteste, die mich faszinierten – friedliche Demonstrationen für Selbstbestimmung, Demokratie, für die Rechte von Albaner*innen. Ich schrieb „Republik Kosovo" in mein Schulheft – inspiriert von den Demonstrant*innen, die genau das forderten.

Dann wurden mein Vater und ich von der Polizei angehalten. Sie wollten meine Hefte sehen und entdeckten diesen Satz. Ich erinnere mich genau an den Zorn der Beamten. Sie fragten: „Wer hat dir das beigebracht?" Ich sagte, ich hätte es im Fernsehen gesehen, in den Nachrichten – und dass wir doch nur

For some time after the war, they were protected by KFOR.[1] Now it's the Kosovar police. It is a complex yet fertile context in which to stage an opera about a fundamentally impossible love story.

AZ: In December, you were talking about the opera and the huge inspiration you found during your last visit to Kosovo. Separately, you were speaking about the invitation from Hamburger Bahnhof and your uncertainties. I could feel that what was going on in Germany, the backdrop to your invitation from the museum, was scratching at something you had experienced. You were visibly uncomfortable, having already lived through the legislation of culture and speech during your childhood, and where it ultimately ended up.

Later in January, you participated in a workshop I co-led as part of *Transmediale* in Berlin.[2] You shared a story from before the war in 1999, when your father worried about what you were drawing in your schoolbook…

PH: By 1998, maybe '97, Kosovo was full of what they called paramilitary police to "increase security for Serbs". This was part of Milošević's plan. There were many steps towards what ultimately happened, but the first one was establishing that the Kosovar Albanians were a security threat. These Serbian forces began conducting random searches on the street. At the same time, there were student protests, which fascinated me. They were peaceful demonstrations about self-determination, democracy and the rights of ethnic Albanians.

I wrote 'Kosovo Republic' in my notebook one day, because the protests were calling for Kosovo to be free and an independent republic.

Then the police stopped me and my father. They wanted to check what was written in my notebooks and they found this slogan. I remember very clearly how absolutely annoying

gleiche Rechte wollten. Ich war damals vielleicht elf oder zwölf Jahre alt. Mein Vater hätte dafür verhaftet, geschlagen oder sogar getötet werden können. Sie schrien ihn an – und doch ließen sie uns gehen. Später sagte er: „Wir müssen vorsichtig sein. Es ist nicht die Zeit, um so etwas zu schreiben...“

Im Workshop habe ich dann auch von unserem Grenzübertritt nach Albanien im Jahr 1999 erzählt. Mein Vater wurde wie viele andere Männer festgenommen, wir anderen kamen ins Geflüchtetenlager Kükes II. Dort traf ich den italienischen Psychologen Giacomo Poli, der humanitäre Hilfe leistete. Und plötzlich – das war das Gegenteil meiner früheren Erfahrung – wurden wir ermutigt, unsere Geschichten zu erzählen. Ich wurde für das Schreiben von „Republik Kosovo“ nicht bestraft, sondern dazu ermutigt. Zeichnen wurde zum Raum der Selbstentfaltung. Die Menschen hörten zu. Wir durften erzählen, was wir erlebt hatten.

AZ: Diese Geschichte zeigt auf berührende Weise die Extreme – besonders aus der Sicht eines Kindes, das gerade beginnt, Meinungsfreiheit zu begreifen und sich über Sprache, Zeichnungen, Kleidung auszudrücken. Und von einem Moment auf den anderen trittst du aus einer Welt des Schweigens und der Vorsicht in eine Welt, in der man dich auffordert, laut und deutlich zu sprechen. Das ist eine ziemlich einzigartige Erfahrung des Erwachsenwerdens.

PH: Ja, genau. Ich bin in Runik aufgewachsen, einem Dorf gleich neben Syrigana im Nordwesten des Kosovo. Das Kulturhaus dort wurde 1991 geschlossen, die Zensur begann aber schon 1989. Ich wurde 1986 geboren. 2008 wurde die Unabhängigkeit des Kosovo erklärt – aber ich kehre seither immer wieder zurück, weil ich Teil dieser neuen Realität sein will. Die Kultur kehrt zurück. Ich will mitgestalten, miterleben, mit Freude dort leben, Teil des kollektiven Gedächtnisses sein, an den Diskursen teilnehmen, die durch kulturelle Veranstaltungen entstehen.

that was to the police. They asked us, 'Who told you to write this?' And I responded that I saw it on TV, in the news and stuff. And I was making this argument to them that we simply wanted equal rights. I was very young, probably eleven or twelve. But my father could have been imprisoned, beaten or even killed over that. They screamed at my father but for whatever reason, they let us go. I remember him saying, 'We have to be so careful, we should not write these things. This is not the time to write these things...'

In the workshop I explained and compared also how, during the war in 1999, my family crossed the border over to Albania. Aside from my father who was, like all Albanian men, detained and imprisoned, we went to the refugee camp, Kükes II, where I met an Italian psychologist on a humanitarian mission, Dr Giacomo Poli.

There, I experienced the exact opposite situation: suddenly, not only could we express what we lived through, we were encouraged to do so by Dr Poli and others.

We were being rewarded for writing 'Kosovo Republic' or creating messages calling for freedom. Drawing was a space for self-expression. People were listening to us and we could share with the world what we just experienced on the other side of the border.

AZ: That story really helps illustrate the extremes of this situation: especially your thinking at eleven or twelve, which is the age where we start to understand freedom

---

1 KFOR ist der Name der NATO-Friedenstruppen, die seit der Intervention von 1999 im Kosovo stationiert und Teil des Militärs geworden sind; KFOR ist die Abkürzung für Kosovo Force.

2 "Children's Drawings as Evidence Part II", co-geleitet von Amy Zion und Thomas Keenan, *Transmediale,* Silent Green, Berlin, 30. Januar 2025.

---

2 "Children's Drawings as Evidence Part II", co-led by Amy Zion and Thomas Keenan, *Transmediale,* Silent Green, Berlin, 30 January 2025.

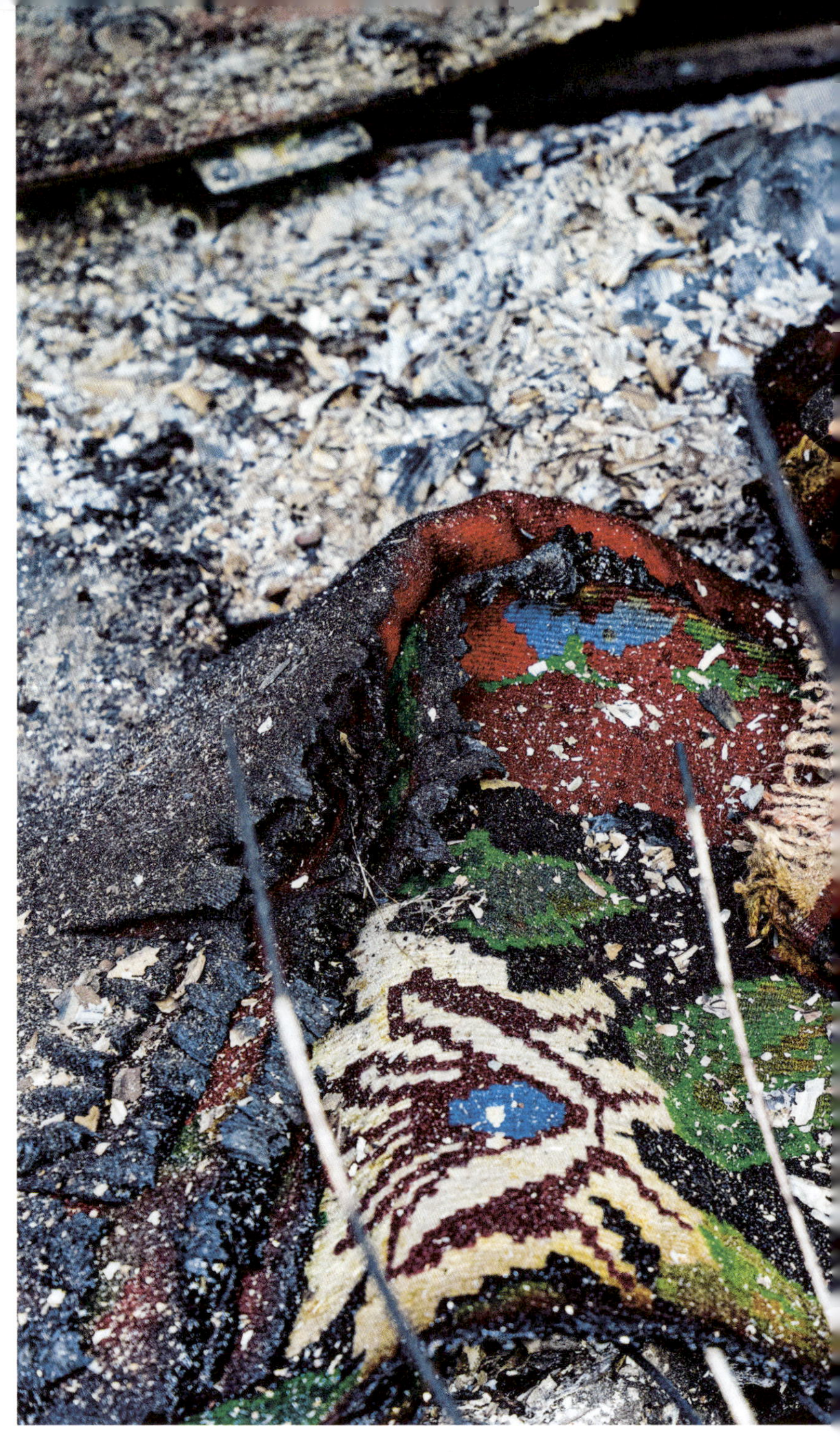

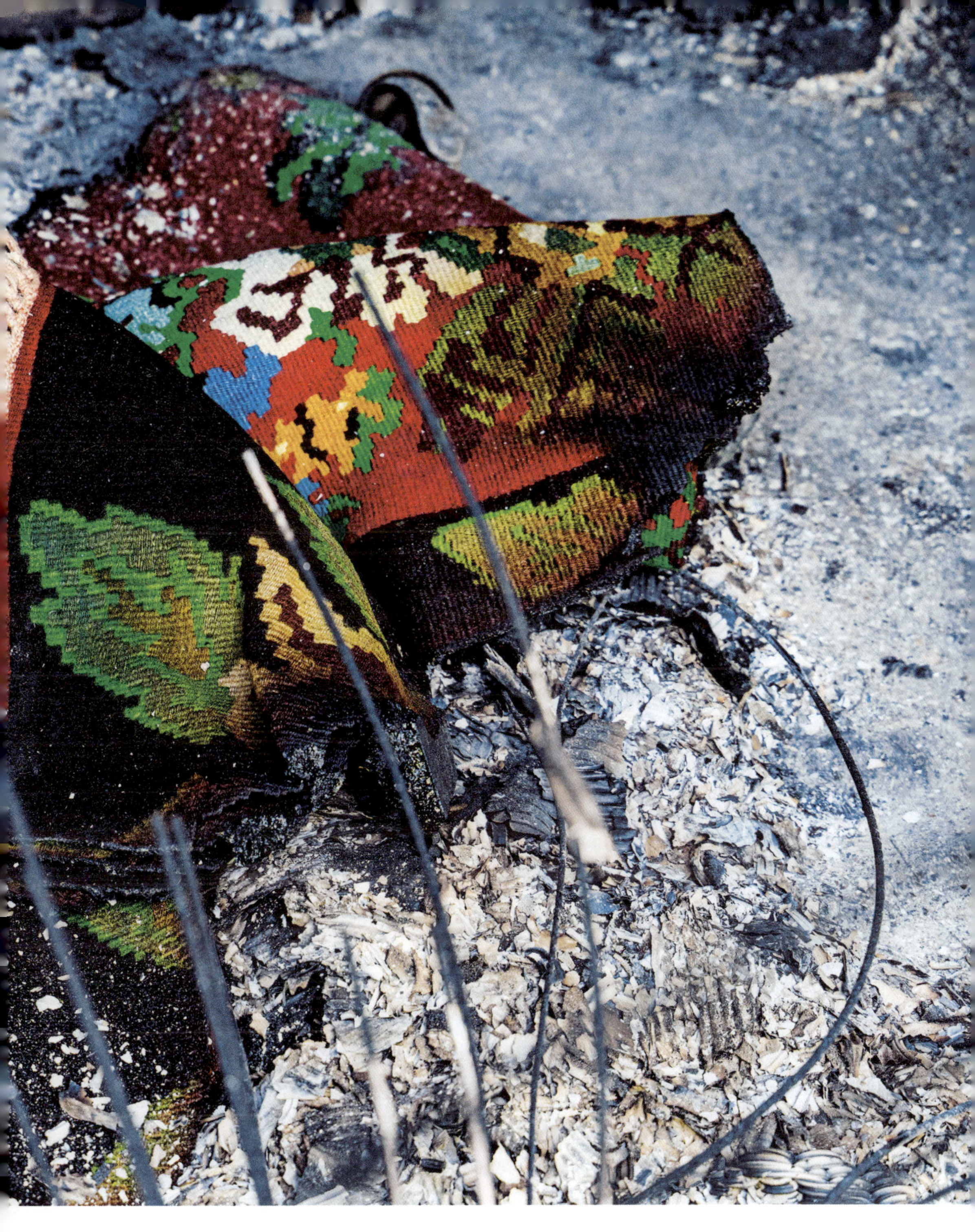

Verbrannte Überreste eines kosovarischen Kelim Teppichs nach einem Brandanschlag / Charred remains of a Kosovar Qilim carpet after an arson attack, **Syrigana, 2025**

AZ: Und so kam es, dass du im November bei einem Familienbesuch begannst, über ein neues Projekt nachzudenken. Du fuhrst zu dem Felsen in Syrigana – und plötzlich hattest du die Vision einer Oper, die genau dort stattfinden könnte…

PH: Ja, was mich immer wieder fasziniert, ist dieser Moment, in dem sich verschiedene Welten zu überlappen scheinen – intuitiv. Zwischen dem Kosovo und Deutschland. Zwischen der Kosovo Philharmonic und dem Hamburger Bahnhof. Zwischen einer Opernproduktion und einem Ort ohne jegliche Infrastruktur, wo Kunst nicht nur gewünscht, sondern dringend gebraucht wird. Zwischen kulturellen Fragestellungen und ungelösten ethnischen Konflikten im Kosovo, aber auch zwischen der Diaspora in Deutschland und den Menschen im Kosovo und all denjenigen, die die Ausstellung sehen werden.

Was Deutschland betrifft, so gibt es nach wie vor eine große kosovarische Diaspora, mittlerweile schon über mehrere Generationen hinweg, die immer noch starke Bindungen zwischen beiden Orten pflegen. Wir befinden uns gerade in einer spannenden Phase. Wir waren noch nie so verbunden wie heute – der Kosovo hat zum ersten Mal eine Visaliberalisierung eingeführt, was es einfacher macht, in Kontakt zu bleiben und zu reisen. Dennoch sind wir in institutionellen und kulturellen Einrichtungen in Deutschland nach wie vor kaum vertreten.

Ich sehe in dieser Ausstellung so viel Potenzial, all diese Welten zusammenzubringen, etwas wie eine Oper im Kosovo zu ermöglichen, die von Catherine Nichols kuratiert, von der Kosovo Philharmonic in Auftrag gegeben und von einer unglaublichen Konstellation aus Teams und Menschen produziert würde. Dann stellte ich mir vor, eine Oper nach Berlin zu bringen und sie in eine immersive Installation zu verwandeln, die Show mit einer Aktivierung der Räume des Museums und der Stadt zu beenden, indem das Orchester hier auftritt… Es war das erste Mal, dass ich versuchte, eine Geschichte im Format einer Oper zu erzählen – dem unpraktischsten,

of expression, where we are finding ourselves through what we say and what we draw, what we wear. But for you, from one day to the next, you went from this very reasonable apprehension towards freedom of expression to being given art supplies and being encouraged to express absolutely anything you wanted. That's a pretty unique adolescent experience.

PH: Yeah. It is. Growing up in my village, Runik, which is next to Syrigana, in the northwest of Kosovo close to the border with Serbia, the House of Culture closed in '91. But the censorship started already in '89. I was born in '86. Eventually, we achieved independence in 2008, but why I insist on going back is to take part in what is developing within this new reality: culture is back. I want to be part of this emerging society more and more, and live in it with joy, to actually be part of building collective memory and participate in the discourse that gets developed through cultural events.

AZ: And so in November, you were on a regular visit to the region, grappling with what to do for this exhibition. You went to the rock in Syrigana and started to imagine staging an opera on it…

PH: **What really fascinates me is when I can intuitively grasp the possibility of colliding worlds:** a world between the context of Kosovo and Germany, between the Kosovo Philharmonic and Hamburger Bahnhof in Berlin, between the Kosovo Philharmonic and doing an opera in an open space totally void of infrastructure, a place where we really want and need art and space for expression, between the cultural context and unresolved ethnic issues in Kosovo, but also the diaspora of Kosovars in Berlin and Germany and everyone who will see the exhibition.

Regarding Germany, there remains a huge population of the Kosovar diaspora, a few generations by now, who still keep strong ties between two places. This is an exciting moment we are in right now. We have never been more

unerwartetsten Format überhaupt. Gleichzeitig war ich überzeugt, dass diese Geschichte erzählt werden konnte.

Aber ich hatte keine Ahnung, wie ich das Ganze umsetzen sollte, keine Ahnung, ob es wirklich funktionieren würde. Da war nur diese Geschichte über eine unmögliche Liebe, über die Anfänge der Menschheit und darüber, wer zuerst da war. Ich hatte gerade den Felsen Gjyteti in Syrigana besucht, mit dieser seltsamen Nacherzählung von Adam und Eva im Kopf, in der sie in Syrigana ankommen, Menschen finden und diese Menschen ihnen eine Hochzeit ausrichten. Erinnerungen an Hochzeiten aus meiner Kindheit kamen an die Oberfläche, und ich begann, alles als Oper vor mir zu sehen. Ich wollte eine epische Liebesgeschichte und Reise aus dem Garten Eden nach dem Verlust des Paradieses zum Leben erwecken – das Bild von Adam und Eva, die balkanische Gastfreundschaft erfahren: eine riesige Opernzeremonie mit Brot, Salz, Herz und *defa*.[3]

AZ: **Kommen wir nun zur Oper selbst – zur Geschichte und dazu, wie sich die gesamte Produktion in einem intensiven Gemeinschaftsprozess entwickelt hat. Das war notwendig, um innerhalb kürzester Zeit eine vollständige Opernproduktion – mit talentierten Darsteller*innen und dem nationalen Philharmonieorchester – in den ländlichen Hügeln auf die Beine zu stellen.**

Eine Fähigkeit, die du als Künstler im Laufe der Jahre perfektioniert hast, ist es, Träume zu ‚verkaufen‘. Das heißt: Du musstest für immer größere Produktionen immer mehr Menschen begeistern – meist sehr schnell – und sie davon überzeugen, sich auf etwas einzulassen. Meine Rolle in der Oper bestand letztlich hauptsächlich darin, die Handlung zu gestalten. Denn ab einem gewissen Punkt existierte keine Synopsis mehr, mit der man all den Beteiligten das Projekt erklären konnte. Ich geriet in Panik und fragte mich, wie ich mit diesem Traum ‚Kinkenputzen‘ gehen sollte – ohne eine zusammenhängende Geschichte.

connected – Kosovo has visa liberalisation for the first time, which makes it easier to stay in touch and to travel. Yet we still have very little representation in institutional and cultural places in Germany.

I saw so much potential in this show to bring all these worlds together, to facilitate something like an opera in Kosovo that would be curated by Catherine Nichols, commissioned by the Kosovo Philharmonic, produced by an incredible mix of teams and people. Then to imagine bringing an opera and transforming it into an immersive installation in Berlin, ending the show by activating the spaces of the museum and the city by hosting the orchestra here… This was my first time trying to tell a story in the format of an opera – the most impractical, unexpected format. At the same time, I had a crystal-clear feeling that it could be told.

But I had no idea how to make it happen, no idea if it would really happen, only this feeling of having a story about an impossible love, about the beginnings of humanity and who came first. I had just visited the stone, which is called Gjyteti, in Syrigana, with this oddball retelling of Adam and Eve in mind, in which they arrive in Syrigana, find people, and those people throw them a wedding. Memories of weddings from my childhood were flooding back to me, and I started to see it all come together as an opera.

I wanted to bring to life an epic love story and journey from the Garden of Eden, after paradise was lost – the image of Adam and Eve receiving Balkan hospitality: a huge operatic ceremony with bread, salt, heart and *defa*.[3]

AZ: So then let's address the opera itself – the story and how the whole production developed as a deeply collaborative process. This was necessary in order to make

---

3 A *defa* is a traditional Albanian percussion instrument, bearing resemblance to a tambourine.

PH: Ja, das stimmt. Die Geschichte basiert auf einem lokalen Mythos – oder vielleicht sollte man eher sagen: einem Gerücht, denn ich habe es nur von einer einzigen Person gehört. Aber es war eine schöne Möglichkeit, unser Verständnis des schriftlich überlieferten Ursprungs der Menschheit, also der biblischen Genesis, infrage zu stellen. Ich wollte mit diesem grundlegenden Mythos spielen, den alle drei abrahamitischen Religionen teilen, und ihn durch eine surreale, fast schon respektlose Erzählung herausfordern – eine Geschichte, die ich in einem Café gehört habe.

AZ: Du meinst das Interview, das du im Rahmen der Arbeit *RU* (2017) geführt hast, die auch Teil deiner aktuellen Ausstellung ist. Es ist das letzte Gespräch, mit einem Freund aus deiner Grundschulzeit, Gëzim Dauti. Er sammelt mit großer Begeisterung neolithische Artefakte aus der Region und interessiert sich für Archäologie und das Erzählen von Geschichten. In einem fast verschwörerischen Ton erzählt er dir, dass Adam und Eva – nachdem sie aus dem Paradies vertrieben worden waren – auf der Suche nach einem Ort zum Heiraten um die Welt reisten. Sie ließen sich schließlich in Syrigana nieder, wo sie von den Dorfbewohner*innen empfangen und verheiratet wurden.[4] Das Ganze ist eine amüsante, paradoxe und vielleicht sogar blasphemische Geschichte – denn sie impliziert, dass Adam und Eva nicht die ersten Menschen waren. Sie stießen auf ein neolithisches Dorf in dem Gebiet, das wir heute als Kosovo kennen, und die Einheimischen organisierten für sie eine Hochzeit.

Mit dieser Ausgangsidee hattest du mich sofort. Ich liebe die Vorstellung, dass Adam und Eva in einem neolithischen Dorf geheiratet haben – also noch vor den heiligen Schriften und vor unserer jüdisch-christlich-islamischen Zeitrechnung.

PH: Haha, ja, das fasst es ganz gut zusammen.

an opera from zero to a refined production by a talented cast and the national philharmonic in the rural hillsides so quickly.

One of the skills you've honed as an artist over the years is that you've figured out how to be a salesman of dreams. Meaning, taking on larger and larger productions has required you to get people on board, usually really quickly, and to have them really buy into something, collectively. My role in the opera, for instance, ended up being largely about shaping the plot. Because at a certain point there was no synopsis to share with various people you needed to make it happen. I was getting panicky thinking, how will you go "door-to-door" selling this dream without a coherent plot?

PH: Yes, this is true. The story is based on a local myth – maybe we should call it a rumour, since I heard this from one person – as a way to question what we understand of the written, Old Testament origin story and the beginning of humanity from a religious perspective. It's a way to play with that foundational myth that the three Abrahamic religions all share, and then twist it with a surreal, iconoclastic story I heard in a coffee shop.

AZ: You're referring to an interview you did as part of the work *RU* (2017), which is part of this present exhibition, it's the last conversation included with a friend of yours since elementary school, Gëzim Dauti. He has collected local Neolithic fragments and is passionate about archaeology and storytelling. In a kind of whisper tone, he confides to you that when Adam and Eve were expelled from Paradise, they went around the world in search of a place to get married. They settled in Syrigana, where the local villagers welcomed them and married them.[4] This was a funny and paradoxical, perhaps sacrilegious story, because it implies that Adam and Eve were not the first humans. They stumbled upon the Neolithic village in what we today call Kosovo and these local people threw them a wedding.

AZ: Irgendwann dachte ich auch an ihre beiden Söhne – Kain und Abel – die so etwas wie die Blaupause für menschliche Feindseligkeit und Gewalt darstellen. Die berühmte Stelle in der Genesis, als Gott Kain fragt: „Wo ist dein Bruder?" – obwohl er die Antwort natürlich schon kennt (weil er Gott ist). Kain lügt und antwortet: „Ich weiß es nicht. Bin ich der Hüter meines Bruders?" Ich fand es faszinierend, dass Syrigana ein Ort mit einem Felsen (er spielt auch in der Oper eine zentrale Rolle) ist, der – zwei Teile eines gespaltenen Dorfes trennt, dessen Bewohner*innen in scheinbar endlosen Spannungen und Konflikten gefangen sind.

Die Figur des Schneiders stammt aus einer weiteren, späteren Geschichte aus dem Alten Testament, ebenfalls in der Genesis: die Hochzeit von Jakob und Lea. Jakob betrank sich in seiner Hochzeitsnacht und heiratete seine Braut, ohne den Schleier von ihrem Gesicht zu lüften. Als er am nächsten Morgen aufwachte, stellte er fest, dass er hereingelegt worden war und Lea geheiratet hatte, die ältere und weniger attraktive Schwester. Ich dachte mir: Was wäre, wenn Fuchs und Hahn heiraten wollen, aber dann etwas dazwischen kommt, das alles durcheinanderbringt? Es ist schließlich eine Oper, und eine Oper braucht Drama.

PH: Ja, am Anfang hat mich die Idee des Schneiders schockiert. Aber dann wurde mir klar, dass er auch die Gestalt der Schlange aus dem Garten Eden annehmen könnte – eine allgemeine, negative Kraft, die in vielen Formen im realen Leben existiert und der man sich auf die eine oder andere Weise stellen muss.

Apropos: Während wir das Drehbuch schrieben – und parallel alle anderen Teile der Oper produziert wurden –, bin ich immer wieder nach Syrigana gereist. Viele fragten mich: „Hast du keine Angst?" oder „Sind die Serb*innen damit einverstanden?"

You had me immediately with this starting point. I love the idea that Adam and Eve were married in a Neolithic village that existed before the scriptures, basically, before our Judeo-Christian-Islamic idea of time.

PH: Haha, yes, that sums it up doesn't it…

AZ: At a certain point it also occurred to me that Adam and Eve's two sons were Cain and Abel, which is the blueprint for human animosity and war – the famous line, also in Genesis, when God asks Cain where his brother is, of course already knowing the answer (because he is God). Cain lies, says he doesn't know, and adds, 'Am I my brother's keeper?' I thought that was so interesting, Syrigana being a place with a rock (which figures prominently in the opera) between two parts of a divided village with neighbours caught up in seemingly endless tension and conflict.

The Tailor character came from a different story from the Old Testament, later on in Genesis, the marriage of Jacob and Leah. Jacob got drunk on his wedding night, and he married his bride with the veil over her face. He woke up the next morning and realised that he had been tricked into marrying Leah, the older and less attractive sister. I thought, what if Fox and Rooster want to get married, but actually, there's this sort of element that comes in and shakes things

---

3 Eine *defa* ist ein traditionelles albanisches Perkussionsinstrument, das einem Tamburin ähnelt.
4 In Gzims Originalversion heiraten Adam und Eva in Runik; Halilaj stellte sich die Geschichte im nahe gelegenen Syrigana vor.

---

4 In Gzim's original version, Adam and Eve are married in Runik; Halilaj imagined the story in nearby Syrigana.

Ich traf mich mit einigen Serb*innen – mit dem Bürgermeister, mit Polizist*innen serbischer Herkunft und auch mit Mitgliedern der albanischen Community.

AZ: Du hattest also nicht das Gefühl, dass ethnische Spannungen das Projekt gefährden könnten?

PH: Nein, nicht in erster Linie. Die Spannungen, die ich spürte, hatten mehr mit den logistischen Herausforderungen zu tun – nicht mit ethnischen Konflikten. Das Kulturhaus der Region liegt seit den Anschlägen in den frühen 1990er-Jahren in Trümmern. Früher gab es dort kleine Musikgruppen, doch das endete mit dem Krieg. Heute gibt es keine offiziellen Kulturveranstaltungen mehr. Natürlich wird gemeinsam gefeiert – in den Tee- oder Kaffeehäusern. Aber es fehlt eine organisierte Struktur. Gerade deshalb war es so bedeutsam, mitten im Dorf eine Oper aufzuführen. Es gibt dort so viele Geschichten, und die Menschen haben ein echtes Bedürfnis nach etwas Kollektivem, Organisiertem, Kulturellem.

Viele erinnerten sich auch noch an *Shkrepëtima*, die Aufführung, die ich 2018 in den Ruinen des Kulturhauses inszeniert habe. Sie kam sehr gut an – die Leute reden noch immer darüber. Und als ich mit den Menschen vor Ort sprach, sagten sie: „Wir versammeln uns noch immer, wir machen noch immer Musik." Aussagen wie diese haben mich tief bewegt. Sie erinnerten mich daran, dass ich auf dem richtigen Weg war. Es war kein einfaches Projekt, aber das hat mir den Mut gegeben, weiterzumachen.

AZ: Die Schwierigkeiten, mit denen du bei der Entstehung und Inszenierung dieser Oper zu kämpfen hattest, hingen also hauptsächlich mit der mangelnden lokalen Infrastruktur zusammen – und damit, dass du Partnerschaften zwischen Institutionen aus verschiedenen Teilen der Welt aufbauen musstest, um das Projekt überhaupt realisieren zu können. Wir haben über die Wendungen in der

up. It's an opera, after all, and an opera has to have drama.

PH: Yes, at first the tailor scandalised me, but then I realised they could take the form of the snake from the Garden of Eden, a general negative force that exists in all facets of real life and must be confronted in some way or another.

Speaking of which, while we were writing the script and every other part of the opera was being produced in parallel, I was going back and forth to Syrigana. A lot of people were asking me, are you not afraid? Are the Serbs fine with this? I met with a few Serbs, with the mayor and some of the police who are Serbs, and also with members of the Albanian community.

AZ: So you didn't have the impression that there would be tension over the opera?

PH: No, I felt tension from mounting such an event in a context where we don't have any support structures, rather than for ethnic reasons: the House of Culture for the region is still in ruins since it was attacked in the early '90s, and in Syrigana there used to be small groups of local musicians but that ended with the war, too, and it never returned. So it is a region where there have been no organised cultural events happening. Local people of course play music together. They have parties and they use the *çajtore* [teahouse] communally, but nothing official. So there were clear signs of the importance of staging an opera in the middle of the village. The richness of stories and the people's wish to have something that is organised and therefore shared, collective and cultural.

They also have the recent memory of *Shkrepëtima,* a performance I staged on what was left of the House of Culture in 2018. It was very well received at the time and people are still talking about it, so everyone was very enthusiastic about having another performance like that in the region. And when I met locals, they would remind me that they still gather, still have music, and that this is so important because the music here kept our stories and identity alive when we didn't have the means to write history or keep physical records. Those sorts of things touched

Handlung der Oper gesprochen, aber es gab auch eine äußerst tragische Wendung in der Woche vor der Premiere...

PH: **Was dann geschah, kam völlig unerwartet. Acht Tage vor der Premiere – die Requisiten waren fertiggestellt, die ersten Proben hatten begonnen – hatten wir zwei große Metallcontainer angemietet. Fast alles, was wir im Kosovo oder in Berlin produziert hatten, war dort untergebracht. Die Container standen direkt hinter dem Felsen, damit die Darsteller*innen die Requisiten leicht zu den Szenen bringen und danach wieder abtransportieren konnten. Nachts wurden sie abgeschlossen.**

An einem Morgen, gut eine Woche vor der Premiere, rief mich Ferdinand Pechmann an, der in meinem Studio die Produktion leitete und die ganze Zeit über vor Ort war. Er sagte: „Petrit, wir haben ein ernstes Problem. Sehr schlechte Nachrichten: Die beiden Container, in denen alle Elemente für die Oper gelagert waren, wurden angezündet. Man hat den Brand erst bemerkt, als die letzten Rauchschwaden aufstiegen." Offenbar wurden sie am frühen Morgen gegen fünf Uhr in Brand gesetzt. Alles war zerstört – einfach so.

Zum Glück waren die Masken und Kostüme noch nicht angekommen. Sie wurden entweder noch in Prishtina produziert oder waren auf dem Weg – in Zusammenarbeit mit Lisa Lauren, dem werkstattkollektiv und Hana Zeqa, mit der ich schon bei *Shkrepëtima* zusammengearbeitet hatte. Aber die Requisiten – insbesondere die für die Garten-Eden-Szene: der Birnbaum, die Früchte, die fünf Blüten, die Okarina, die Kelim-Teppiche – alles, was das Paradies verkörperte, war verloren. Auch Werkzeuge und andere Dinge brannten mit, aber diese Requisiten waren die Herzstücke. Es war merkwürdig – in der Oper singen die Vögel, die beiden Sopranistinnen: „Sie sagen, ein Garten, der verloren wurde..."

Wir gehen davon aus, dass es sich um einen politisch motivierten Brandanschlag handelte. Die Täter*innen sprühten nicht nur „SRB" (für Serbien) auf die Container, sondern auch das Kreuz, das im Krieg auf niedergebrannte Häuser im Kosovo gemalt

me so deeply. They reminded me that I was on the right path to do something beautiful here. This was not a simple project, but that gave me the courage to continue.

AZ: So the hardship you were experiencing in creating and staging this opera had mainly to do with the lack of local infrastructure, and the fact that you had to build partnerships between institutions from different parts of the world in order to just make the thing happen. We spoke about plot twists within the opera itself, but in the span of production, there was a very unfortunate turn of events the week before the premiere...

PH: What happened was completely unexpected. Eight days before the premiere of *Syrigana* – after finishing the props, starting to do the first rehearsals – we rented two large metal shipping containers. Almost everything that we produced either in Kosovo or in Berlin, we stored in these units on the site and closed them up at night. They were just behind the rock where it was easy for actors to go to bring the props in and out of the scenes.

That morning, a little more than a week out, I received a call from Ferdinand Pechmann, who oversees production in my studio and who was on site the whole time for the opera, that, 'Well Petrit, we have a very big problem and very bad news:

the two containers holding all of the elements for the opera were set on fire, and discovered only when the last gusts of smoke were rising out.'

It seems they were burned earlier that morning around 5 a.m. Everything was incinerated, just like that.

Luckily, the masks and the costumes had not yet arrived. The costumes done in collaboration with Lisa Lauren and werkstattkollektiv and in Kosovo with Hana Zeqa, with whom I worked previously for the birds of *Shkrepëtima*, were still on their way or in Prishtina. Oddly, what

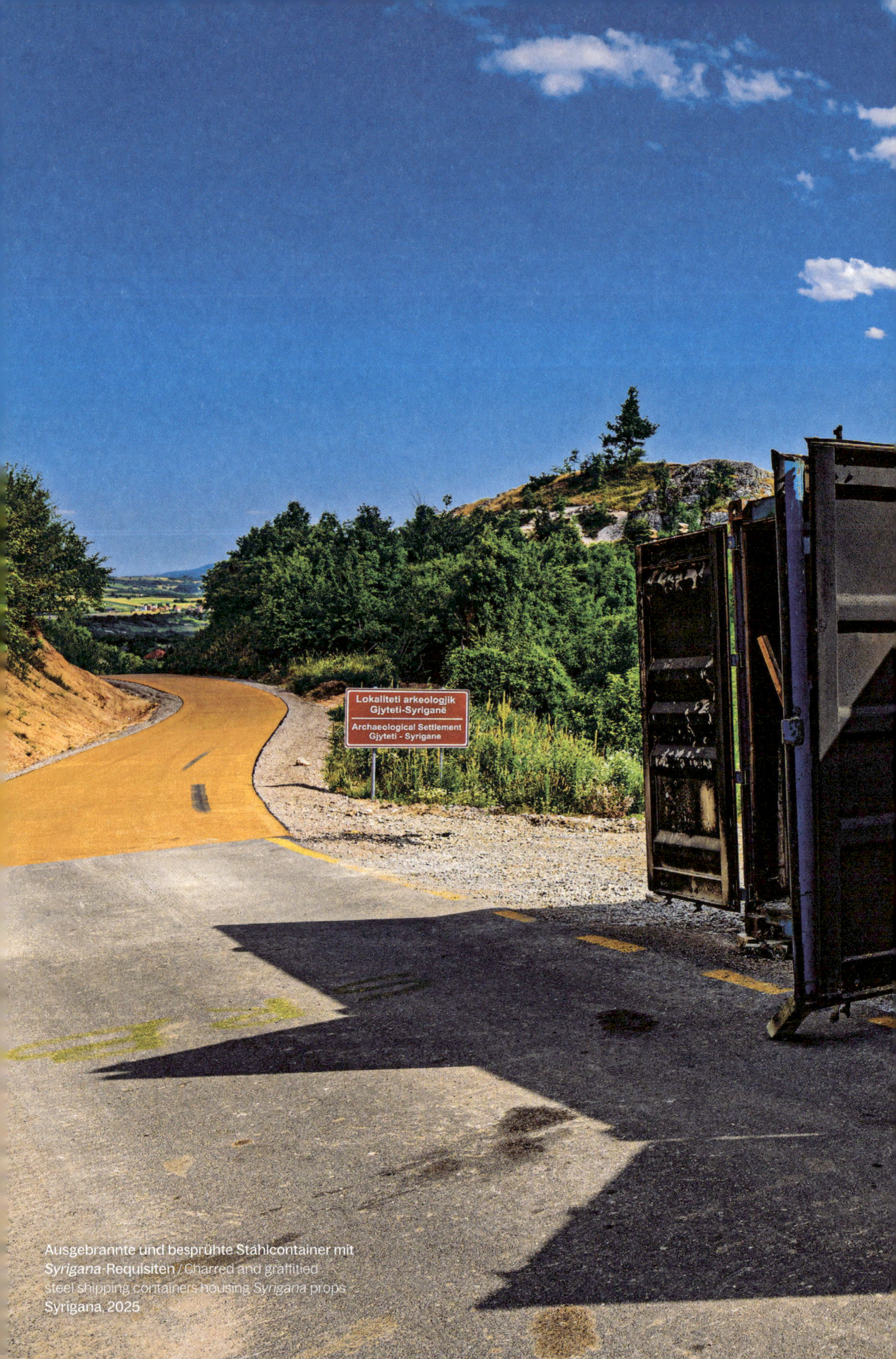

Ausgebrannte und besprühte Stahlcontainer mit
Syrigana-Requisiten / Charred and graffitied
steel shipping containers housing *Syrigana* props
Syrigana, 2025

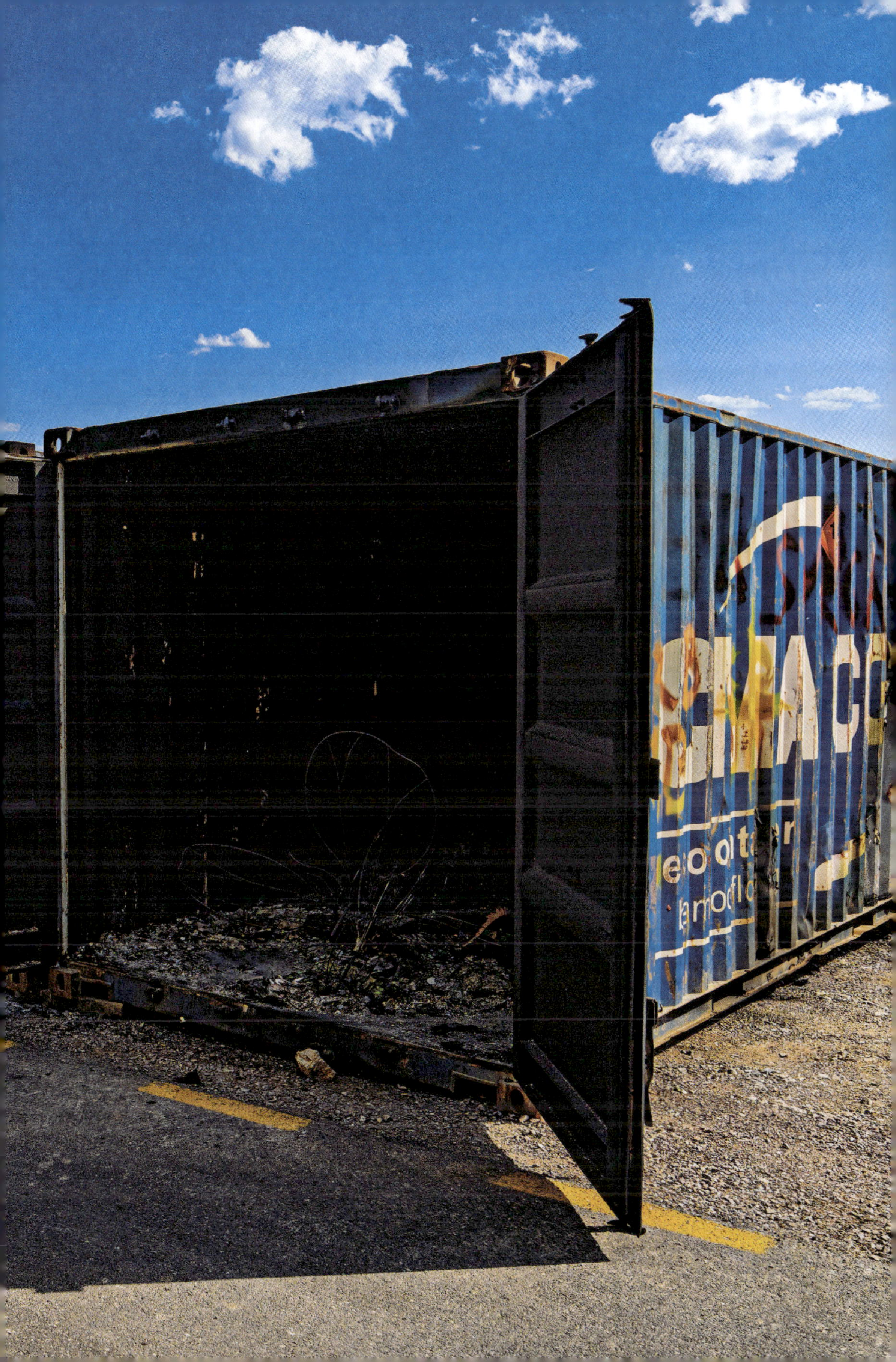
CMA CG
e o ta
amofl

wurde, sowie Graffiti wie „Kill you" – auf Englisch. Als ich die Bilder sah, brach für mich für einen Moment die Welt zusammen. Es war extrem schwer, das zu verarbeiten. Ich hatte das Glück, im Krieg keine Angehörigen zu verlieren. Aber wir kehrten damals in niedergebrannte Häuser zurück. Und nun war da dieses Gefühl: Egal, wie sehr man sich in den letzten 26 Jahren eingeredet hat, dass das Schlimmste hinter einem liegt – die Realität ist immer noch brutal. Dieser Anschlag war ein gezielter Versuch, ein Kulturprojekt zu zerstören – eines der wenigen seit dem Krieg.

AZ: **Als ich davon erfuhr, fragte ich mich ob wir zu naiv gewesen waren; ob wir die Risiken, die ein solches Projektes birgt, unterschätzt hatten.**

PH: **An dem Morgen sprach ich mit dem Kulturminister. Seine Reaktion war im Grunde: „Willkommen in unserer Realität, mein Lieber. Wenn man Kultur in fragilen Regionen machen will, wo ethnische Konflikte über Generationen bestehen und Menschen eng beieinander leben, dann passiert so etwas. Aber lassen Sie sich davon nicht abhalten." Er sagte, er würde mit der Polizei sprechen – sie kamen auch tatsächlich und sicherten die Produktion rund um die Uhr.**

Bis heute wissen wir nicht, wer genau hinter dem Feuer steckte und mit welcher Absicht es gelegt wurde. Klar ist: Monate an Arbeit, unzählige Produktionsstunden, enorme Investitionen – all das war in einer Nacht zerstört worden. Und uns blieb kaum Zeit, um das emotional oder praktisch zu verarbeiten. Wir mussten sofort alles neu organisieren: eine neue Birne, Ersatz für die KFOR-Hubschrauber, neue Teppiche, neue Werkzeuge, die Metallblumen reinigen, die Blütenblätter aus Berlin holen, die eigentlich für die Ausstellung gedacht waren... Ich nahm mir einen Moment, um allein zu sein, und ich weinte viel. Dann rief ich wichtige Menschen an – Catherine, meine Mutter, den Kulturminister, den Bürgermeister von Syrigana, mein Studioteam. Am Ende wurde mir klar: Es lag an mir zu entscheiden, ob uns das auseinanderbringen würde.

burned were the props for the Garden of Eden scene, so the pear tree, the pear fruit and the five pear blossoms, the ocarina, the Qilim carpets, in other words all the props for the scenes that take place in paradise. There were tools and other items lost, but those props were the main elements of the opera. It was just oddly like the line in the opera when the birds, the two sopranos, narrate the story: 'They say, a garden that was lost …'

We suspect that it was a politically motivated arson because not only did the perpetrators write 'SRB', as in Serbia, on the containers, but they added this cross that they put on all the burnt houses in Kosovo during the war, and more graffiti like 'Kill you' written in English.

And when I saw these images, honestly, the sky fell down for me for a moment; it was very hard to see and live this situation.

Luckily my family did not lose anyone during the war but we returned to burned-out houses. And it was very harsh to understand that, actually, no matter how much illusion I live with now, since the war, thinking that the worst is behind us, and how much has changed and developed in the past 26 years, and even though we are on a new path forward, it is still a somewhat brutal context. This was an attempt to stop, to destroy a whole cultural project, one of the few since the war.

AZ: Yes, when I heard the news I wondered if we had all been totally naïve in not considering the security risks for such a project.

PH: That morning, I had a call with the Minister of Culture. His response was basically: 'Welcome to our reality, dear. If you want to produce culture in very fragile places, where there are longstanding ethnic conflicts between Kosovar Serbs and Albanians, and where they live so close together, this is what happens most of the time. But this should not stop you. In other words: We totally support you, I will speak with the police and they will get you more security.' And then the police showed up and really took care of everyone.

Wir hatten monatelang an etwas gearbeitet, das für mich – und viele andere – größer war als das, was da passiert war.

Meine Intuition sagte mir: Wir müssen alles, was möglich ist, neu machen. Wenn die Polizei Sicherheit garantieren kann, wenn die Schauspieler*innen sich sicher fühlen, wenn niemand aus dem Team gefährdet ist – dann geben wir nicht auf. Wir machen keine große Sache daraus, aber wir lassen uns auch nicht einschüchtern. Wir machen die Oper. Denn allein die Realisierung war der größte Sieg über diesen Akt der Gewalt.

Ich bin unglaublich dankbar für die Solidarität – von Catherine, dem Team, den Menschen vor Ort. Es hat uns zusammengeschweißt. Es hat dem Projekt noch mehr Bedeutung verliehen. Die Darsteller*innen waren vielleicht verunsichert – aber niemand hat auch nur einen Moment überlegt, auszusteigen.

Und bei der Premiere kamen mehr als 1.200 Menschen auf den Hügel – viele aus dem Dorf und der Region, aber auch aus dem ganzen Kosovo. Sogar Familien aus der Diaspora – aus Deutschland und anderen Ländern – hatten ihren Sommerurlaub um dieses Ereignis herum geplant. Es war magisch: Ich sah alte Klassenkamerad*innen aus der Grundschule, Freund*innen aus Schweden, Bekannte aus Berlin. Es war die erste kulturelle Veranstaltung dieser Größenordnung seit dem Krieg – der Tag gehörte den Menschen dort. Viele von ihnen hatten nie wieder zurückgefunden, seit ihre Häuser zerstört worden waren.

AZ: Deine Mutter ist in Syrigana aufgewachsen, richtig?

PH: Ja.

AZ: Du hast mir erzählt, dass es in der Zeit Jugoslawiens nicht die Spannungen gab, die später kamen – dass deine Mutter tatsächlich alle Kinder aus dem Dorf kannte, ob albanisch oder serbisch, und dass sie alle miteinander spielten. Die soziale Ordnung war eine völlig andere.

We still don't know who set the fire or exactly why. The reality was that months and months of production and work and a huge amount of effort literally went up in smoke and was gone in one night. And there was very, very little time to process this emotionally, and also physically, to remake everything, the pear, the two KFOR helicopters, to find more carpets, to buy replacement tools, to clean the metal flower structures, to bring the flowers and petals from Berlin that were prepared for the exhibition… But I took a moment to myself and I cried a lot. Then I called and consulted a few key people: Catherine, my mum, the Minister of Culture, the mayor of Syrigana, my studio team… I realised it was ultimately up to me to decide if this would break us apart. We had been working for months on something that was way more meaningful to me and to many people than what happened that day.

My intuition was, let's remake everything that we can. And if the police can assure us that we are secure and if the actors can feel safe again, and they are protecting us and the public day and night, if I can feel assured that nothing will happen to my crew… then I thought, let's not give up.

Let's not make this a big deal but also, let's not allow ourselves to be intimidated or silenced. Let's just make the opera. Because making this cultural event was the biggest win we could have over that act of violence.

I am really grateful that, from Catherine, to the team, to the citizens, everyone was super sympathetic about what happened, but it pulled us together. It gave even more meaning to the event and made clear how important it was to make this experience happen. The actors may have been worried but they never for a moment considered not continuing.

And when the opera premiered, there were more than 1,200 people on the hillside that night. Mostly they came from the village and the region around the towns and cities from all over Kosovo

PH: Ja. Die geopolitische Situation im jugoslawischen Sozialismus war alles andere als ideal – besonders für die albanische Bevölkerung – aber sie war anders. Besser als unter Milošević, besser als alles vor Tito.

Meine Mutter wuchs gemeinsam mit der serbischen Bevölkerung auf. Sie sprach Serbisch, Serb*innen sprachen Albanisch. Das änderte sich in der nächsten Generation. Sprache wurde zur Barriere. Ich selbst spreche zum Beispiel kein Serbisch. Früher nutzten alle gemeinsam das Kulturhaus, spielten Fußball, musizierten. Dann, in den 1990er-Jahren, verbreitete das Milošević-Regime gezielt nationalistische Propaganda über die Medien. Es ist schwer, sich dem als Einzelperson zu entziehen – ganz gleich, wie man persönlich denkt. Mit der Zeit vertiefte sich der nationalistische Riss, der durch die Gesellschaft ging.

Nach dem Krieg hat meine Familie das Haus in Syrigana nie wieder aufgebaut. Deshalb fühlte sich der Abend der Oper fast wie eine Rückkehr an. Auch das erste Zusammentreffen der Zuschauer*innen am Fuß des Hügels und der gemeinsame Aufstieg zur Bühne – das Publikum bewegte sich mitten durch die Szenen. Ich wollte bewusst alle Grenzen und Barrieren auflösen. Auch wenn es eine Oper war, sollte sie inklusiv sein – nichts Elitäres, Unverständliches. Nicht die Bühne dort und das Publikum hier.

Wir haben die Oper daher auch in drei Sprachen übersetzt – Englisch, Albanisch und Serbisch. Um so viele wie möglich einzuschließen. Ich weiß nicht, wie viele Serb*innen tatsächlich gekommen sind, aber serbische Polizist*innen waren da. Und ein serbischer Hirte war ebenfalls im Publikum. Selbst wenn nur wenige kamen – in einem kleinen Dorf ist es ein starkes Signal, inklusiv zu sein.

AZ: Ja, die Übertitel, die neben der Bühne eingeblendet wurden, waren in drei Sprachen. Die Hauptsprache der Oper aber war ‚Tierisch'. Es gab Passagen auf Englisch und Albanisch, aber hauptsächlich handelte es sich um eine Sprache aus einer anderen Welt.

too, but also there were families who came from the diaspora – from Germany and all over the world – and planned their summer holiday in Kosovo around the event. It was so magical to reconnect with former classmates that night, people I hadn't seen since I was attending elementary school there in Syrigana. I also met some friends who came from Sweden… a lot of friends and people came from Berlin too, of course. This was the first sort of cultural event of this scale since the war to gather so many people in Syrigana. This was their day, a huge gathering, because many of them never came back after the war, when their homes were destroyed.

AZ: Your mother grew up in Syrigana, right?

PH: Yes.

AZ: You told me that during the Yugoslavian era, there wasn't the kind of tension that came later, that she actually knew all the kids from the village, whether from the Albanian or Serbian community, and they played together and it was a completely different social arrangement.

PH: Yes. The wider geopolitical reality of Yugoslavian socialism was not an ideal situation either, but a very different one. For the Albanian community, it was never ideal, but still, it was better than what Milošević brought, and it was better than anything that came before Tito.

For one, during that period, my mum grew up alongside the Serbian population, speaking Serbian, and with Serbs knowing Albanian. That changed one generation later. Language is a great barrier – I don't speak Serbian, for example. Second, they would play together, they would share the House of Culture, they would play music or football together… And then in the 1990s, the Milošević regime was intent on building nationalist narratives and spreading propaganda through the media. As an individual, whatever your position, that's very difficult to resist. And over the years, this nationalist divide became bigger and bigger.

After the war, my mum's family never rebuilt their house in Syrigana. It really felt like the night

PH: Genau. Das war wichtig – als Antwort auf die Frage, welche Sprache man wählen sollte. Denn Albanisch, Serbisch oder Englisch – jede dieser Entscheidungen hätte eine exklusive Wirkung gehabt. Deshalb entschied ich mich dafür, Tiere in die Hauptrollen zu setzen. Die Geschichte von Adam und Eva wurde von einem Fuchs und einem Hahn gespielt – erzählt von zwei Vögeln, zwei Sopranistinnen. Die Sopranistinnen sangen nicht nur wie Vögel, sondern sprachen auch wie Vögel sprechen würden. Ihre Stimmen waren nicht-menschlich. Mir war es wichtig, einen Raum für alle zu schaffen, in dem Sprache keine ethnisch motivierte Position einnimmt.

Als ich Nina Guo, eine der beiden Sopranistinnen, die die Vokalpartitur komponiert hat, traf und ihr die Rolle, die ich mir vorstellte, erklärte, sagte sie: „Das ist ein Traumjob für mich als Sopranistin, die sich für experimentelle Musik interessiert." Das war ein großes Glück für uns.

AZ: Die beiden Projekte – dein Impuls, eine Oper zu schreiben, und die Einladung zu einer Ausstellung im Hamburger Bahnhof – wurden gewissermaßen zum Anlass für das jeweils andere, auf sehr schöne und produktive Weise. Denn für einen Künstler, der ein Leben wie du geführt hat, ist es nicht einfach zu wissen, wie man sich im aktuellen politischen Klima in Deutschland einbringen kann. Die Art von Resonanz zwischen zwei Orten und Zeiten, die du mit diesem Projekt herstellst, scheint deine Antwort auf diese drängende Frage zu sein.

PH: Ja. Ich habe palettenweise Rohbau-Ruinen des Kulturhauses in Runik, die ich seit der Inszenierung von *Shkrepëtima* im Jahr 2018 aufbewahrt habe, ins Museum gebracht und in die Installation integriert. Sie sind einfach nach Materialien sortiert und auf Paletten gestapelt, wo sie darauf warten, Ende des Jahres wieder aufgebaut oder wiederverwendet zu werden. Es ist sehr bewegend, etwas an einen Ort zu bringen, von dem ich hoffe, dass er in 30 Jahren noch immer ein wichtiges Haus für

of the opera, somehow, especially with the initial gathering at the bottom of the hill, and the parade up to the stage with the public moving among the actors... I tried to blur boundaries and borders as much as possible with these gestures. Even though it is an opera, it was inclusive, not something elitist that you can't understand, where you sit here and the stage is there...

The reason we translated the opera into three languages – English, Albanian and Serbian – was to be inclusive. I don't know how many Serbs actually came, but there were Serbian members of the police, and there was a shepherd who came. Even if just a few Serbs came, it's so important to be inclusive, especially in such a small village.

AZ: Yes, the titles (which were flashing next to the stage) were in three languages. But the main language of the opera, however, was in fact, "animal". There were parts in English, parts in Albanian, but it was primarily an otherworldly language.

PH: Yes. It was super important, a response to the idea that if you were to perform the opera just in Albanian, or Serbian or English, all of these choices would also be exclusive positions. That's why I decided to cast animals in the main roles in the first place. To have Adam and Eve's story played by a fox and a rooster, and their story told by two birds, two sopranos.

By having the sopranos not just be but also speak like birds, to take on other-than-human voices, was an attempt to build space for everyone, where language is not taking some kind of ethnically motivated position.

When I met Nina Guo, one of the two sopranos, who composed the vocal score, and explained the role I had in mind, she said, 'This is a dream job for me as a soprano who is into experimental music.' We were lucky with that.

Kultur sein wird. Ich brauchte einen Weg, um irgendwie eine Tür zu öffnen, um mich dieser Ausstellung zu nähern.

Es ist wichtig, hier zu sein und diese Ausstellung zu machen, Raum einzunehmen und unsere Sichtweisen zu teilen – es ist auch ein großes Privileg. An einer bestimmten Stelle in *Syrigana*, nachdem der Schneider ihre Hochzeit ruiniert hat, müssen die Adam- und Eva-Figuren, Fuchs und Hahn, entscheiden, ob sie bleiben oder gehen sollen. Hahn sagt: „Schau dir die Blumen an, lass uns noch eine Nacht bleiben. Geben wir dem Ganzen noch einmal eine Chance. Bleiben wir hier." Als wir hörten, dass die beiden Container verbrannt waren, war es wichtig, nicht aufzugeben und die Oper nicht abzusagen. Und zu bleiben. „Bleib, bleib, bleib...", wie sie in der Oper singen...

AZ: The two projects – your impulse to make an opera and the invitation to do an exhibition at Hamburger Bahnhof – one became an excuse for the other in a way, in a very beautiful and productive way. Because it's not easy for an artist who has lived the life you've lived to know how to participate in the current political climate in Germany. The sort of reverberation between two places and times you set up through this project seems to be your way to answer this looming question.

PH: Yeah. The ruins of the House of Culture that I kept since we staged *Shkrepëtima* in 2018 – I brought pallets and pallets of ruins to the museum and incorporated them in the installation. They are just divided into materials and stacked on pallets waiting to be rebuilt or reused in the restoration starting at the end of the year. It's very touching to bring something to a place that I hope in 30 more years will still be an incredible house of culture. I needed a path, to open some door somehow to approach this exhibition.

It's important to be here and to do this show, to take up space and share our points of view – it is also a great privilege. At a certain point in *Syrigana*, after the Tailor tries to ruin their wedding, the Adam and Eve characters, Fox and Rooster, have to decide whether to stay or to leave. Rooster says, 'Look at the flowers, let's stay just another night. Let's give it another chance. Let's be here.' When we heard that the two containers had been burned, it was important not to give up and not to cancel the opera. And to stay. 'Stay, stay, stay...', as they sing in the opera...

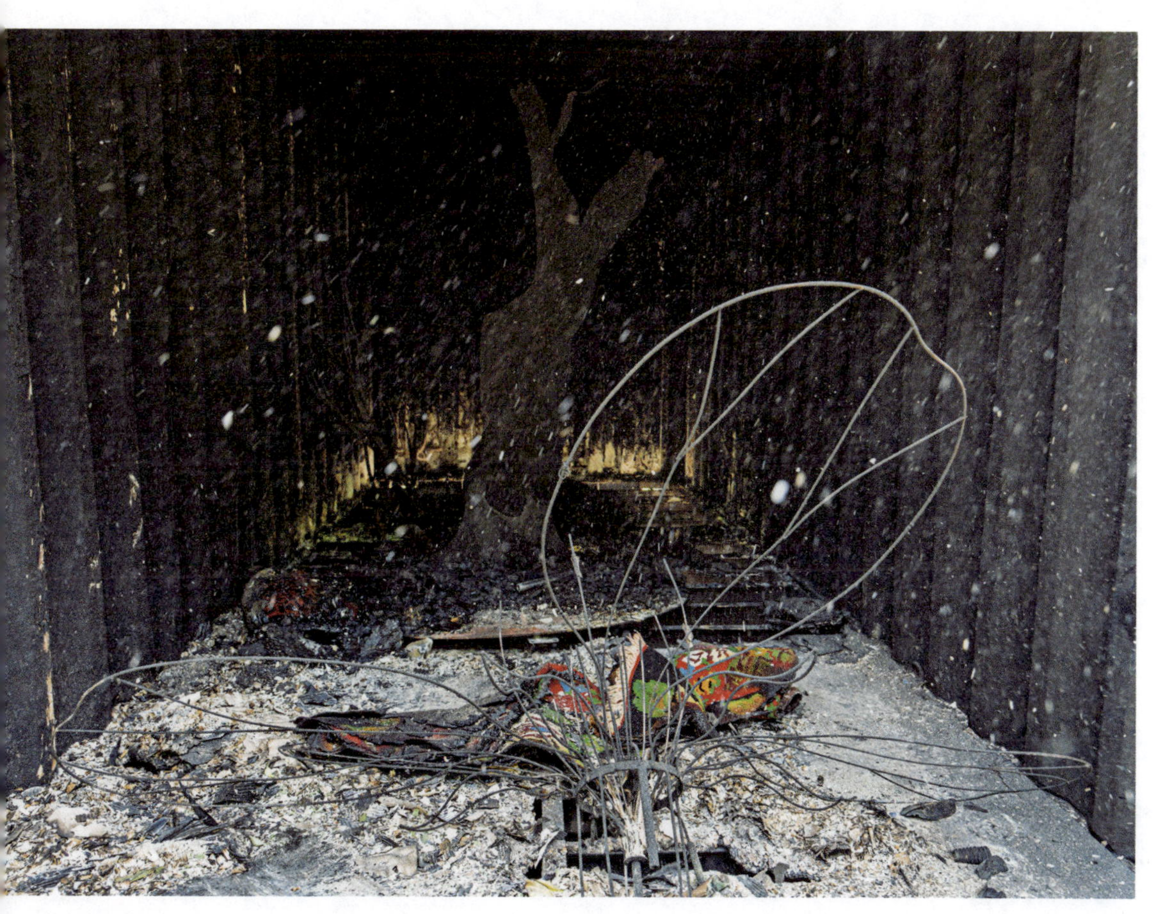

Verbrannte Überreste von *Syrigana*-Requisiten nach einem **Brandanschlag** / Charred remains of *Syrigana* props after an arson attack, **Syrigana, 2025**

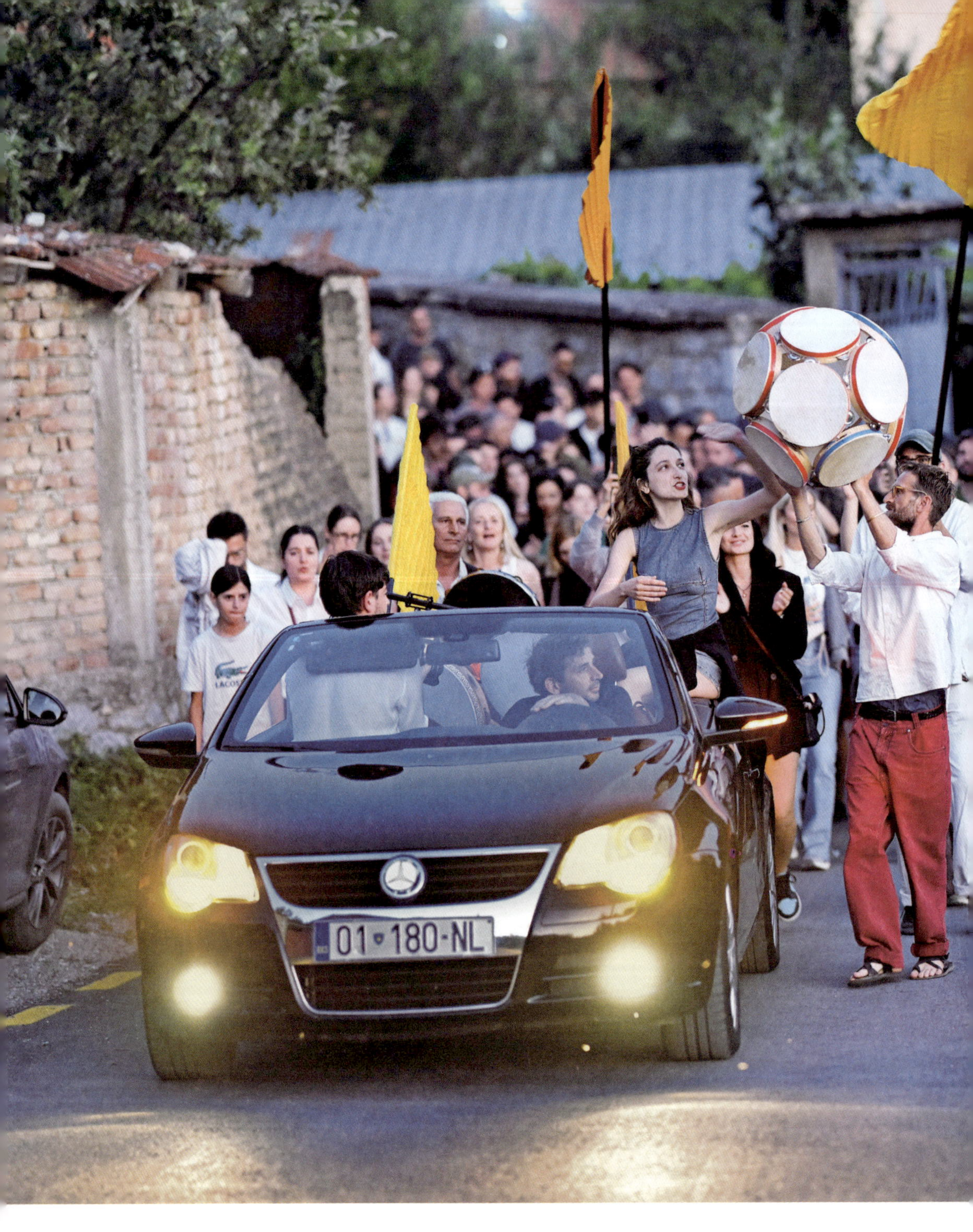

Straßenumzug durch Syrigana hoch zum Gjyteti-Felsen / Parade up the streets of Syrigana towards Gjyteti, **Syrigana, 2025**

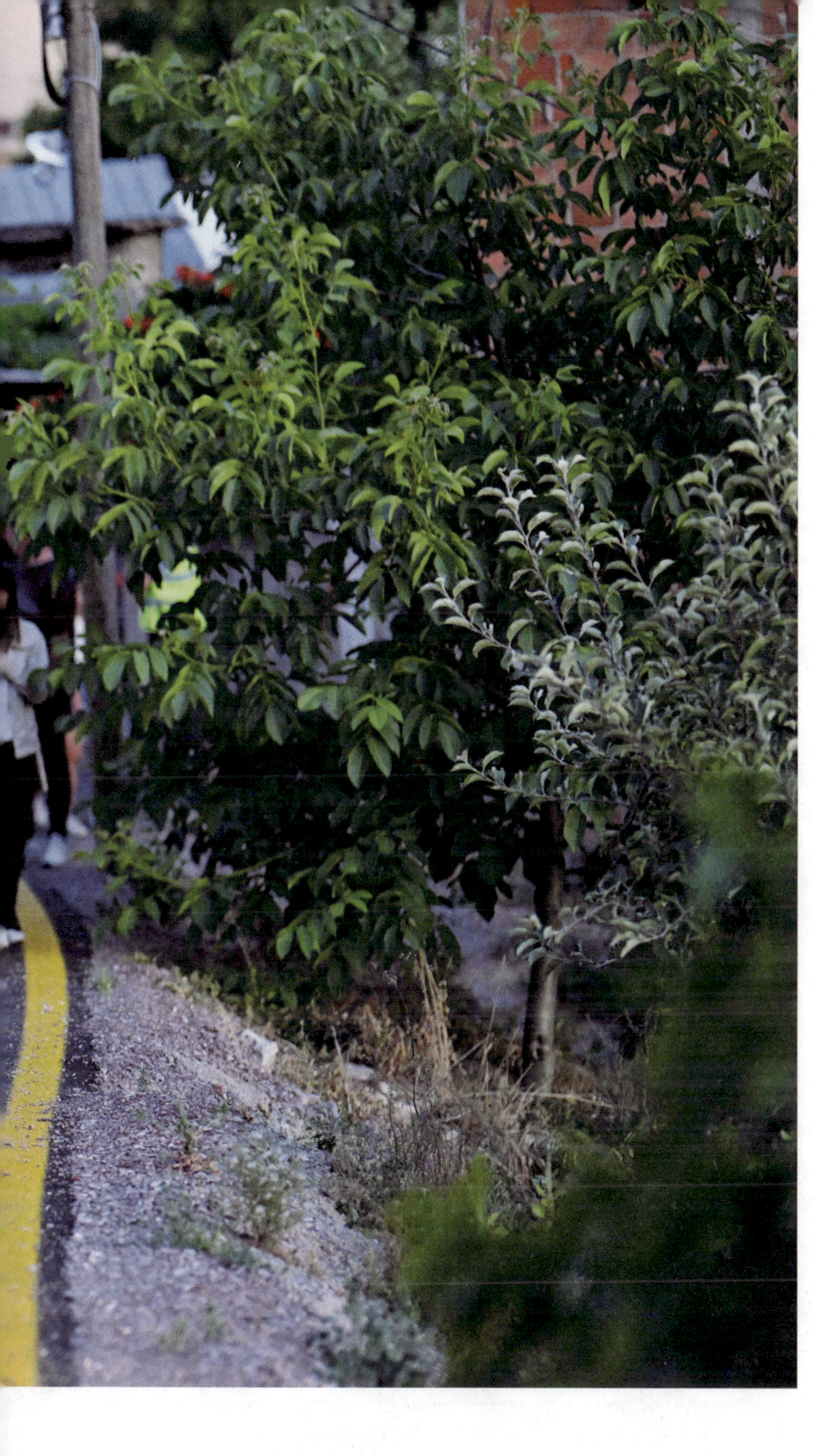

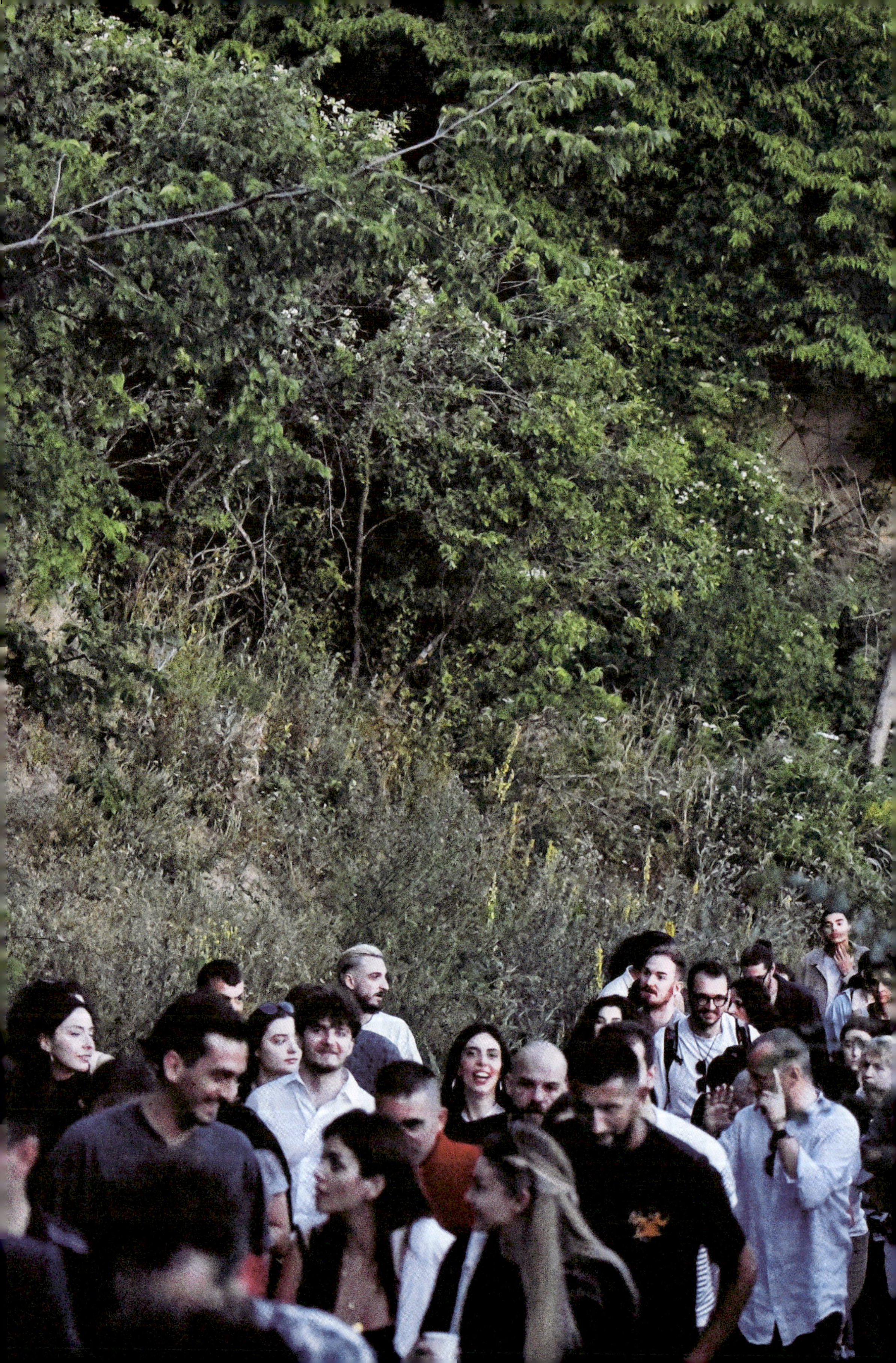

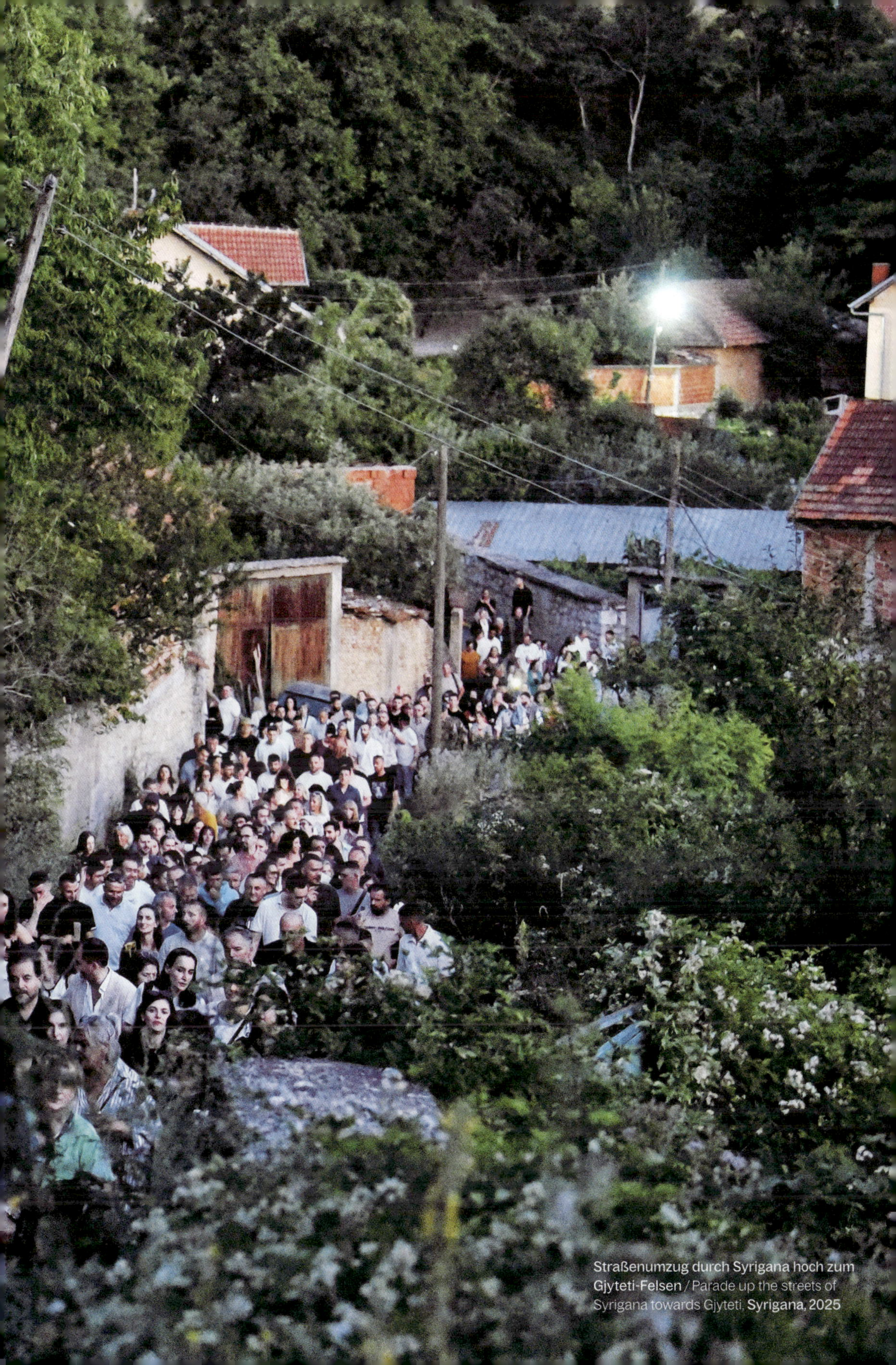

Straßenumzug durch Syrigana hoch zum Gjyteti-Felsen / Parade up the streets of Syrigana towards Gjyteti, Syrigana, 2025

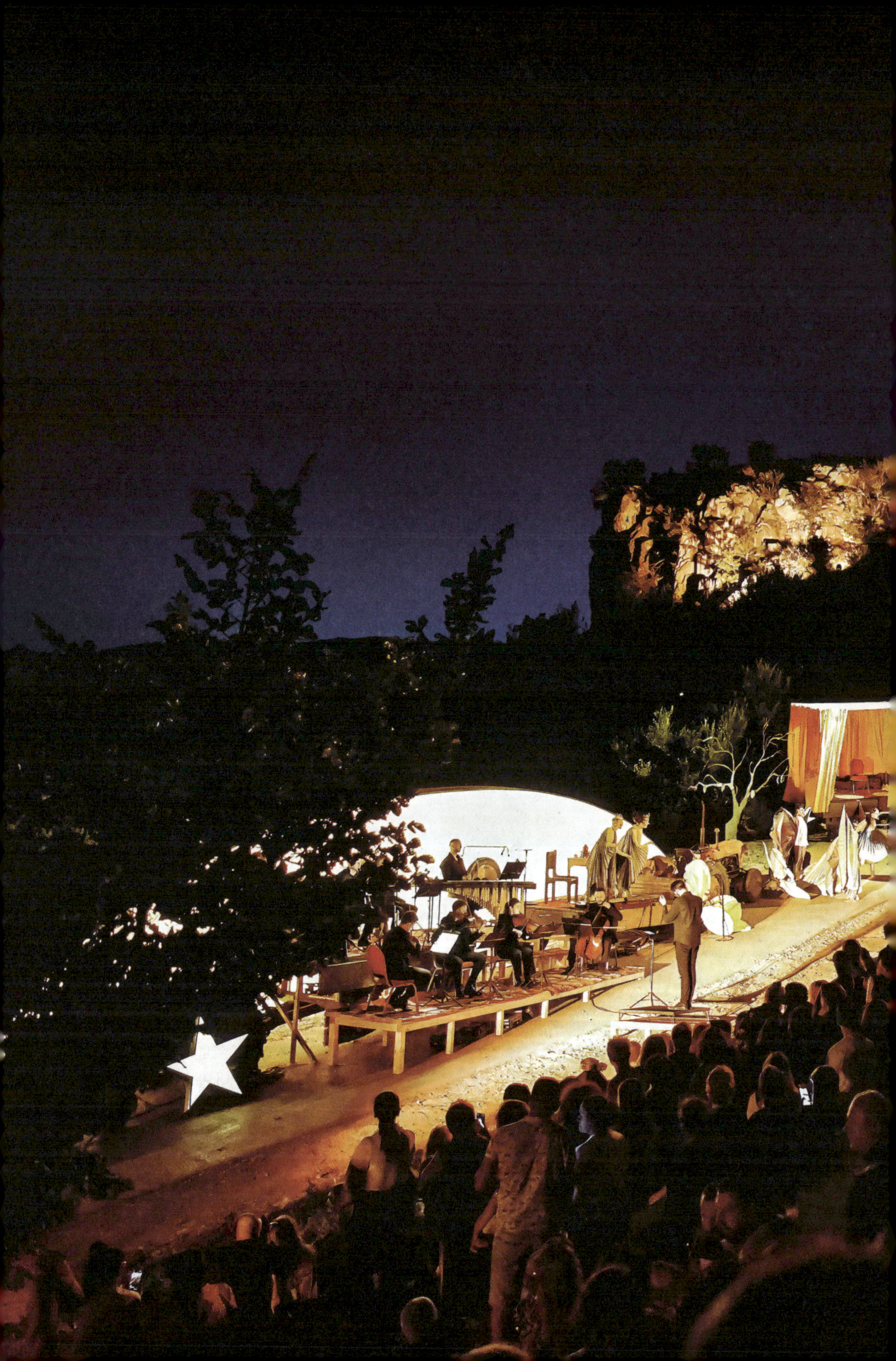

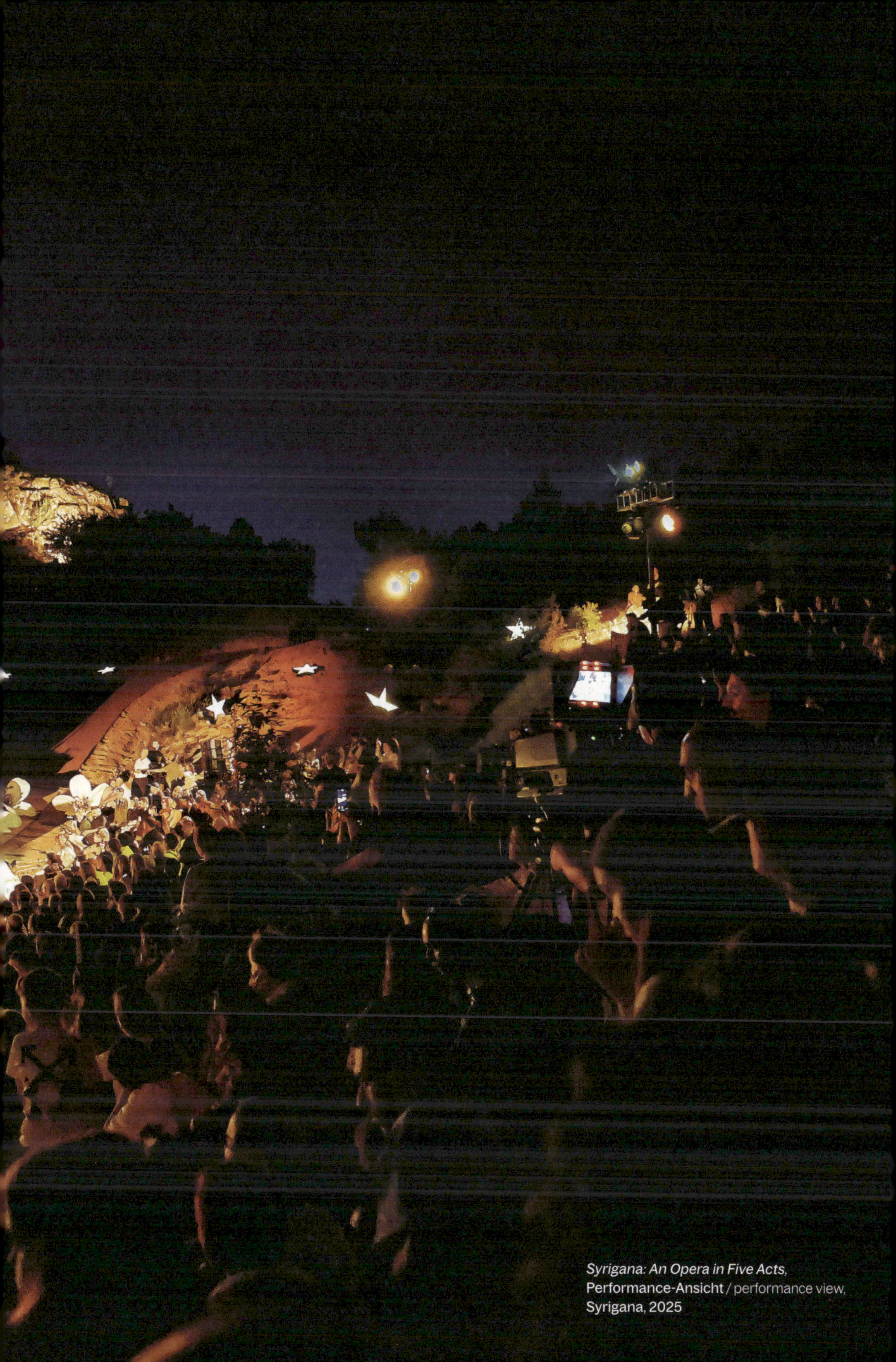

Syrigana: An Opera in Five Acts,
Performance-Ansicht / performance view,
Syrigana, 2025

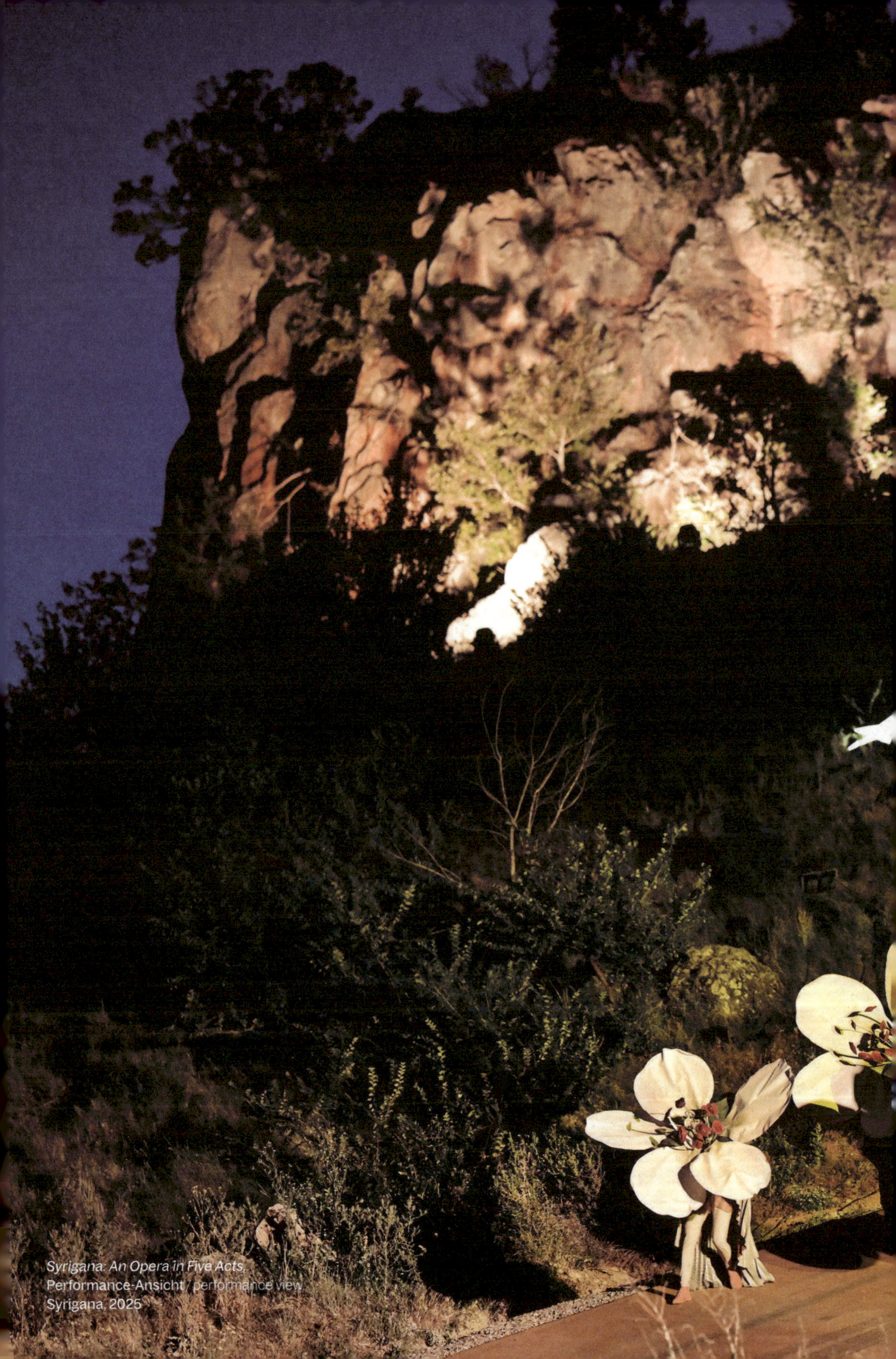

Syrigana: An Opera in Five Acts,
Performance-Ansicht / performance view
Syrigana, 2025

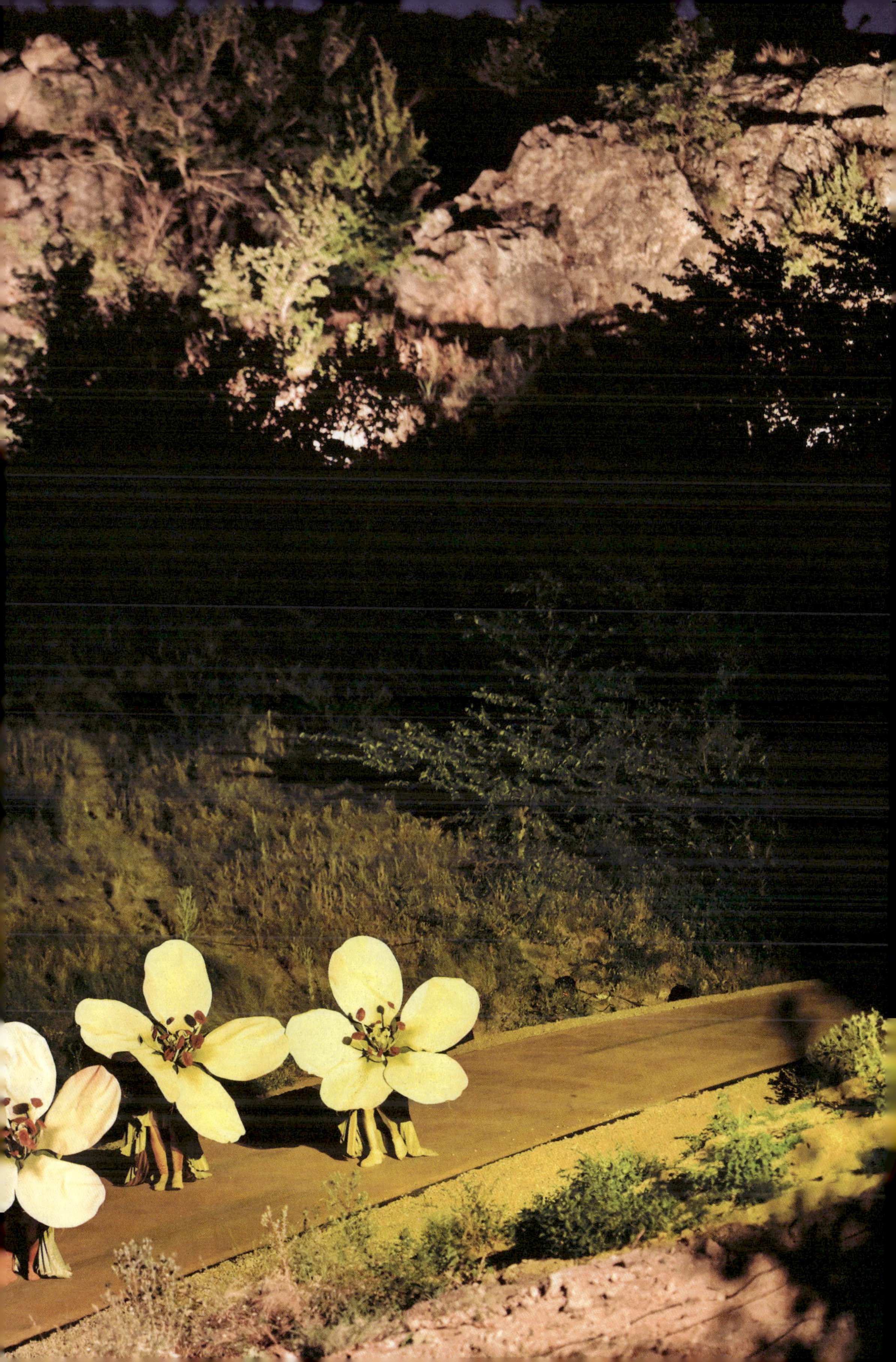

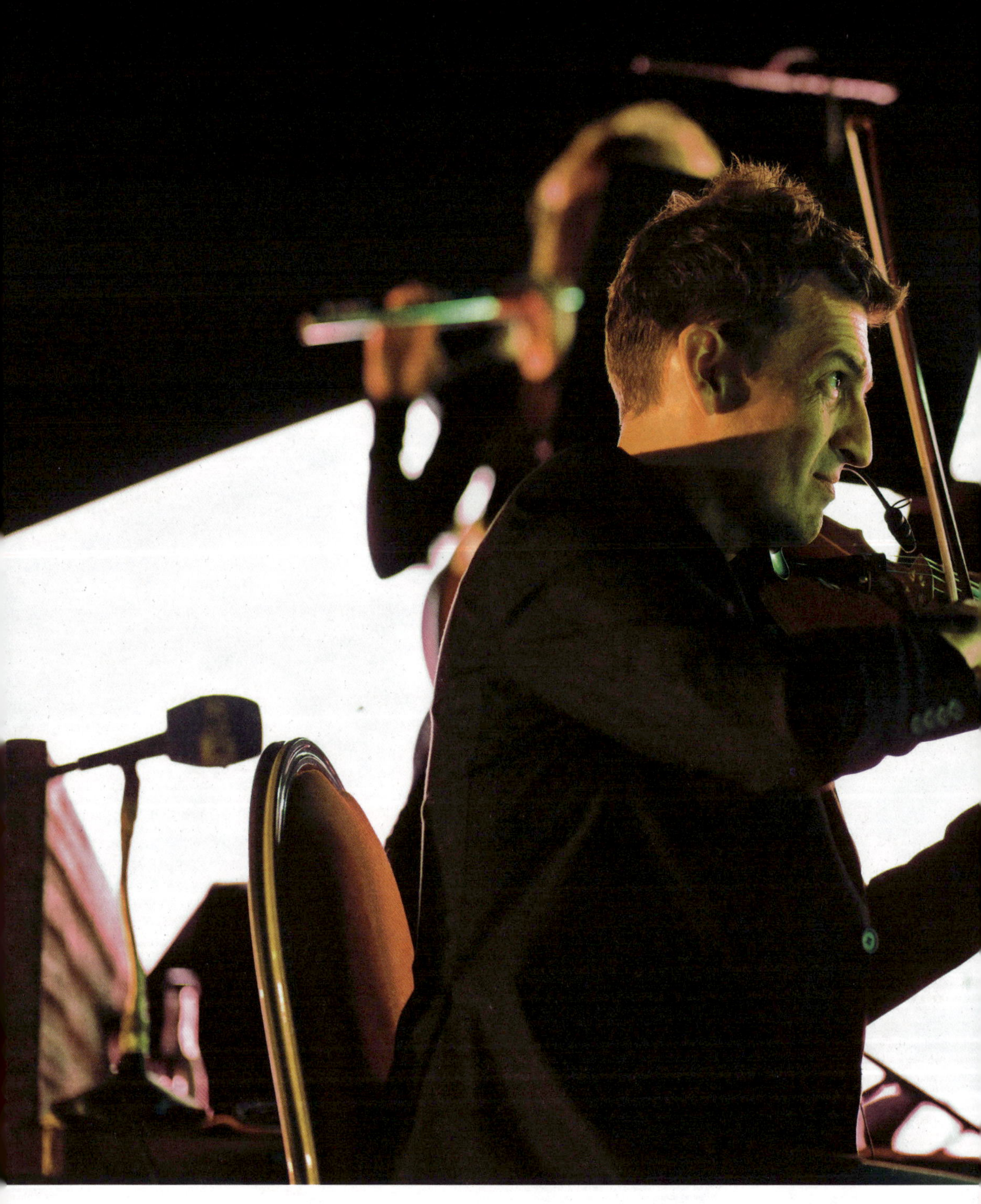

Syrigana: An Opera in Five Acts,
Performance-Ansicht / performance view,
Syrigana, 2025

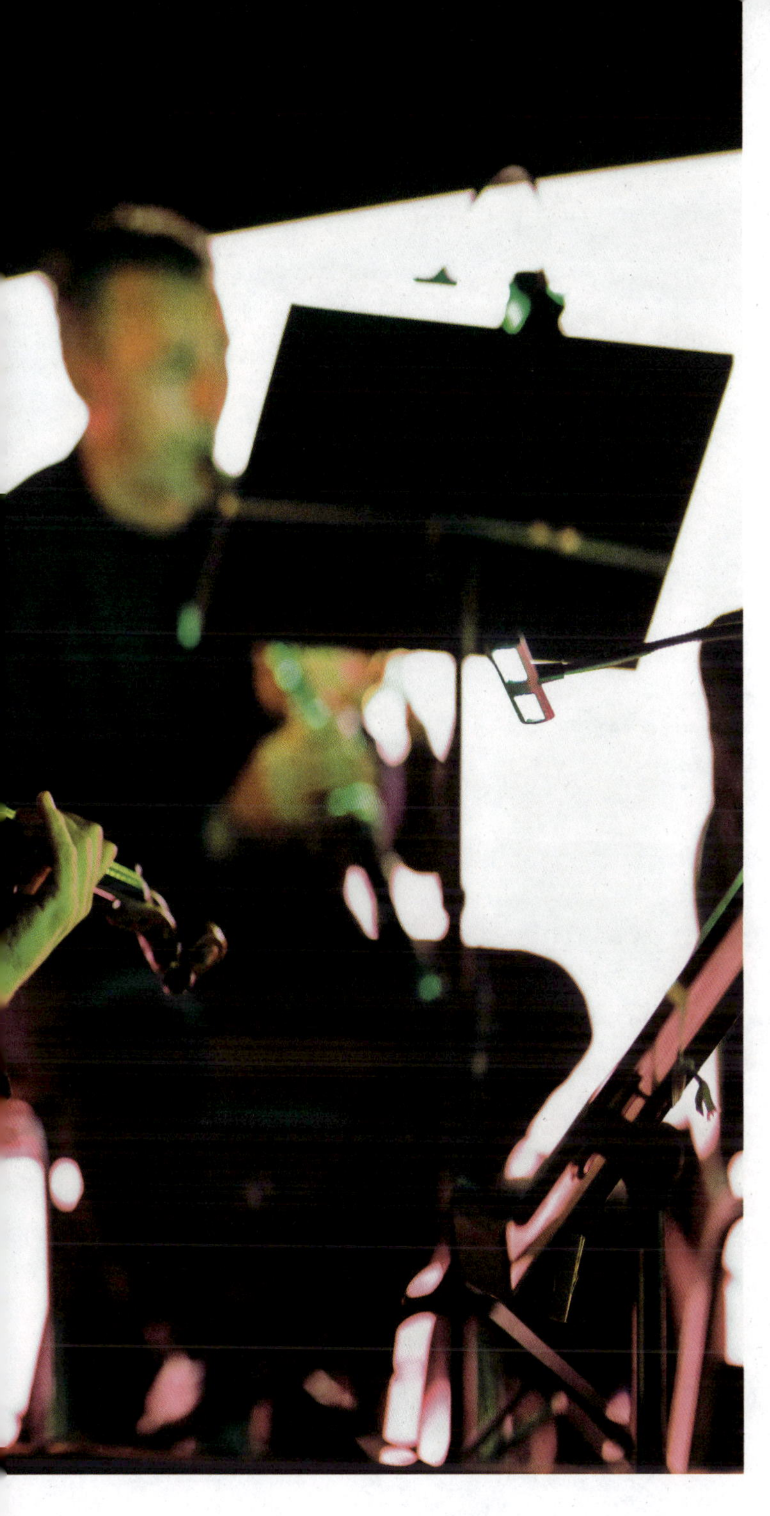

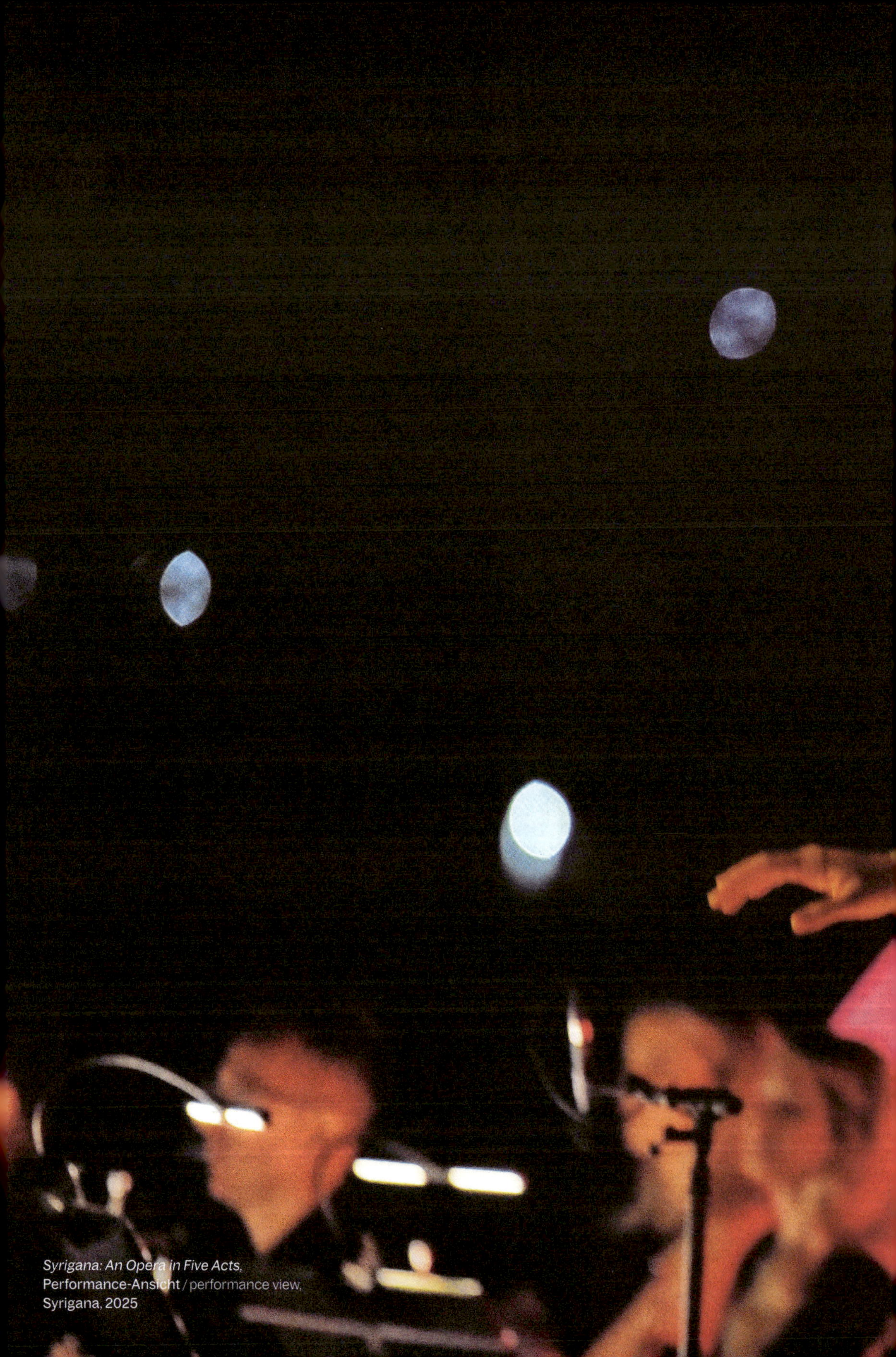

Syrigana: An Opera in Five Acts,
Performance-Ansicht / performance view,
Syrigana, 2025

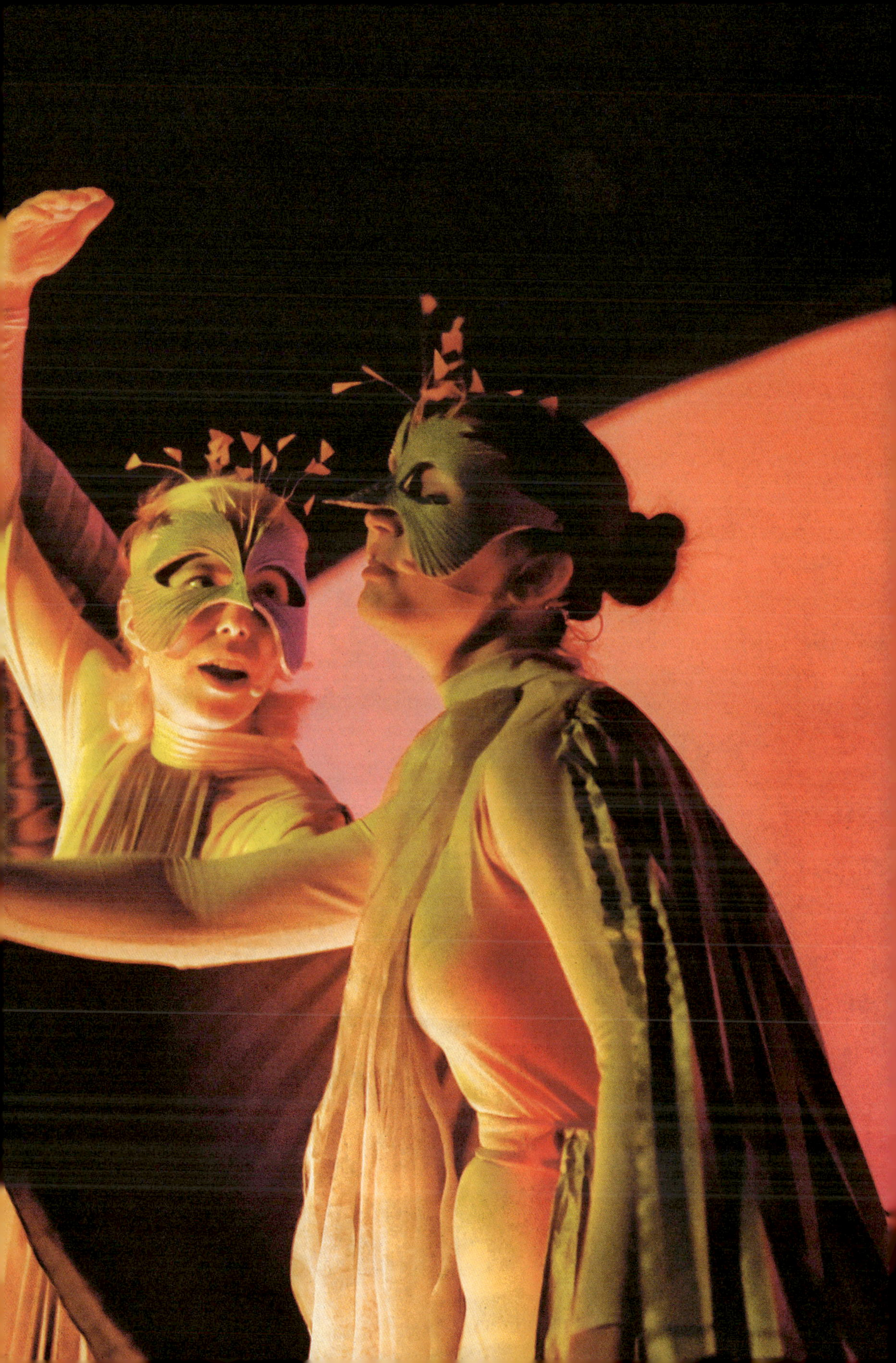

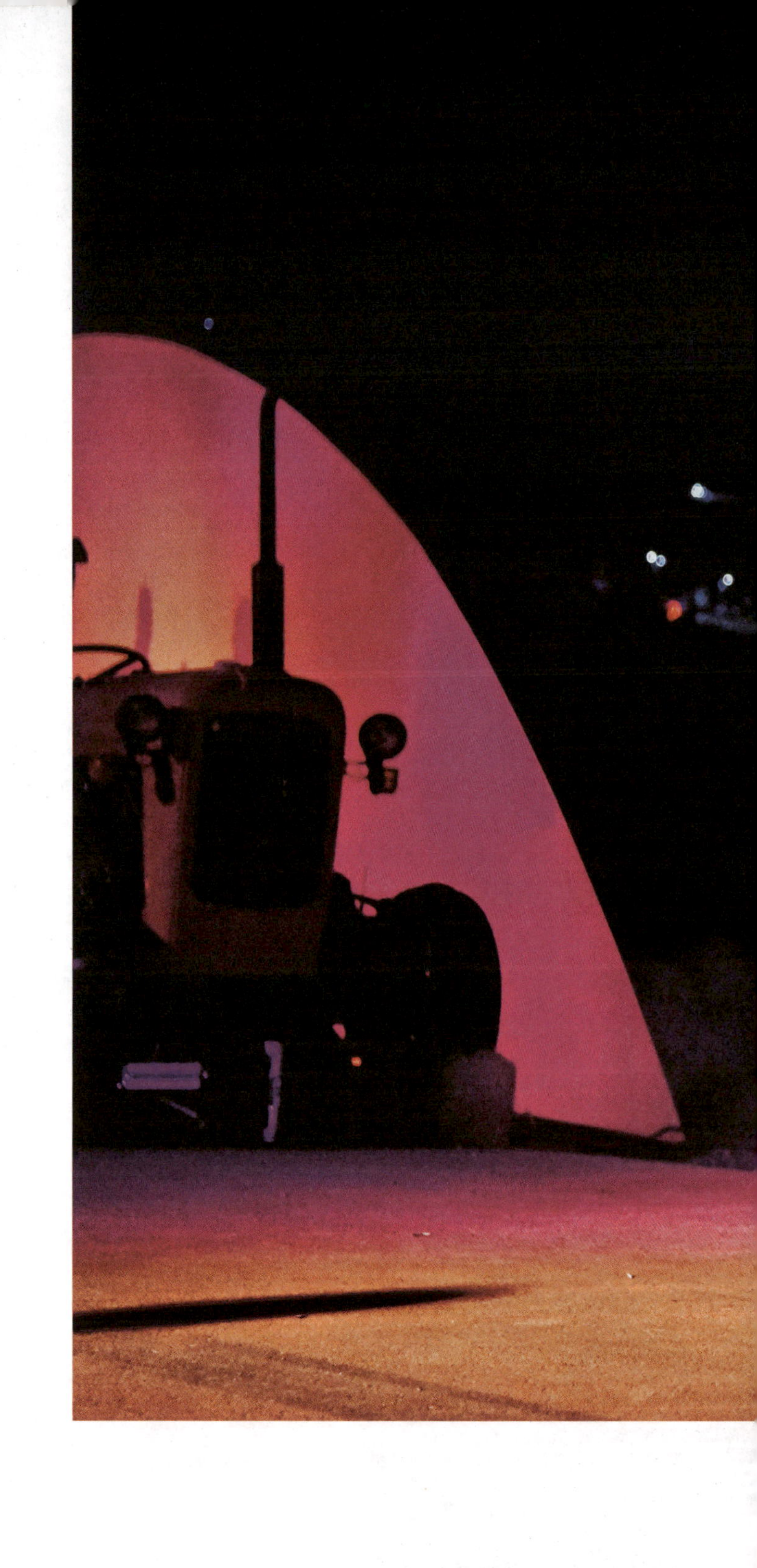

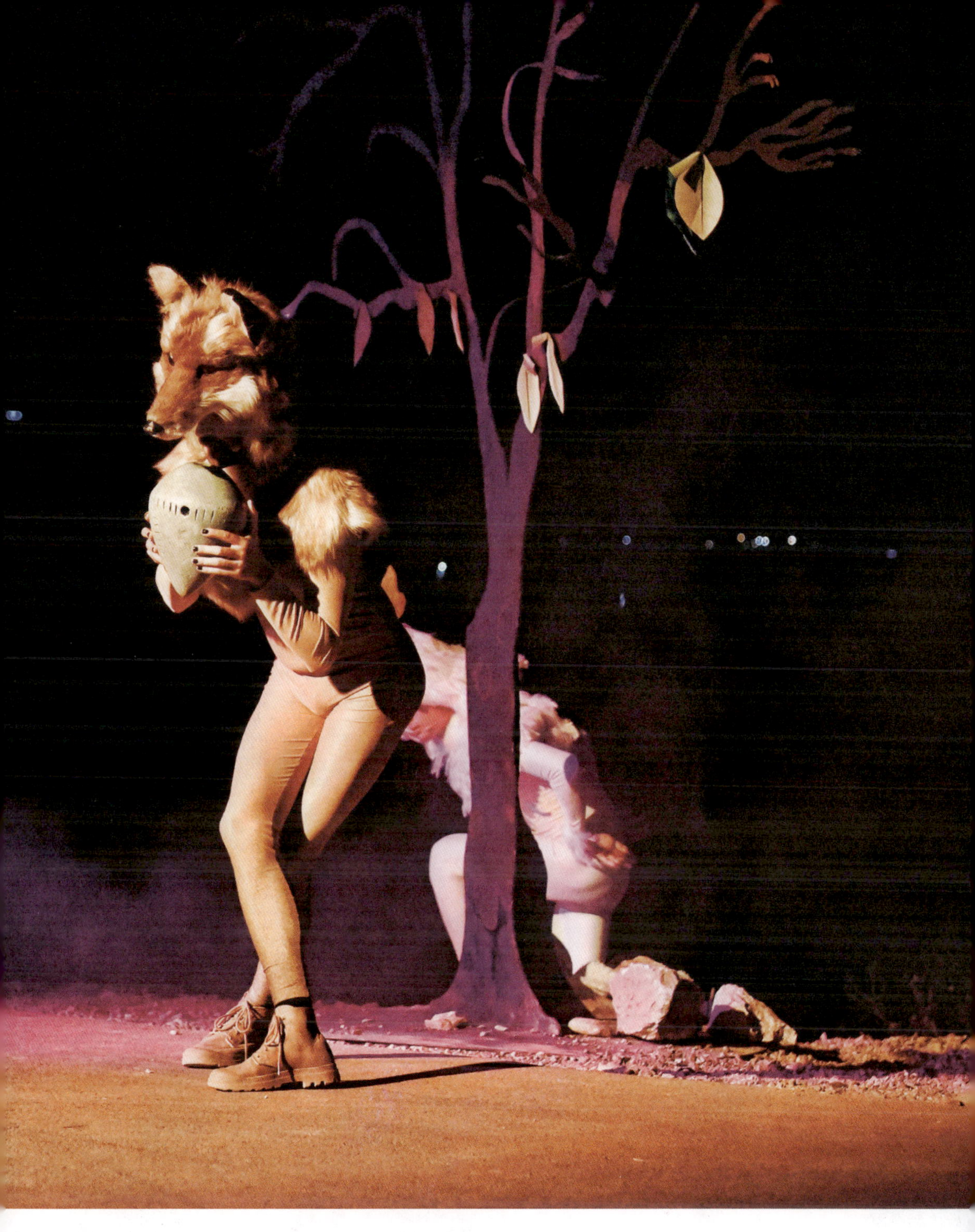

Syrigana: An Opera in Five Acts,
Performance-Ansicht / performance view,
Syrigana, 2025

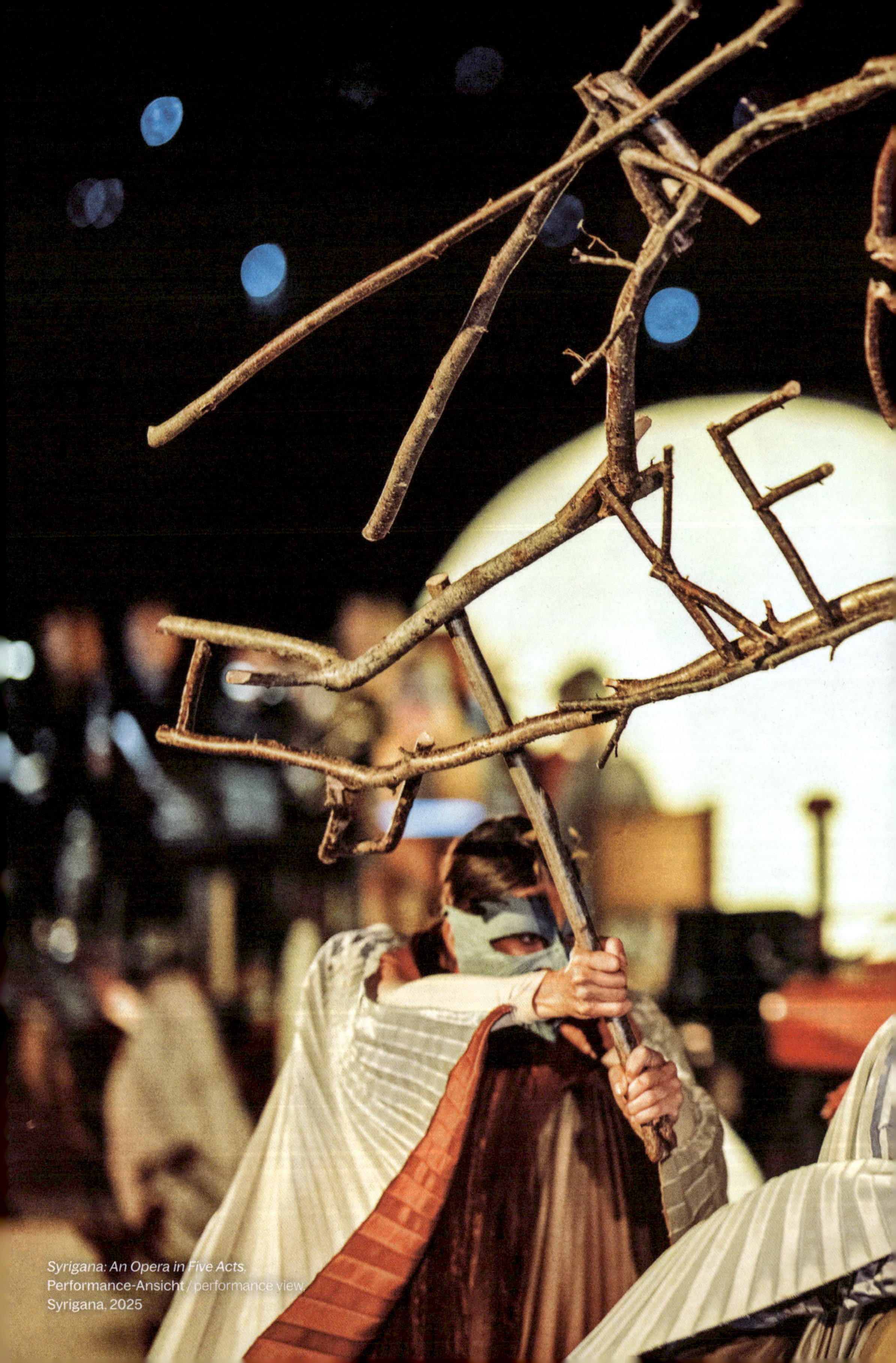

Syrigana: An Opera in Five Acts.
Performance-Ansicht / performance view.
Syrigana, 2025

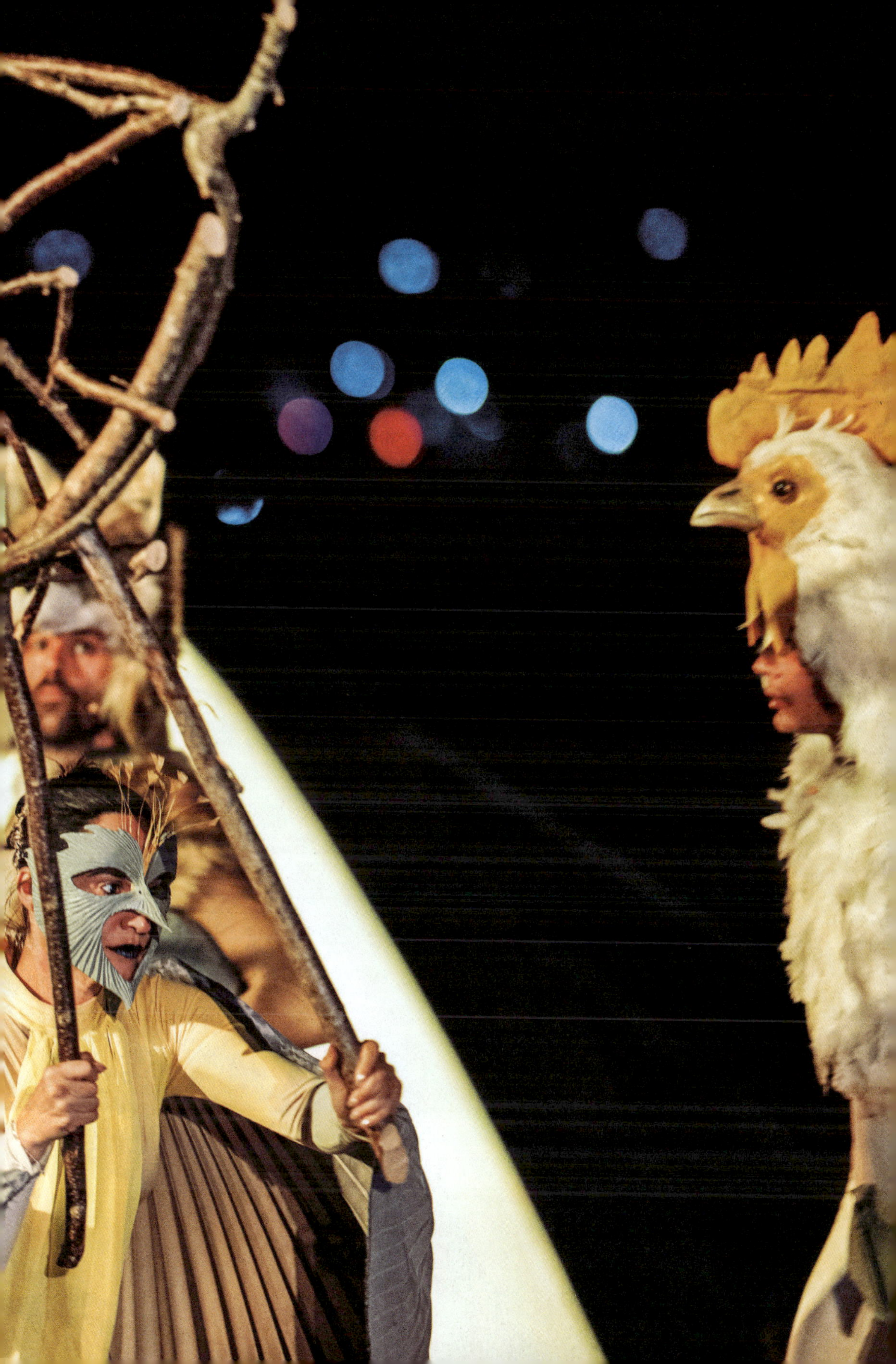

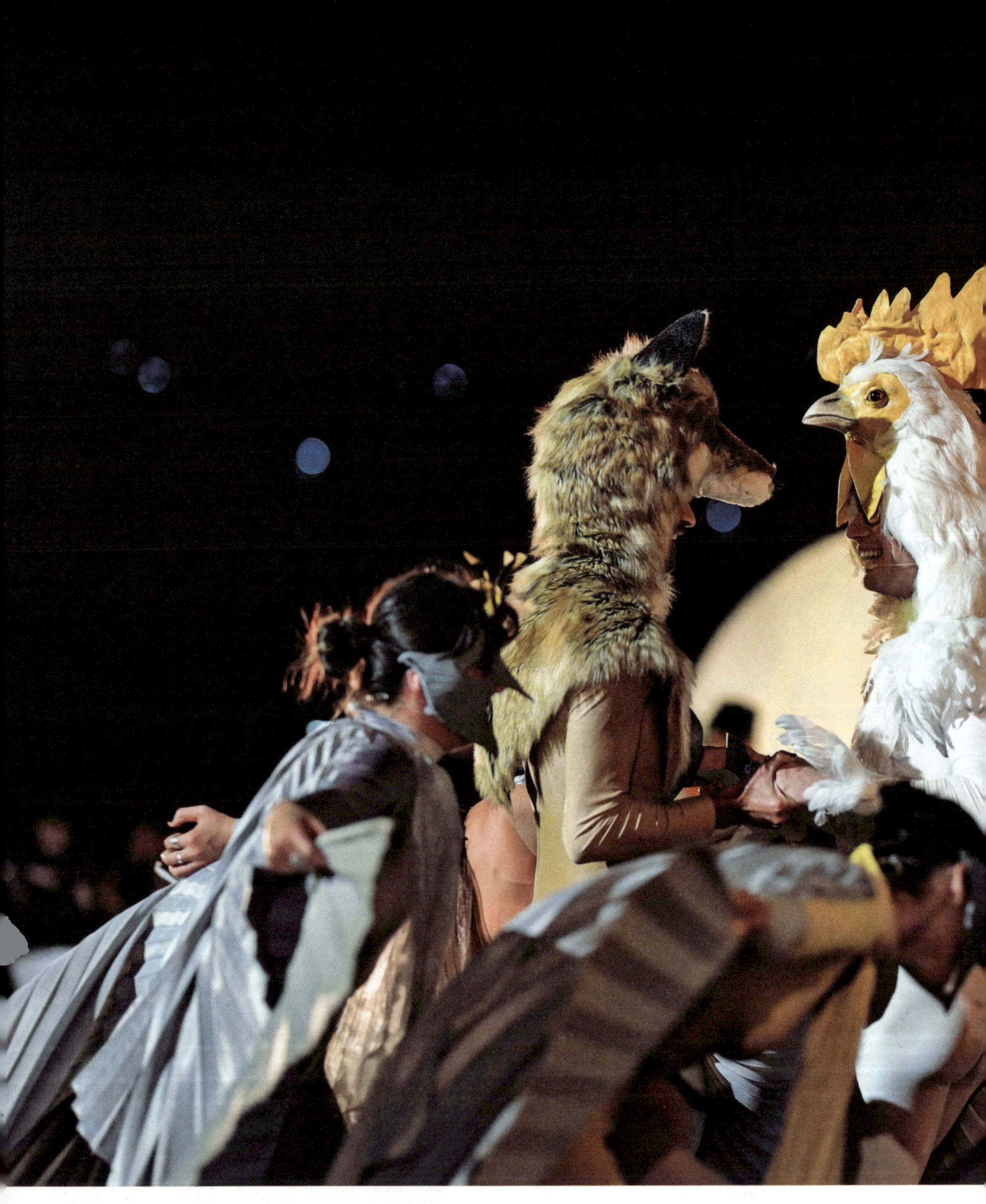

Syrigana: An Opera in Five Acts,
Performance-Ansicht / performance view,
Syrigana, 2025

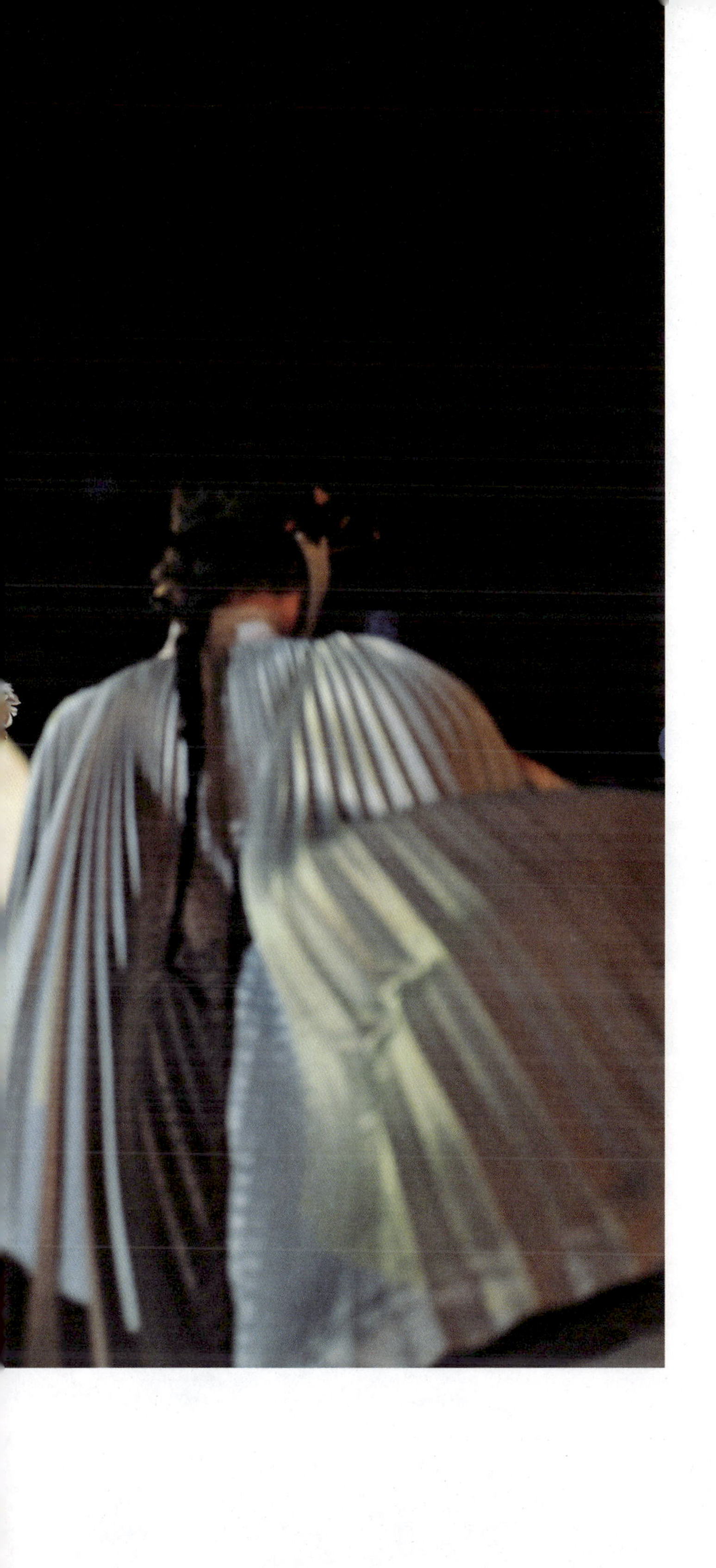

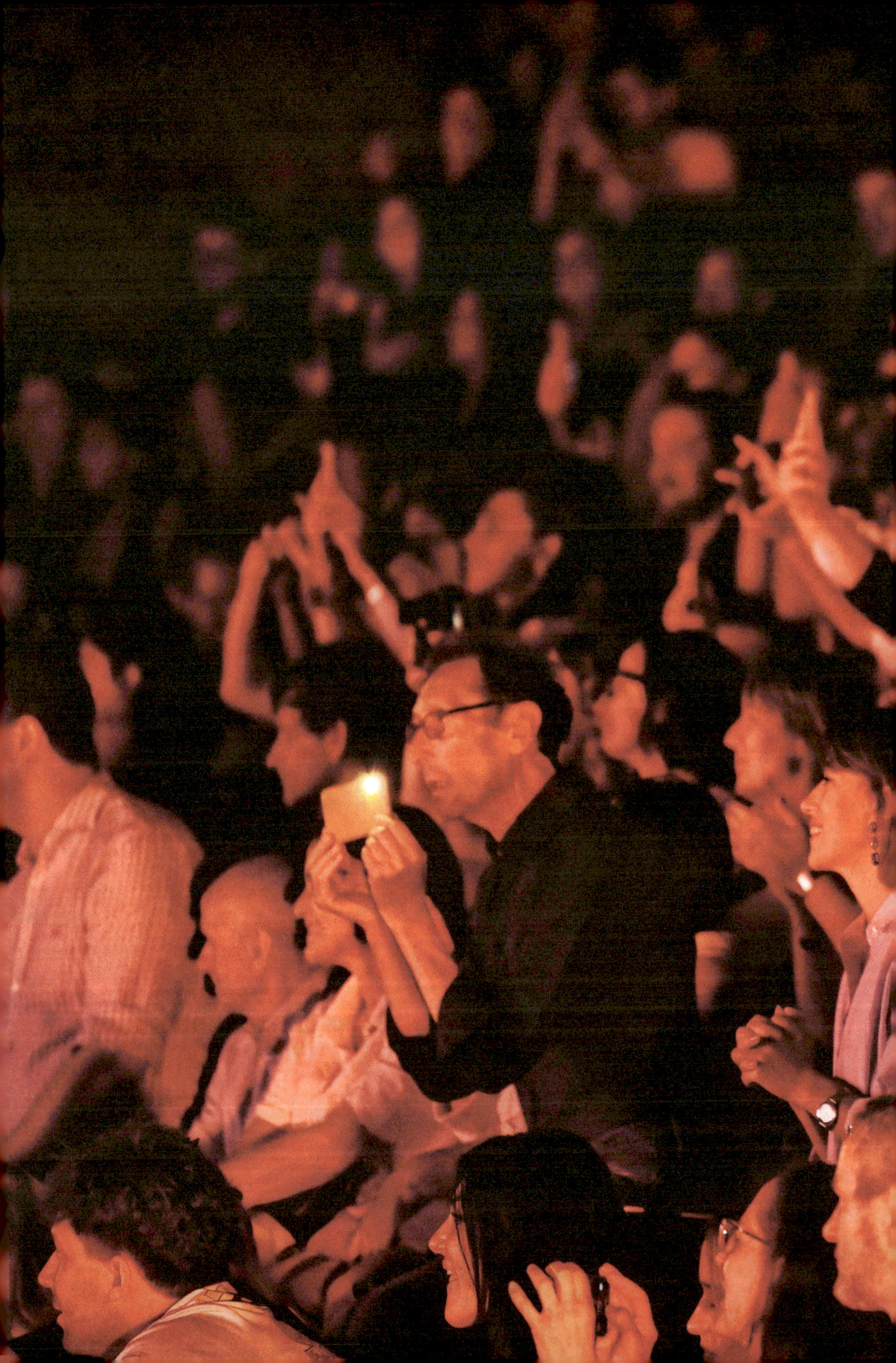

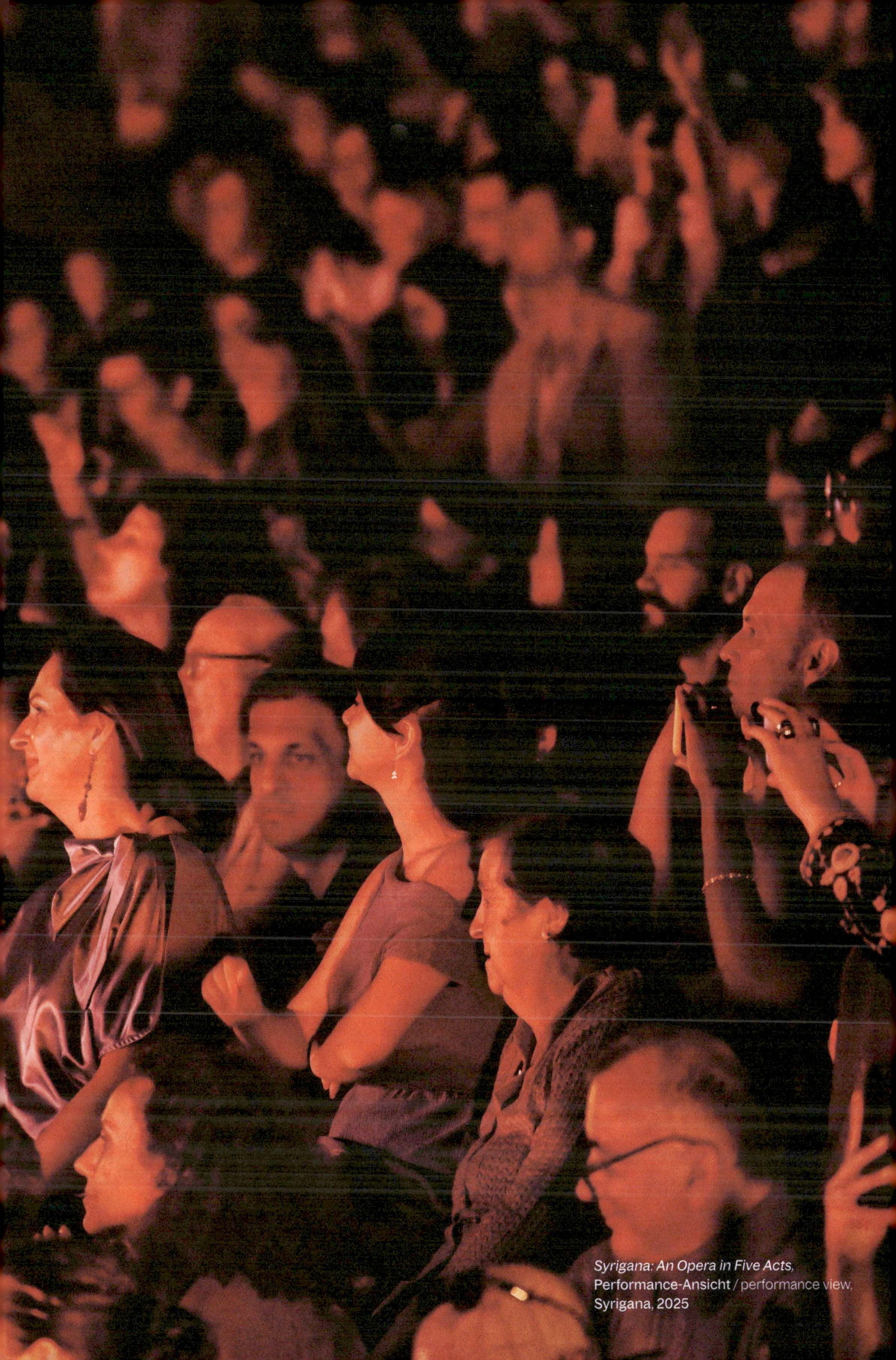

Syrigana: An Opera in Five Acts,
Performance-Ansicht / performance view,
Syrigana, 2025

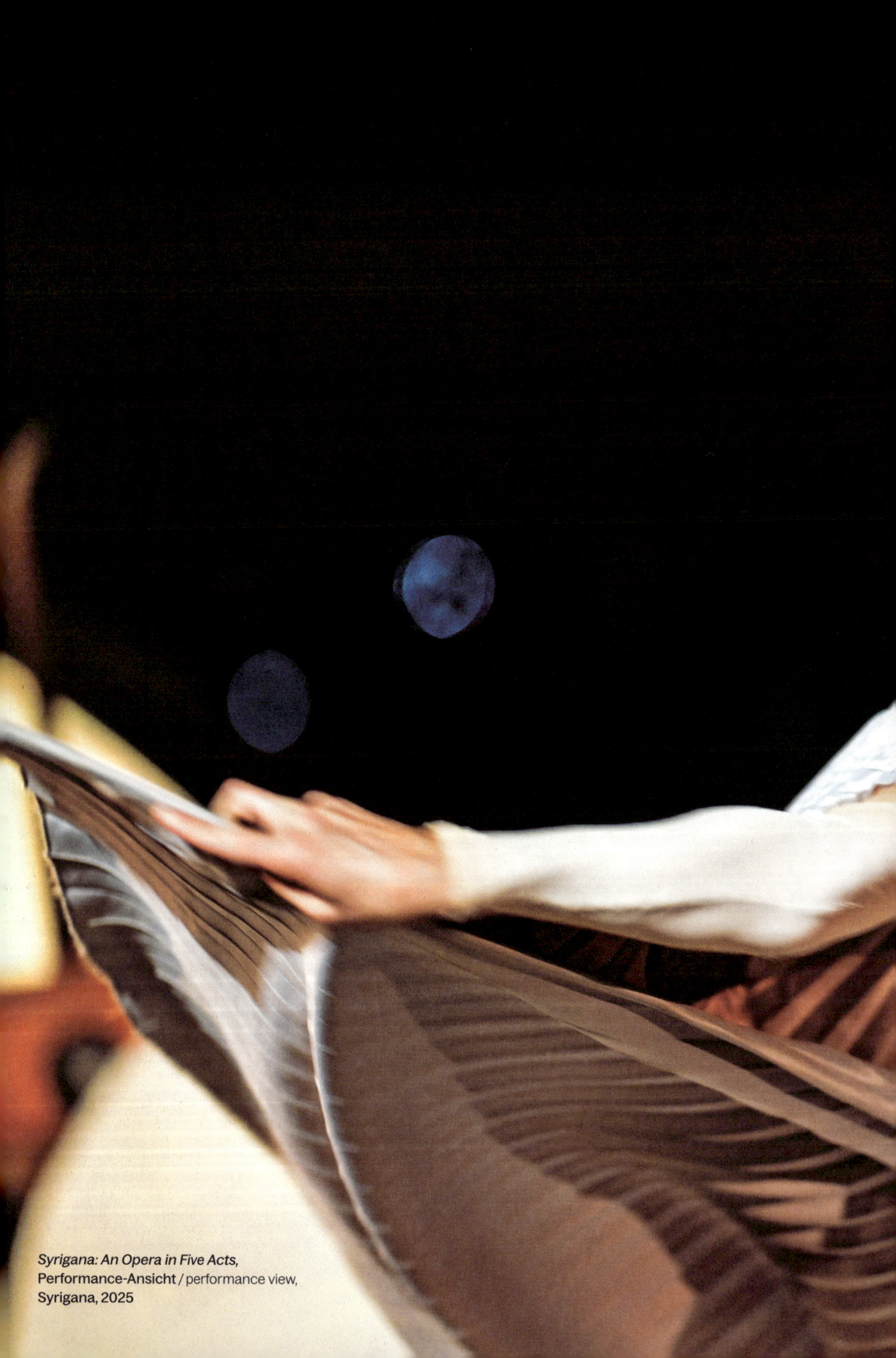

Syrigana: An Opera in Five Acts,
Performance-Ansicht / performance view,
Syrigana, 2025

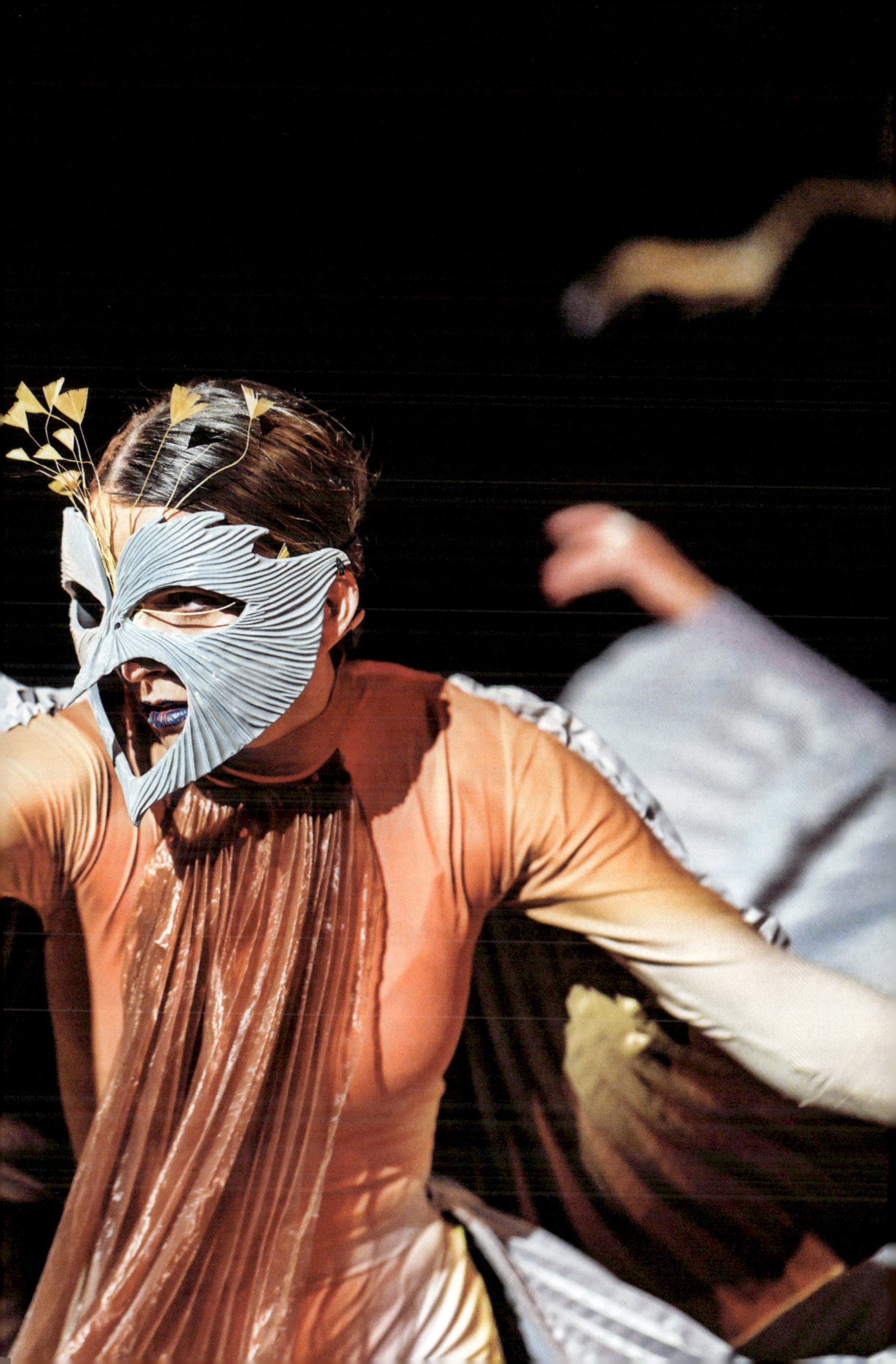

Fitzcarraldo-Träume in Syrigana / Fitzcarraldian Dreams in Syrigana

Lura Limani

Syrigana: An Opera in Five Acts ist Petrit Halilajs bislang ambitionierteste Arbeit. Der Künstler kehrte mit seiner Menagerie blauer Vögel in seine Heimatregion zurück, um sich mit der Fülle an Geschichte(n) zu beschäftigen, die der Ort Syrigana für ihn und die dort ansässigen Menschen in sich birgt. In Kooperation mit dem Philharmonischen Orchester des Kosovos brachte Halilaj ein Ensemble von Künstler*innen zusammen, um gemeinsam eine epische Liebesgeschichte zu inszenieren. Die Premiere des opernähnlichen Werks fand in dem titelgebenden Dorf statt, und der massige Felsen Gjyteti, von dem es heißt, er habe schon in der späten Bronzezeit einer Festung als Ständort gedient, fungierte dabei als eine natürliche Kulisse.

In Syrigana verbindet sich die kulturelle Bedeutung einer historischen Stätte mit der

Syrigana: An Opera in Five Acts is Petrit Halilaj's most ambitious work to date. The artist returned with his menagerie of blue birds to his home region to engage with the multitude of histories the place encompasses for him and his townspeople. In collaboration with the Kosovo Philharmonic Orchestra, Halilaj brought together an ensemble of artists to bring to life an epic love story. It was first enacted in the eponymous village, with the massive boulder of Gjyteti – believed to have been used as a fortress as early as the Late Bronze Age – serving as a natural backdrop.

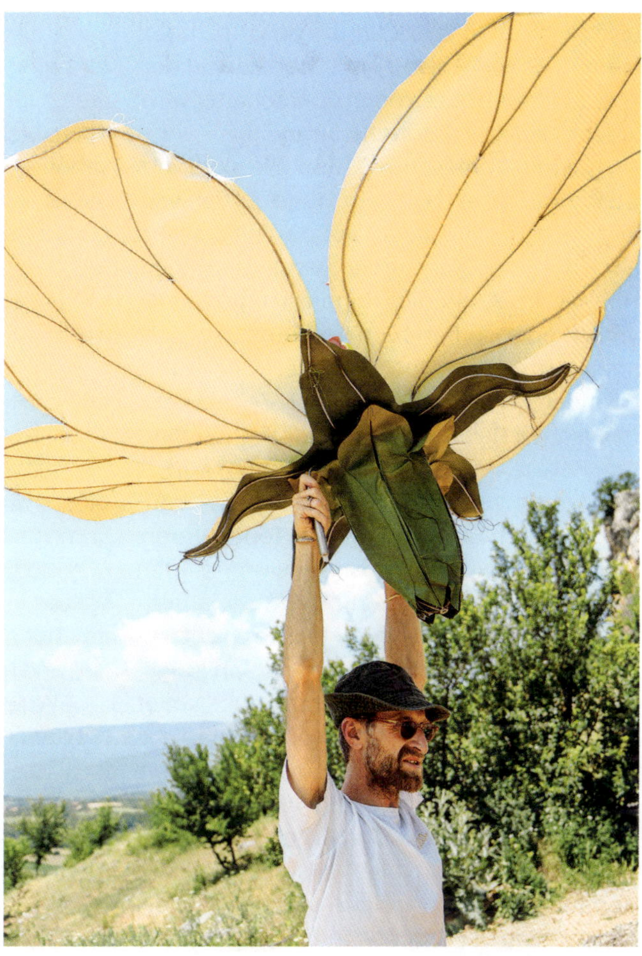

Syrigana: An Opera in Five Acts, **Probenfoto** / rehearsal view, **Syrigana, 2025**

zentralen Rolle, die der Ort in Halilajs Werk und Leben spielt. Die Region, von der angenommen wird, dass dort seit mindestens 3.500 Jahren fortlaufend Menschen ansässig waren, ist als Stätte von archäologischer Bedeutung bislang wenig erforscht. Angesichts der Gefährdung durch Plünderungen wird die Gegend von Ansässigen jedoch nach Kräften verteidigt; die Dorfbewohner*innen sind die ersten, Fragen zu stellen, wenn sie Fremde in der Region umherstreifen sehen. Im Mai betört der Duft von Holunderblüten die Sinne, während man den frisch verlegten Asphalt entlangspaziert, der zu der prähistorischen Festung führt; von dem steil aufsteigenden Felsen bietet sich eine spektakuläre Aussicht auf die Ebenen von Dukagjini und Drenica. Schaut man unten, sieht man die akkuraten Vierecksformen von Gehöften, die von albanischen

Syrigana is a site that intertwines the cultural significance of a historical site with the imaginary and lived personal attachment that Halilaj has to the place. A location believed to have been continuously inhabited for at least the past 3,500 years, Syrigana has been explored very little as an archaeological site. Endangered by looters, the site is ferociously protected by locals who will be the first to query when they see a stranger strolling around. In May, the smell of blooming elderflowers overpowers the senses as one walks on the freshly laid asphalt leading to a rocky outcrop, the prehistoric hillfort that offers spectacular views of the Dukagjini and Drenica plains. Immediately below, one can observe the neat quadrangular farms of Albanian and Serb farmers. Despite the legacy of the war looming large across the Drenica region, they cohabit the village today.

und serbischen Bäuer*innen bewirtschaftet werden. Obwohl die Region Drenica von den Altlasten des Krieges noch überschattet wird, leben sie im Dorf heute zusammen.

Die neu befestigte Straße, die an einem Steinbruch oben auf dem Hügel endet, verläuft durch ein Gebiet, das derzeit – wenn auch nur temporär – unter Schutz gestellt ist. Hier haben Archäolog*innen Artefakte aus verschiedenen Perioden gefunden, von der späten Bronzezeit, der Eisenzeit, der Antike oder dem Mittelalter bis hin zur Zeit des Osmanischen Reichs. Manche der uralten Bauten, Relikte der Wehrmauern zum Beispiel, wurden freigelegt und sind für jeden sichtbar, wie auch Bruchstücke von Töpferwaren. Im unteren Teil der Fundstätte wurden auch die Ruinen einer antiken oder mittelalterlichen Kirche und die Überreste eines nicht weniger alten Friedhofs entdeckt. Erst in jüngster Zeit wurde damit begonnen, das Gebiet archäologisch zu erschließen. Die ersten, die 2022 Ausgrabungen in Syrigana vornahmen, war eine Gruppe um Premtim Alaj, Michael L. Galaty und Erina Baci. Den Ergebnissen ihrer Forschungsarbeit zufolge weist die Verschiedenartigkeit der Tongefäße und Materialien, die während der Grabungen zutage gefördert wurden, darauf hin, dass Syrigana nicht nur eine Festung war, sondern wahrscheinlich ein kontinuierlich besiedelter Ort und Zeuge menschlicher Aktivität.[1]

Auch wenn die Leben der prähistorischen Bewohner*innen Syriganas für die Wissenschaft zumeist noch im Dunkeln liegen, gibt es eine Fülle von Mythen und Legenden über den Ort. Manche glauben, es war einst eine Stadt, die sich den ganzen Weg bis nach Runik erstreckte, das vier Kilometer südöstlich von Syrigana liegt und nicht weniger als neun Kirchen Raum bietet. Einer der Mythen ist aufgrund seines verspielten Witzes besonders einprägsam: Als Adam und Eva aus dem Garten Eden vertrieben wurden, suchten sie nah und fern nach einem Zuhause, bis sie schließlich nach Syrigana kamen und sich dort niederließen. Doch anders als in der konventionellen abrahamitischen Schöpfungsgeschichte wird in der örtlichen Version

The newly-paved road, which leads up to a quarry on top of the hill, runs through an area currently only under temporary protection. There archaeologists have found artefacts from various periods from the Late Bronze Age, Iron Age, Antiquity, the Medieval era to the Ottoman period. Some of the ancient structures, such as remnants of the defensive walls, are visible on the surface, as are bits and pieces of pottery. In the lower part of the site, remains of a possibly ancient or medieval church, and remnants of an equally ancient cemetery, can also be found. According to research being conducted by Premtim Alaj, Michael L. Galaty, Erina Baci and others, who were the first to conduct an excavation in Syrigana as recently as 2022, the diversity of pottery and materials found during the excavations indicate that Syrigana was not simply a fort, but a potential site of continuous occupation and human activity.[1]

While the lives of Syrigana's prehistoric inhabitants may still be a mystery to scientists, the local lore sufficiently makes up for it. Some believe that at some point the town of Syrigana extended all the way to Runik, located four kilometres southeast – big enough to need nine churches. One particular myth stands out for its playfulness: when Adam and Eve were expelled from Eden, they travelled far and wide looking for a home before they settled in Syrigana. But unlike in the conventional Abrahamic telling of the creation myth, the local story has it that when Adam and Eve landed here, to their great surprise, they found Syriganians already roaming the Earth and going about their lives.

Reimagined as a love story between two characters, Fox and Rooster, this myth is also the starting point which propels the plot of *Syrigana* forward. In this comic, tongue-in-cheek retelling, after the Fall, Fox and Rooster, intent on finding a spot to settle down, arrive at Syrigana, where they are met by welcoming locals who immediately start planning their wedding.

For Halilaj, *Syrigana* is a means to playfully explore both ancient and recent history of the village and underscore the urgent need to preserve the archaeological site. Bringing a completely original performance to a rural village, which arguably sees very little of cultural

weiterhin erzählt, dass Adam und Eva bei ihrer Ankunft zu ihrer großen Überraschung auf Syriganer*innen trafen, die die Erde bereits bevölkerten und ihre Leben lebten.

Diese mythische Geschichte inspirierte auch die Handlung in *Syrigana*, die Halilaj als Liebesgeschichte neu imaginiert. In seiner humorvollen, ironisch gefärbten Version des Mythos sind es zwei Figuren namens Fuchs und Hahn, die auf der Suche nach einem Ort sind, an dem sie sich nach dem Sündenfall niederlassen können. Als sie in Syrigana eintreffen, werden sie von gastfreundlichen Syriganer*innen begrüßt, die auf der Stelle damit beginnen, die Hochzeit der beiden zu planen.

Für Halilaj ist *Syrigana* ein Mittel, sowohl die sehr alte als auch die jüngere Geschichte des Dorfes auf spielerische Weise zu erkunden und dies mit dem dringenden Appell zu verbinden, dass die archäologische Fundstätte unbedingt dauerhaft geschützt werden muss. Indem er eine so innovative Performance in ein ländliches Dorf bringt, das heute wenig kulturelles Geschehen zu Gesicht bekommt, erweist Halilaj zudem den kulturellen Unterfangen seinen Respekt, die es in der Region über Jahrzehnte gab. Die Bühne für den Auftritt beispielsweise besteht aus Traktoren-Anhängern und ist somit eine Hommage an die unter der Leitung von Sala Ahmetaj and Murat Dauti gegründete Theatertruppe, die in den 1970er-Jahren mit ganz ähnlichen Transportmitteln durch die Dörfer der Region Drenica zog, um auf den Fahrzeugen Theaterstücke wie *Nita* oder *Hakmarrja* [Die Rache] aufzuführen.

In den traditionellen albanischen Hochzeitsliedern, die in der Produktion immer wieder zu hören sind, eröffnet sich ein Bezug zu Halilajs persönlichen Kindheitserinnerungen. Für Halilaj ist das Dorf Syrigana, der Geburtsort seiner Mutter, mit den ersten Schritten in die Selbstständigkeit verbunden: Er wohnte, während er die erste Klasse besuchte, bei seinen Onkeln mütterlicherseits, da für ihn die Schule in Syrigana von deren Haus zu Fuß erreichbar war. In gewisser Weise, erinnert sich Halilaj, war Syriganas majestätischer Felsen prägend für seine Kindheit, dort

activity today, Halilaj also pays tribute to decades-long cultural endeavours in the area. For example, the performance stage, consisting of tractor trailers, is a reference to the theatre troupe formed by the teachers Sala Ahmetaj and Murat Dauti, who traversed the Drenica villages in the 1970s with similar vehicles, on top of which they performed plays such as *Nita* and *Hakmarrja* [The Revenge].

Traditional wedding songs in Albanian, which speck the production, are also a hint at Halilaj's own personal memories of Syrigana. Being his mother's birthplace, the village denotes Halilaj's first venture away from the family hearth: because the school in Syrigana was a walkable distance, Halilaj moved in with his maternal uncles while attending the first grade. In a way, Halilaj recounts, it is under Syrigana's majestic rock that he came of age, experiencing for the first time the liberties of being away from the patriarchal reach. During this time, Halilaj remembers most fondly attending *kanagjegjs*, traditional bachelorette parties, in which women gather to sing songs and bid farewell to the bride. On one such occasion, Halilaj remembers being distraught as one of his cousins, a bride-to-be, began wailing inconsolably. Traditionally, despite the wedding being a joyful occasion, lamenting is a key element of performance by the bride, who is supposed to mourn leaving her family and home. As a young boy, Halilaj had no idea, and started pestering everyone with questions, so much so that the young woman had to put him aside, lift up her red veil and tell him, 'Shsh, stupid, I'm only pretending!' 'It was like the origin of theatre for me,' Halilaj says.

This interest in theatre remains steadfast in Halilaj's work, whether it is in the stage-like theatricality of his Tate St. Ives show or the one-time performance of *Shkrepëtima*, enacted at the decrepit House of Culture in the next-door village

---

1 E. Baci, P. Alaj, et al. „Preliminary results of excavations at the sites of Lubozhdë and Syrigana, Western Kosovo" in: *Kosovo Arkeologjike* (in Kürze erscheinend).

---

1 Premtim Alaj et al., "Preliminary results of excavations at the sites of Lubozhdë and Syrigana, Western Kosovo" in: *Kosovo Arkeologjike* (forthcoming).

erlebte er zum ersten Mal, was es bedeutet, dem väterlichen Einflussbereich entkommen zu sein. Halilaj denkt gern an diese Zeit zurück; er erzählt auch, dass er oft zu *kanagjegjs* mitgenommen wurde, den traditionellen Junggesellinnenabschieden, bei denen die Frauen zusammenkommen, um Lieder zu singen und die Braut in ihr neues Leben zu entlassen. Halilaj erinnert sich, bei einer dieser Gelegenheiten sehr verstört gewesen zu sein, als eine seiner Cousinen, die zukünftige Braut, vehement zu jammern und zu klagen begann. Obwohl eine Hochzeit ein freudiges Ereignis ist, gehören Klagegesänge zur Tradition: Der Brauch verlangt, dass die Braut ihre Trauer darüber bekundet, dass sie die Familie und ihr elterliches Zuhause verlässt. Als kleiner Junge hatte Halilaj davon keine Ahnung und begann, die Anwesenden mit Fragen zu belästigen und zwar so beharrlich, dass sich die junge Frau veranlasst sah, ihn zur Seite zu nehmen, ihren roten Schleier zu lüften und ihm zu sagen: „Sch! Dummkopf, ich tue nur so als ob." „Das war für mich wie der Ursprung des Theaters", sagt Halilaj.

Das Interesse am Theater sollte ein bleibender Einfluss in Halilajs Arbeit sein, sei es in der bühnenartigen Theatralik seiner Ausstellung in der Tate St. Ives oder der Performance *Shkrepëtima*, die nur ein einziges Mal im Haus der Kultur zu sehen war, einem baufälligen Gebäude in dem nahe bei Syrigana gelegenen Dorf Runik. Auf magische Art und in einer einzigen Nacht erweckte Halilajs Performance 2018 die Ruinen des Kulturzentrums zu neuem Leben und setzte damit ein deutliches Zeichen, wie wichtig es ist, das seit den frühen 1990er-Jahren nicht mehr genutzte Haus zu erhalten. Seitdem setzt sich Halilajs Stiftung Hajde! dafür ein, das Gebäude zu restaurieren und erneut als kulturellen Ort nutzbar zu machen. 2025 sind konkrete Pläne, eine Bibliothek und einen Ausstellungsraum darin unterzubringen, schließlich auf den Weg gebracht worden. Wie im Fall der Performance *Shkrepëtima,* mithilfe derer der Künstler ein ehemaliges kulturelles Zentrum neu aktivierte, um in der Öffentlichkeit Erinnerungen wiederaufleben zu lassen und ein Bewusstsein für

of Runik. In 2018, for a single night, Halilaj's performance magically revived the ruins of the cultural centre, which was abandoned since the early 1990s and highlighted the importance of its preservation. Since then, Halilaj's foundation Hajde! has fought hard to restore the building and functionalise it once again as a cultural space with plans to turn it into a library and gallery being finally underway in 2025. As in the case of *Shkrepëtima,* which activated a space to trigger memories and awareness of the centre's relevance, Halilaj's operatic performance in Syrigana invites the audience to reimagine the space, in its bygone glory and acknowledge the immense potential it contains today.

An inverted Fitzcarraldian figure, Halilaj's homecoming is not led by the grand enterprise to build an opera house deep in the "Amazonian" forest untouched by civilisation as in Herzog's film (1982), but rather an effort of the native son to turn local stories, music, heritage and landscape into one grand performance, which once seen, will be impossible to ignore or neglect.

Written by Halilaj in collaboration with Doruntina Basha, Robert Schulz and Amy Zion, and composed by Lugh O'Neill with contributions by Nina Guo, *Syrigana* is the first-ever commission of the Kosovo Philharmonic, an institution founded in 2000 after the Kosovo war ended. Marking the 25th anniversary of the Philharmonic, the opera is a departure from the institution's traditional way of operating and represents current director Dardan Selimaj's ambition to make it more accessible to wider audiences. The collaboration poses quite a few elements of originality for the institution: in addition to being the first time working with a visual artist in creating a new work, the orchestra's ensemble was also intimately involved in the creative process. Incidentally, it is also the first time that an opera is being staged in Kosovo at the specific site for which it was written, marking a new chapter in Kosovo's operatic and cultural history.

die Relevanz eines solchen Raumes zu schaffen, lädt auch Halilajs opernähnliche Performance in Syrigana das Publikum ein, sich an die vergangenen Sternstunden des Ortes zu erinnern um zu erkennen, welch immenses Potenzial er heute besitzt.

Im Unterschied zu Fitzcarraldo ist Halilajs Heimkehr nicht von dem kühnen Unterfangen geleitet, ein Opernhaus an einem von der Zivilisation noch unberührten Fleckchen Erde zu bauen, tief im Amazonasgebiet, wie wir es aus Herzogs Film (1982) kennen. Hier haben wir es vielmehr mit den Bestrebungen eines Einheimischen, die Geschichte(n), Musik, Überlieferungen und Landschaft des Ortes zu einer groß angelegten Performance zu verweben, die – wurde sie einmal gesehen – unmöglich ignoriert oder missachtet werden kann.

Syrigana: An Opera in Five Acts wurde von Halilaj gemeinsam mit Doruntina Basha, Robert Schulz und Amy Zion geschrieben, und die Komposition stammt von Lugh O'Neill, mit Beiträgen von Nina Guo. *Syrigana* ist das allererste Werk, das von der Kosovo Philharmonic, einer 2000 nach Ende des Kosovokrieges gegründeten Institution, je in Auftrag gegeben wurde. Die Oper, die das 25-jährige Jubiläum der Philharmonie markiert, repräsentiert die Abkehr der Institution von traditionelleren Wegen der Operninszenierung und die Bestrebungen des derzeitigen Direktors Dardan Selimaj, ein breiteres Publikum für Oper zu interessieren. Für die Institution verbindet sich die Zusammenarbeit mit einer Reihe neuer Aspekte: Zum ersten Mal arbeitet die Kosovo Philharmonic hier bei der Erschaffung eines neuen Werkes mit einem bildenden Künstler zusammen, und auch das Ensemble des Orchesters war maßgeblich in den kreativen Prozess involviert. Darüber hinaus ist es auch eine Premiere, dass eine Oper an dem spezifischen Ort im Kosovo aufgeführt wird, für den sie geschrieben wurde – und somit markiert *Syrigana: An Opera in Five Acts* ein ganz neues Kapitel in der Opern- und Kulturgeschichte des Kosovos.

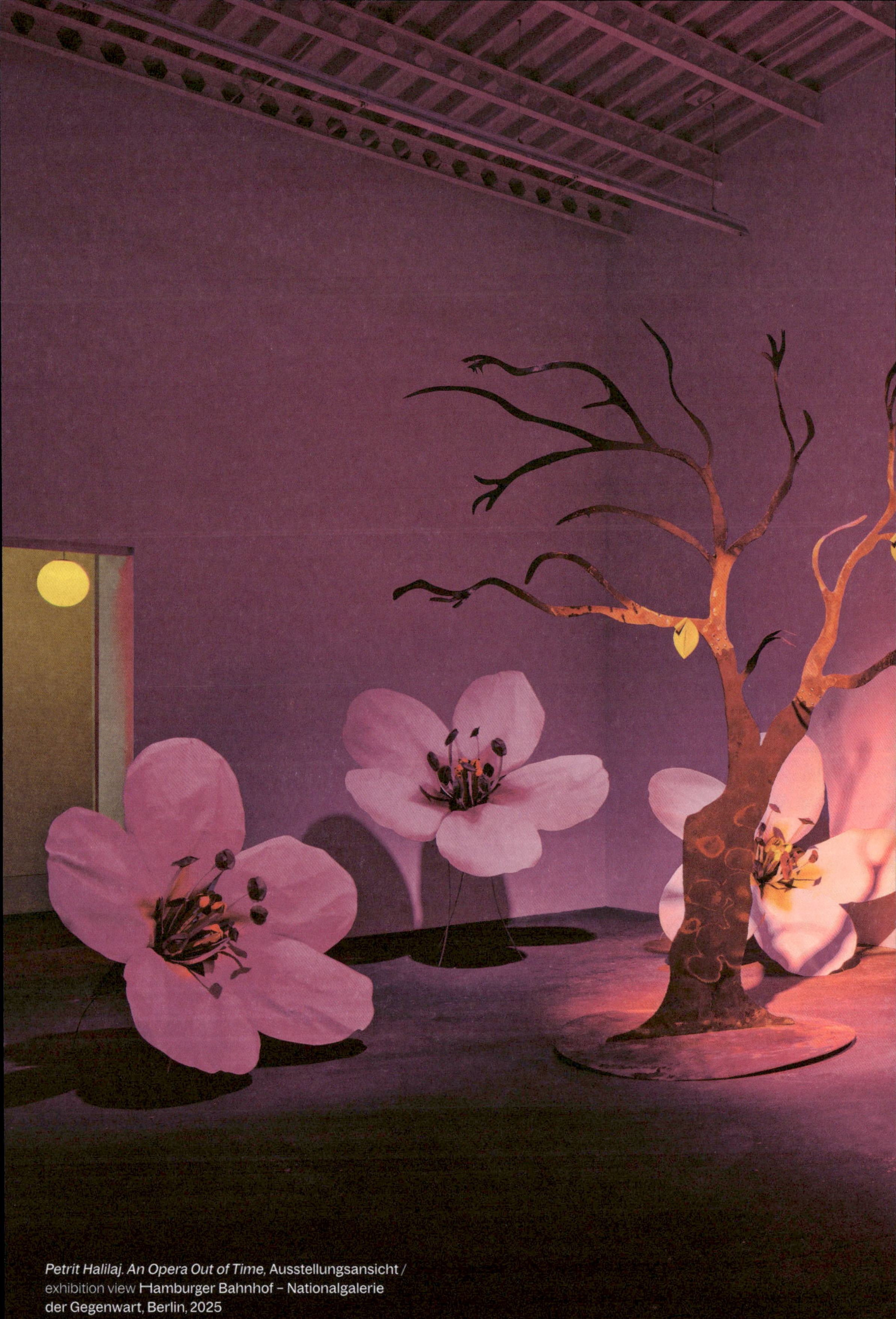

Petrit Halilaj. An Opera Out of Time, Ausstellungsansicht /
exhibition view Hamburger Bahnhof – Nationalgalerie
der Gegenwart, Berlin, 2025

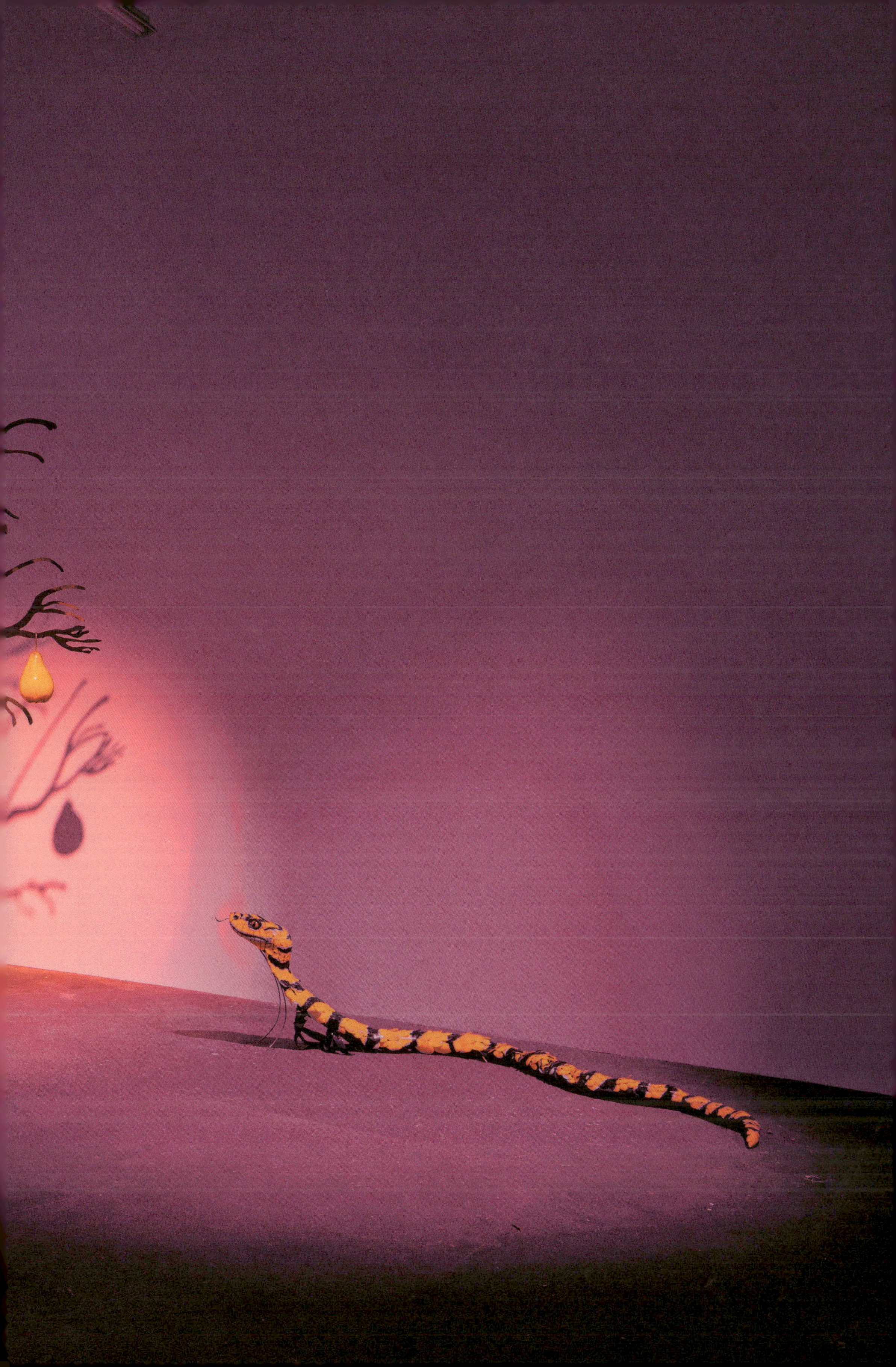

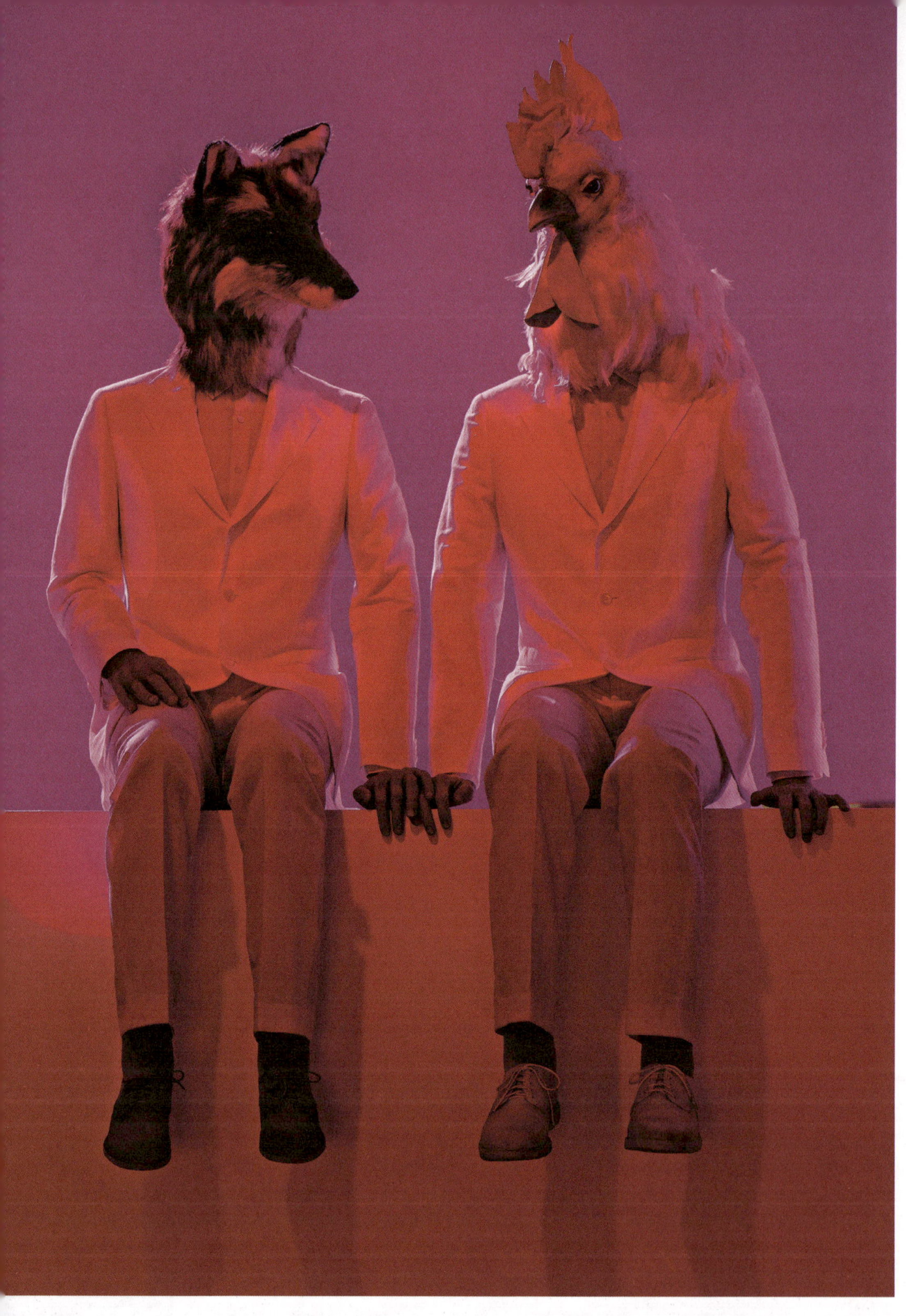

Petrit Halilaj. An Opera Out of Time, Ausstellungsansicht /
exhibition view Hamburger Bahnhof – Nationalgalerie
der Gegenwart, Berlin, 2025

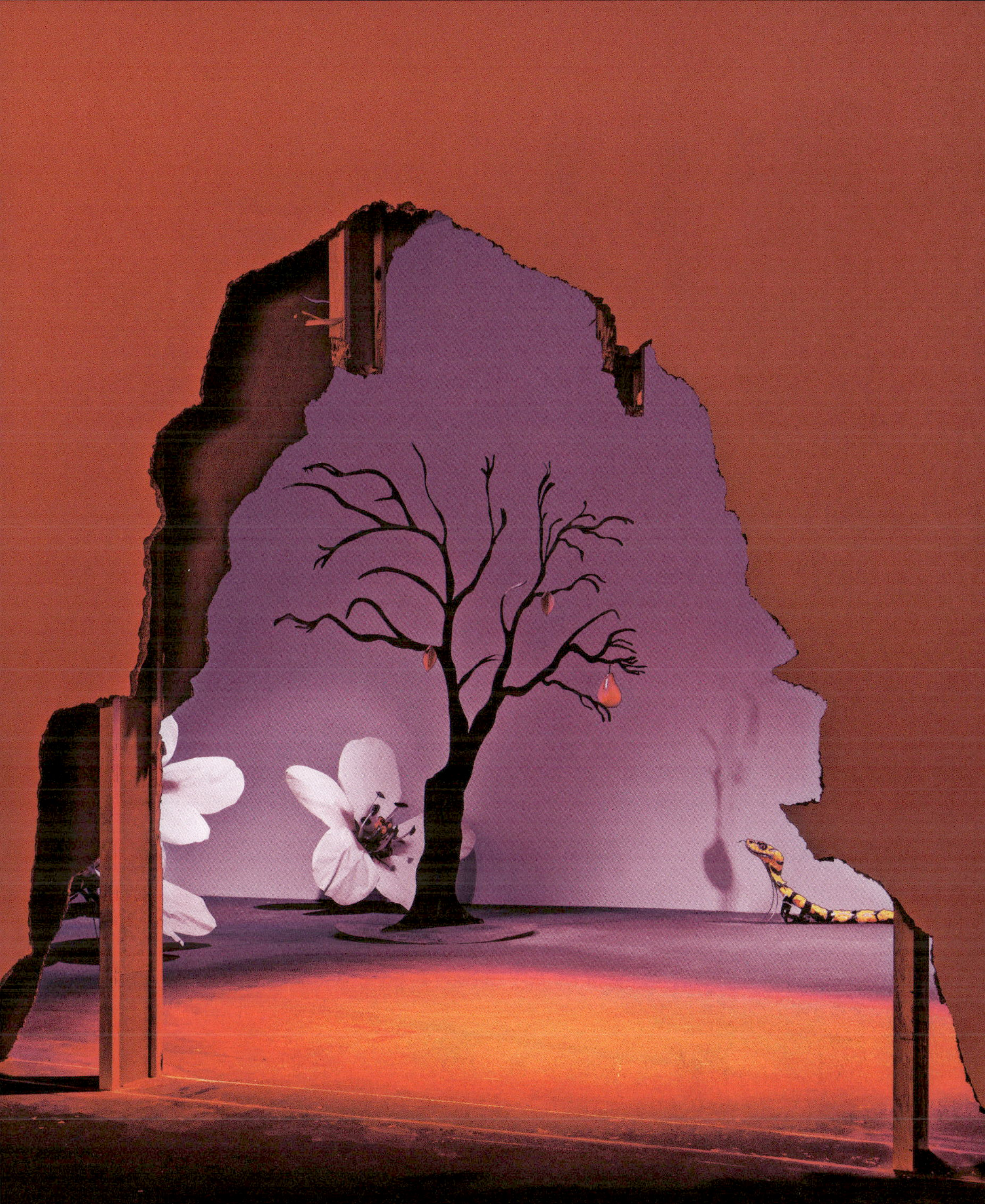

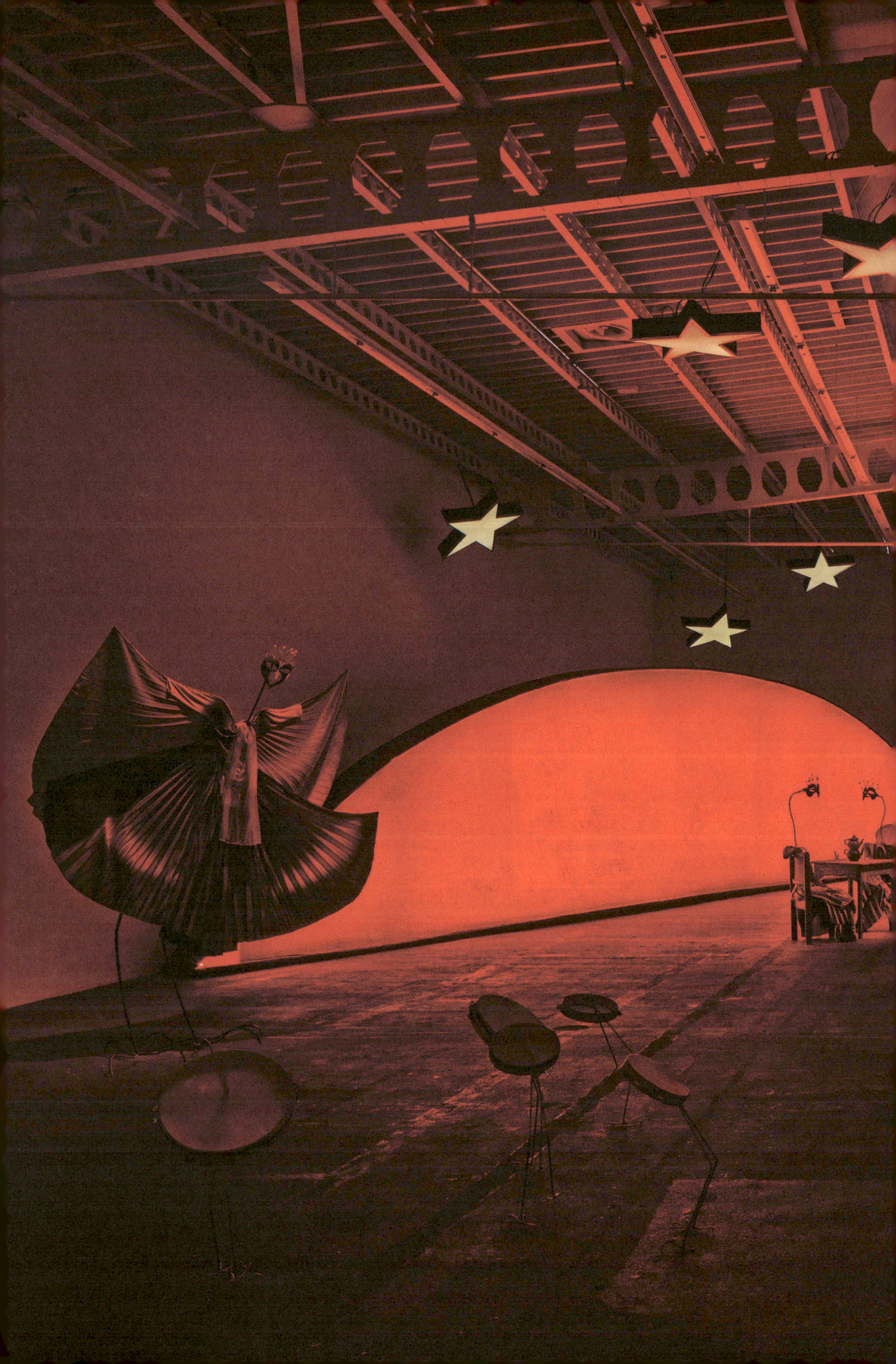

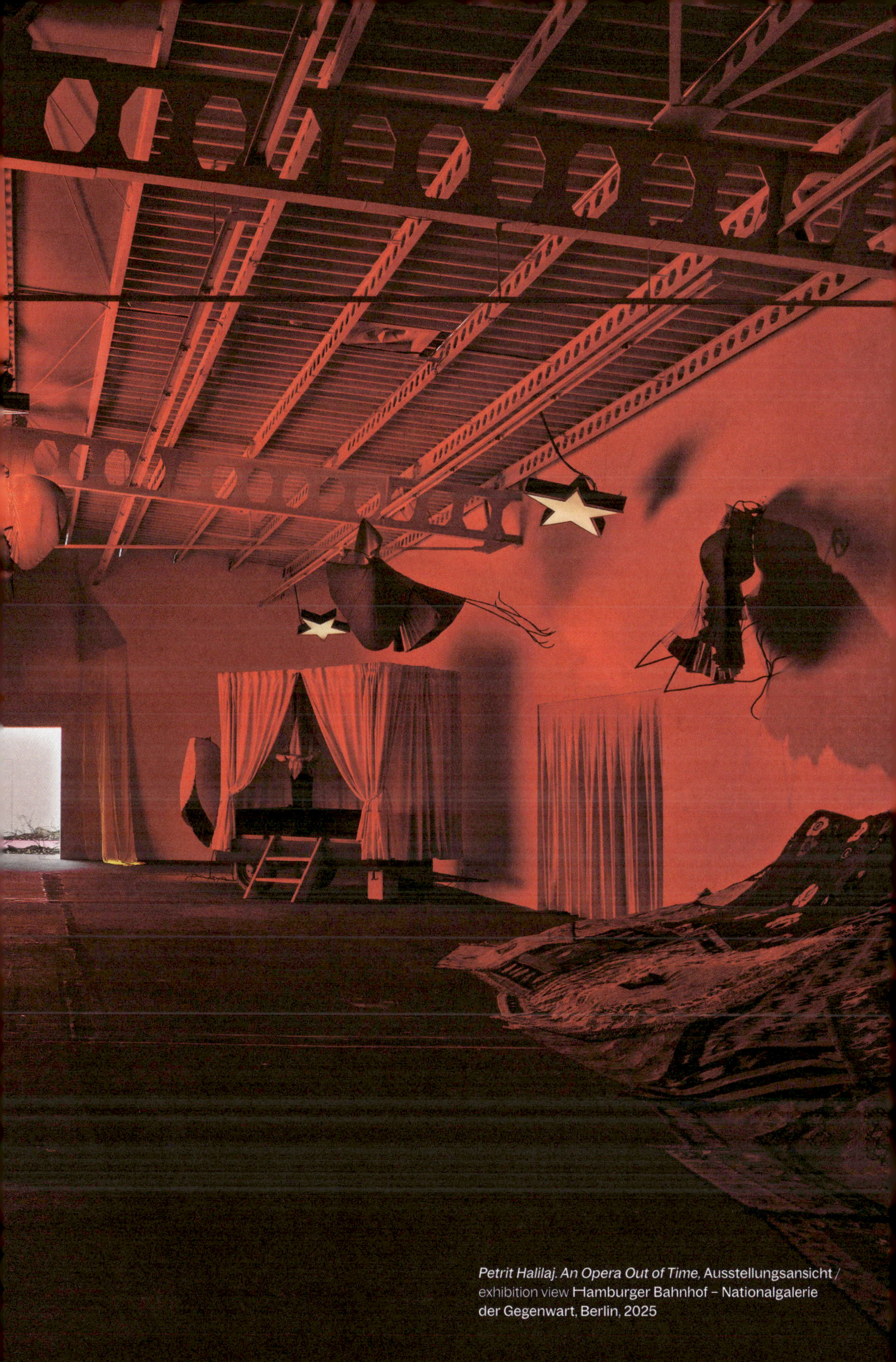

Petrit Halilaj. An Opera Out of Time, Ausstellungsansicht /
exhibition view Hamburger Bahnhof – Nationalgalerie
der Gegenwart, Berlin, 2025

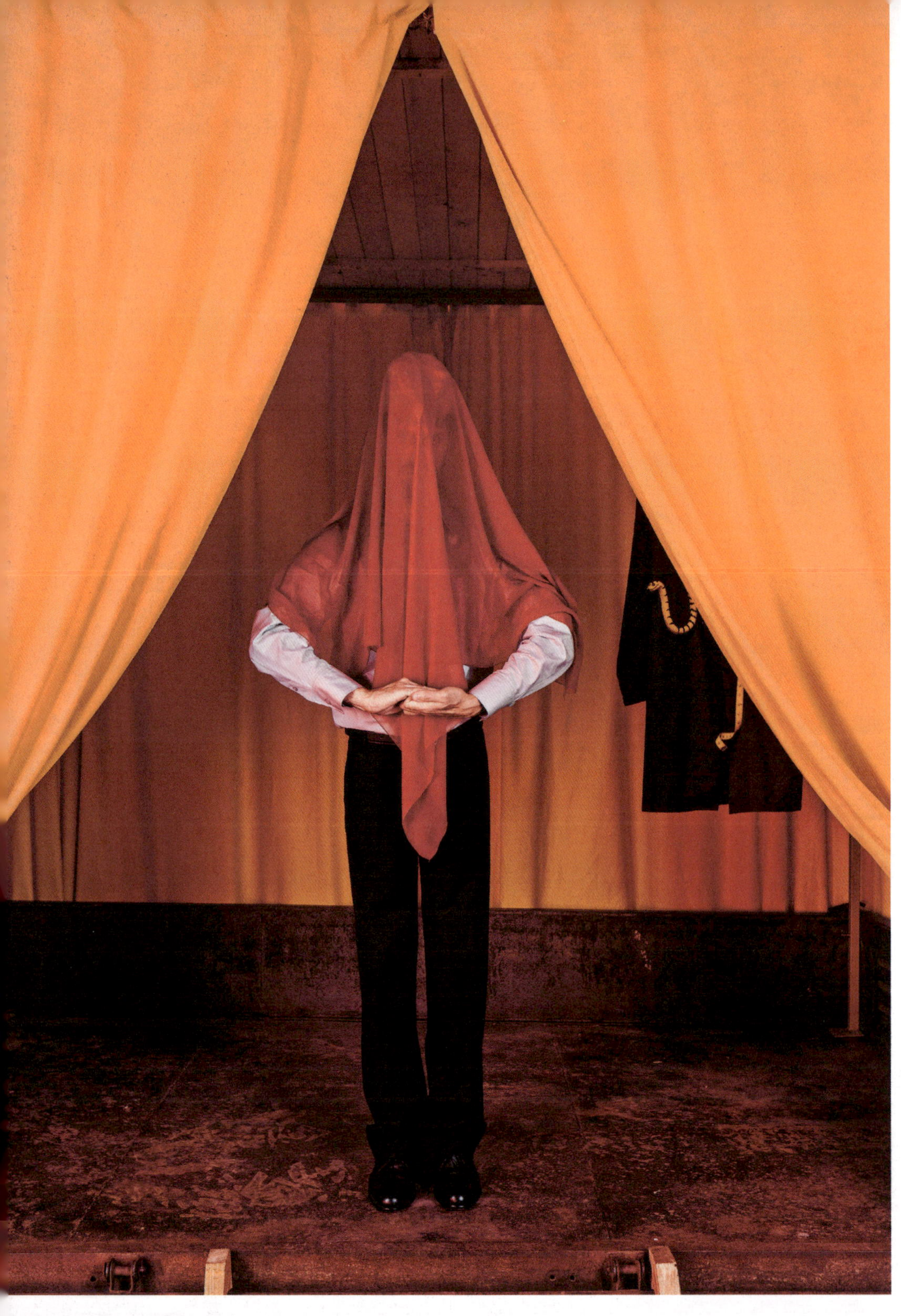

Petrit Halilaj. An Opera Out of Time, Ausstellungsansicht /
exhibition view Hamburger Bahnhof – Nationalgalerie
der Gegenwart, Berlin, 2025

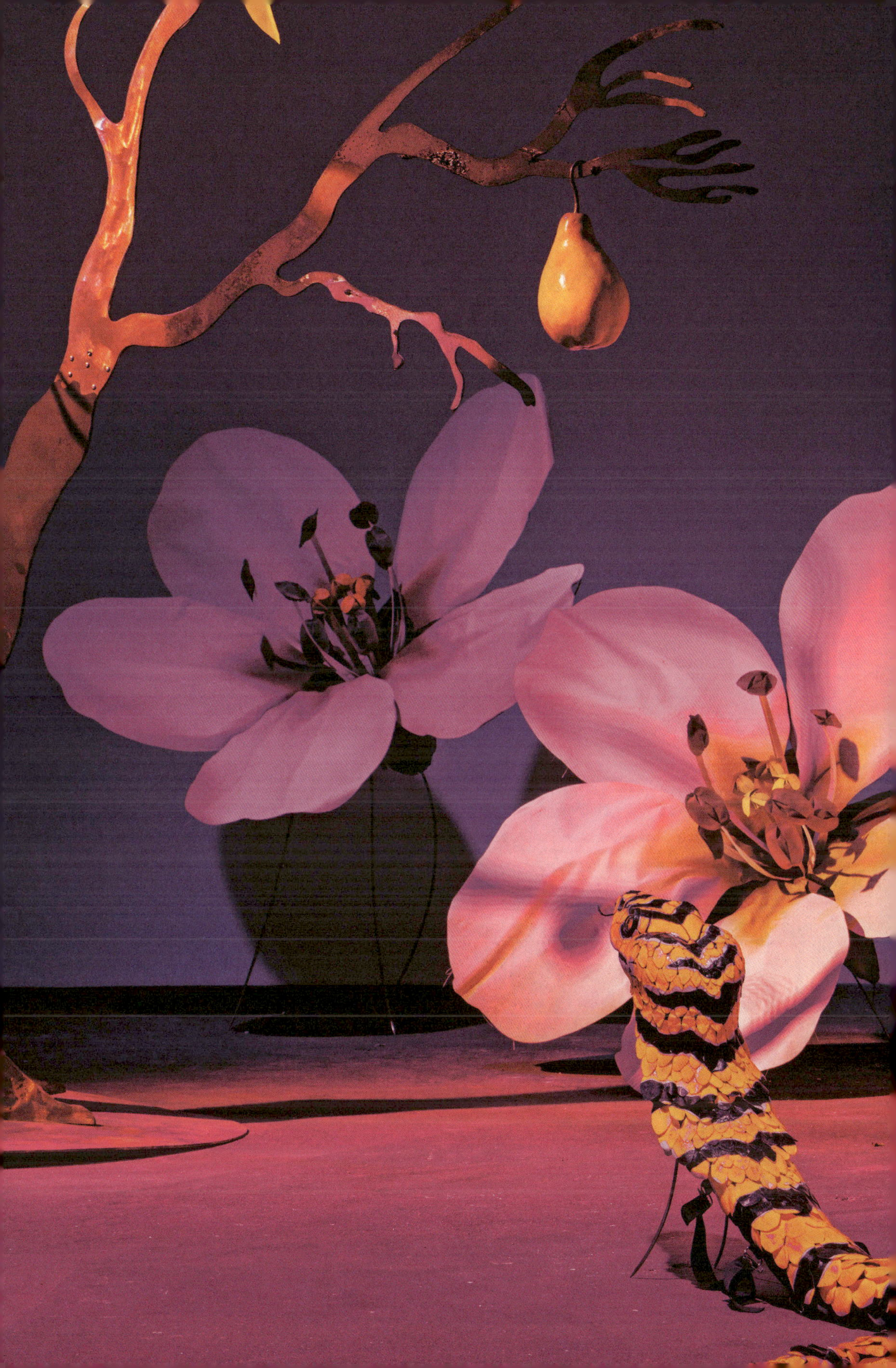

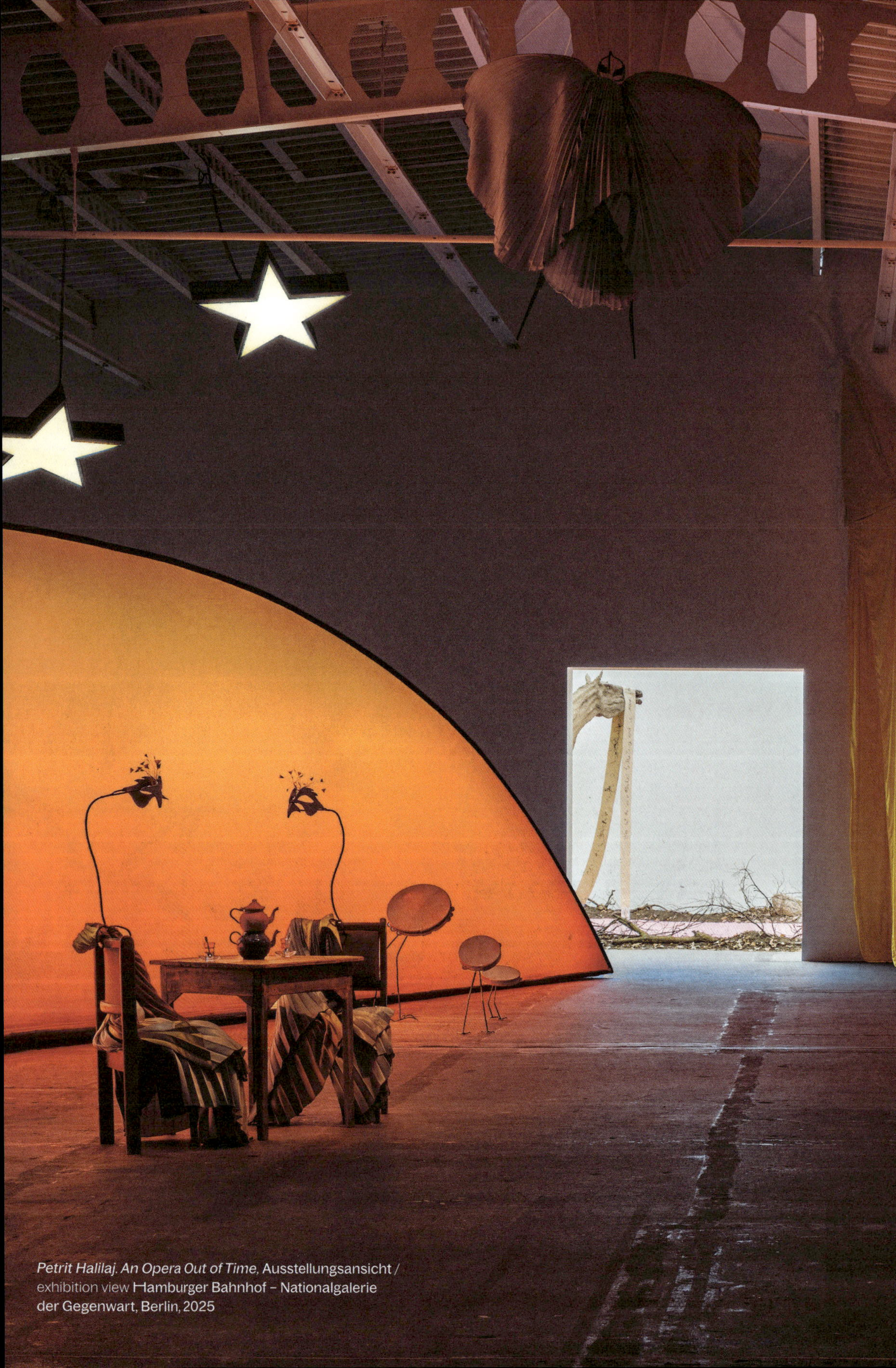

Petrit Halilaj. An Opera Out of Time, Ausstellungsansicht /
exhibition view Hamburger Bahnhof – Nationalgalerie
der Gegenwart, Berlin, 2025

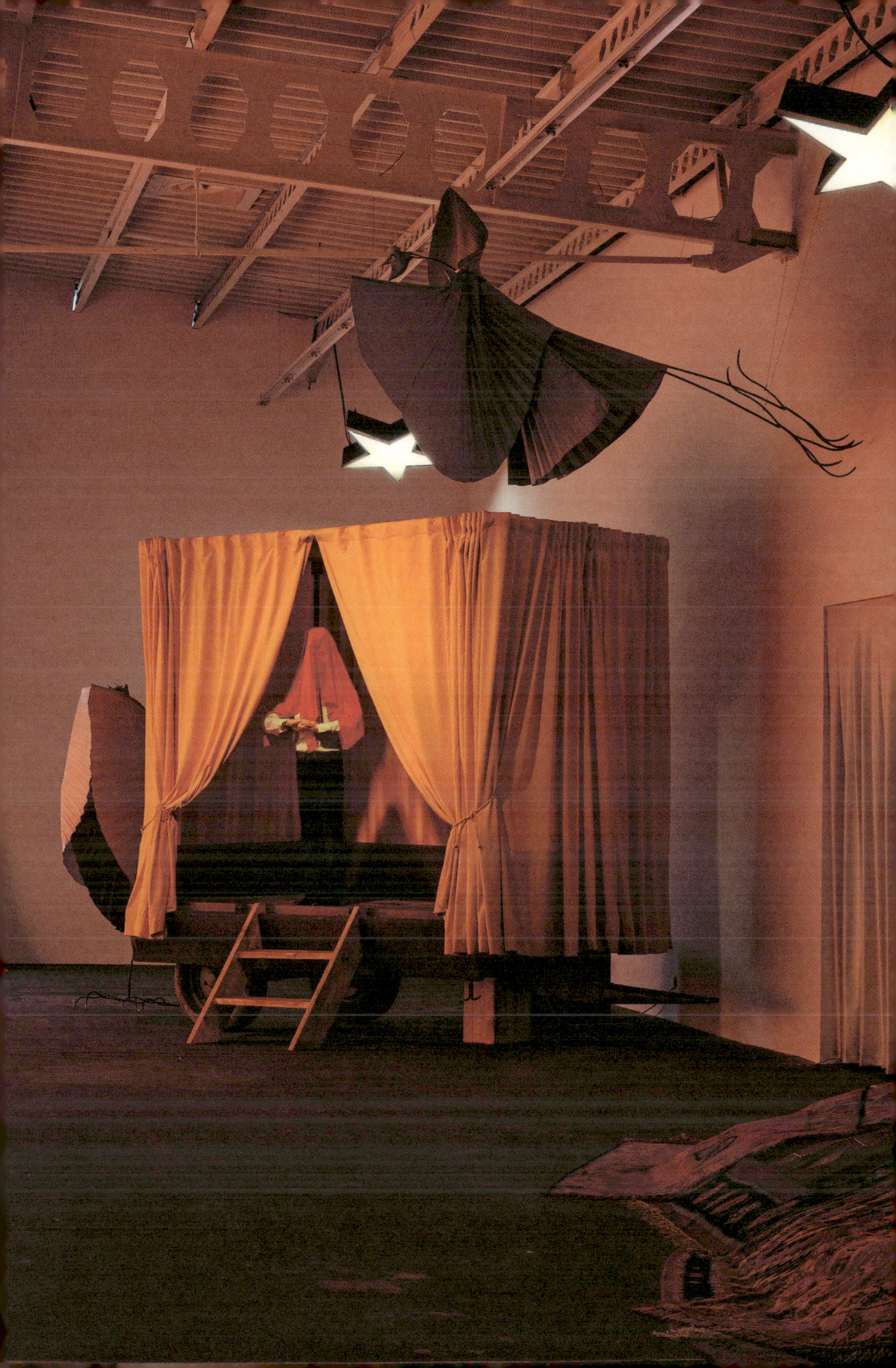

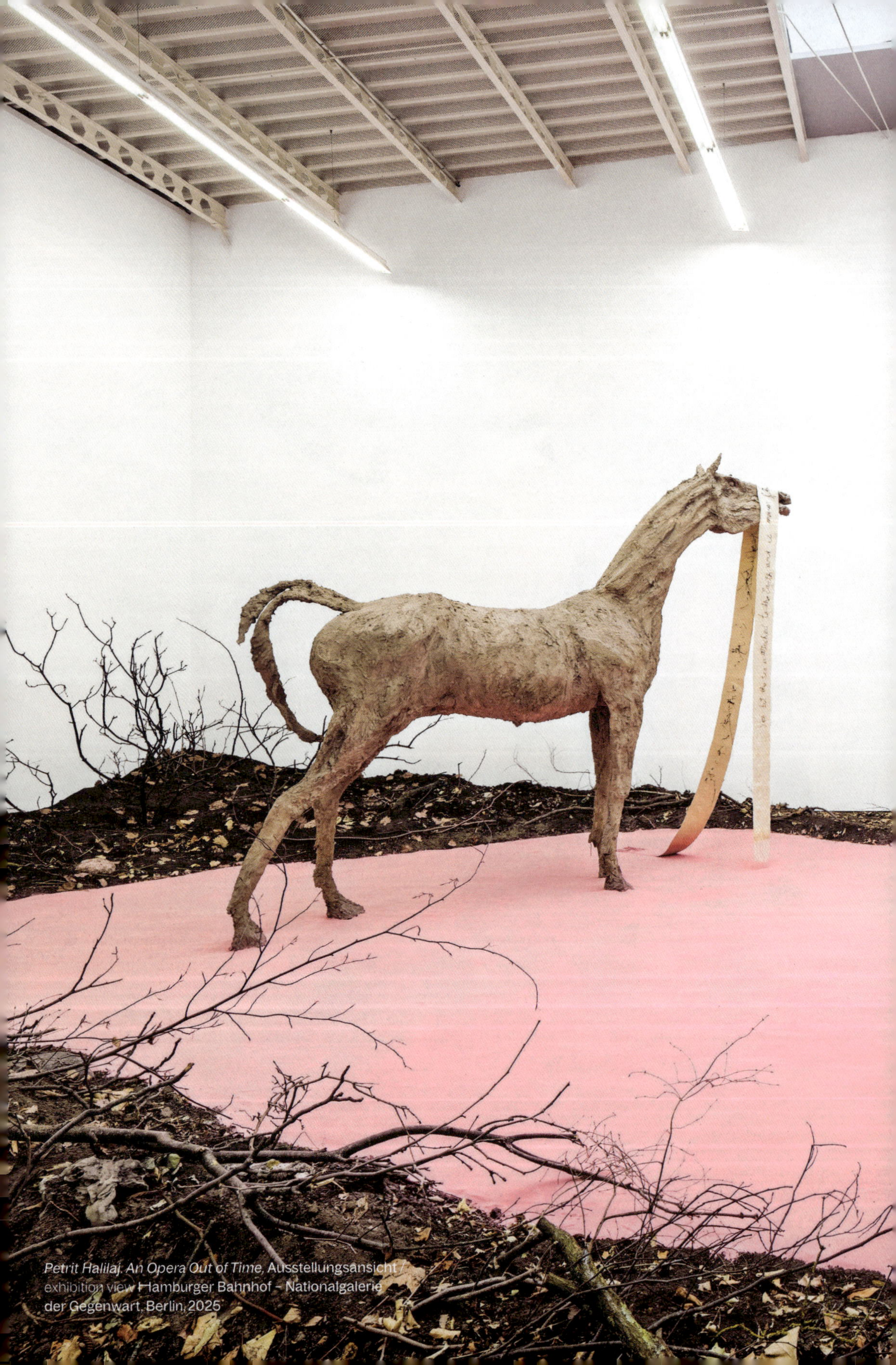

Petrit Halilaj, An Opera Out of Time, Ausstellungsansicht /
exhibition view Hamburger Bahnhof – Nationalgalerie
der Gegenwart, Berlin, 2025

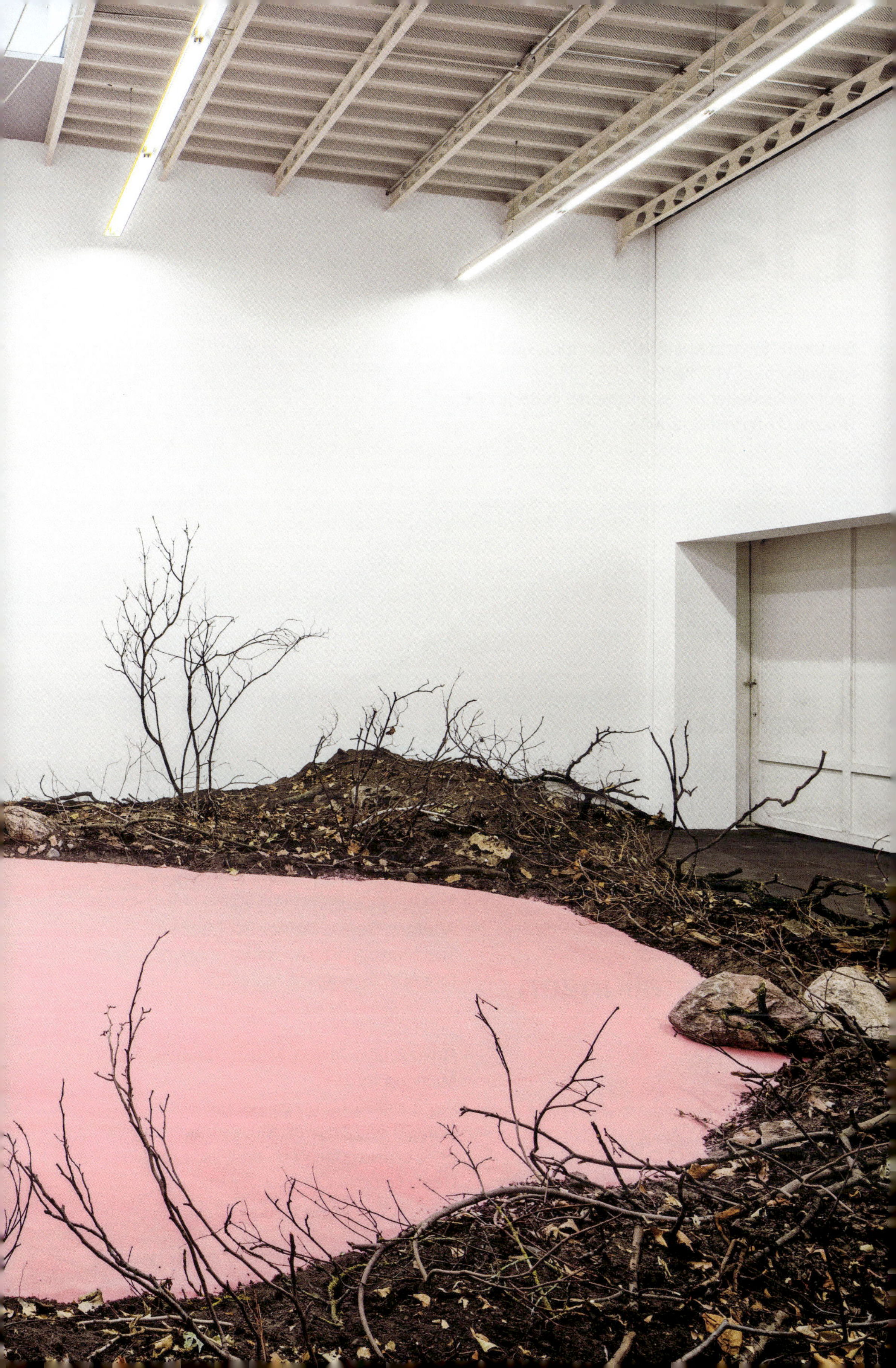

Petrit Halilaj

Geboren / Born in Kostërrc-Skënderaj, KOS
(damals / then YU), 1986
Lebt und arbeitet / Lives and works in Berlin, DE,
Bozzolo, IT & Prishtina, KOS

Ausbildung /
Education

2009
BA in Bildender Kunst / Fine Art,
Accademia di Brera, Mailand / Milan, IT

Ausgewählte
Einzelausstellungen /
Selected Solo
Exhibitions

2025
Petrit Halilaj: An Opera Out of Time.
Hamburger Bahnhof – Nationalgalerie der
Gegenwart, Berlin, DE; Katalog / catalogue
*Alberto Giacometti / Petrit Halilaj: We Built
a Fantastic Palace at Night.* Fondation
Giacometti, Paris, FR; Katalog / catalogue

2024
*Petrit Halilaj & Álvaro Urbano:
Lunar Ensemble for Uprising Seas.*
MACBA, Barcelona, ES
*Premio Strómboli: HEROIC (the)
LANDSCAPE / EROICO (il) PAESAGGIO.*
Chiesa di San Bartolomeo, Stromboli, IT
*The Roof Garden Commission: Petrit Halilaj,
Abetare.* Gerald Cantor Roof Garden,
The Metropolitan Museum of Art, New York
City, NY, US; Katalog / catalogue

2023
Petrit Halilaj: RUNIK. Museo Tamayo,
Mexico City, MX
*Petrit Halilaj: Histoires inachevées /
Unfinished Histories.* Musée international
de la croix-rouge et du croissant-rouge,
Genf / Geneva, CH

2022
*Petrit Halilaj: You used to fly, go everywhere
and wake up those who are asleep.*
Fries Museum, Leeuwarden, NL

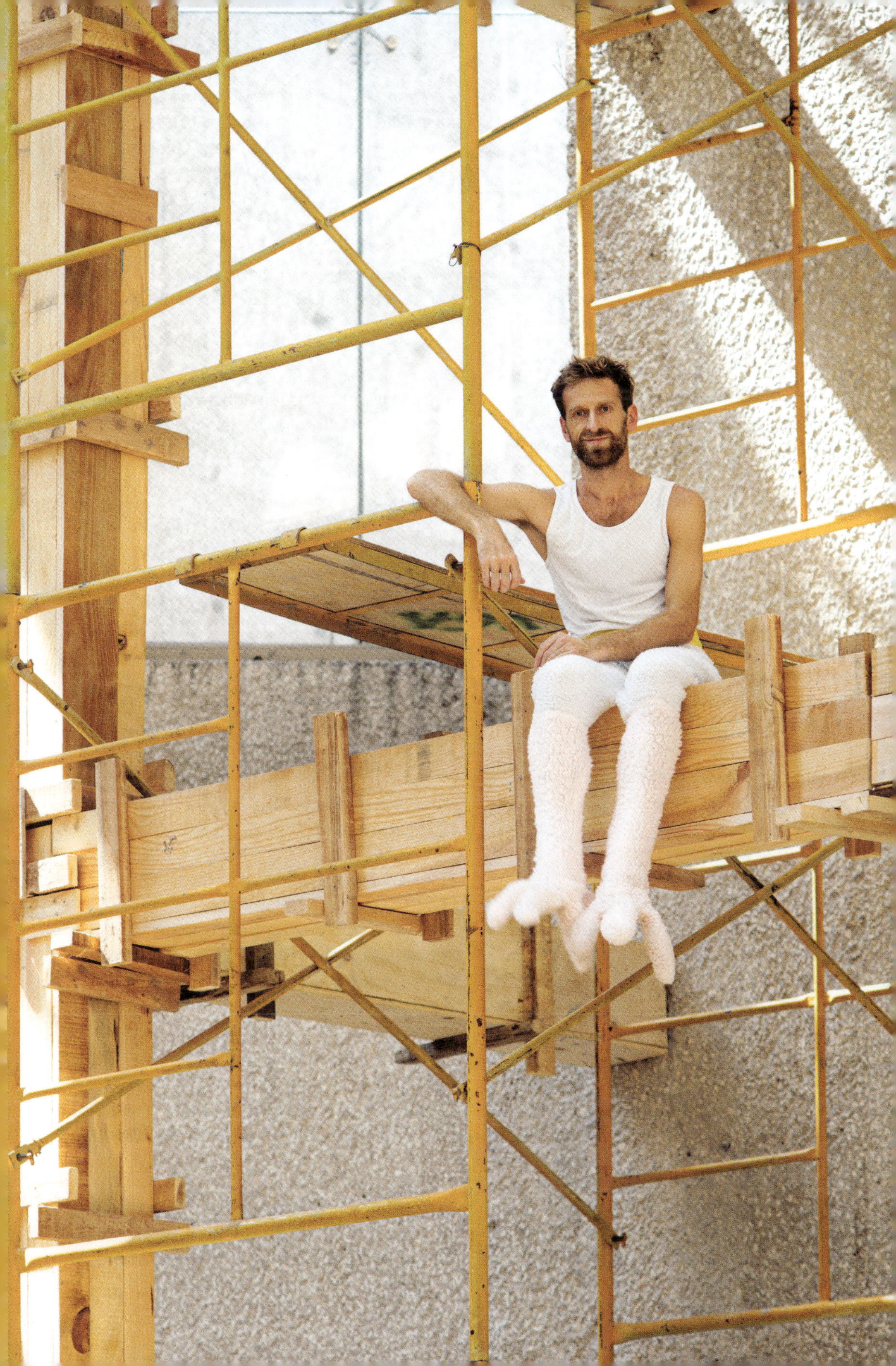

2021
Petrit Halilaj: Very volcanic over this green feather. Tate St Ives, Saint Ives, GB; Katalog / catalogue

2020
Petrit Halilaj: To a raven and hurricanes that from unknown places bring back smells of humans in love. Palacio de Cristal, Museo Reina Sofia, Madrid, ES

2018
Hammer Projects: Petrit Halilaj. Hammer Museum, Los Angeles, CA, US
Petrit Halilaj: Shkrepëtima. Paul Klee Zentrum, Bern, CH (weitere Station / travelled to: Fondazione Merz, Turin, IT); Katalog / catalogue

2015
Petrit Halilaj: Space Shuttle in the Garden. Pirelli HangarBicocca, Mailand / Milan, IT; Katalog / catalogue
Petrit Halilaj: ABETARE. Kölnischer Kunstverein, Köln / Cologne, DE; Katalog / catalogue
Petrit Halilaj: She, fully turning around, became terrestrial. Bundeskunsthalle, Bonn, DE; Katalog / catalogue

2014
Zemër shtype pullën dhe fshima kujtesën / Darling squeeze the button and remove my memory. Galeria e Arteve e Kosovës, Prishtina, KOS; Katalog / catalogue

2013
July 14th? Fondation Galeries Lafayette, Paris, FR
Petrit Halilaj: I'm hungry to keep you close. I want to find the words to resist but in the end there is a locked sphere. The funny thing is that you're not here, nothing is. Kosovo Pavillon / Pavilion, La Biennale di Venezia, Venedig / Venice, IT (weitere Station / travelled to: Kunsthalle Lissabon, Lissabon / Lisbon, PT); Katalog / catalogue

Poisoned by men in need of some love. WIELS Contemporary Art Center, Brüssel / Brussels, BE; Katalog / catalogue
Petrit Halilaj. Sammlung Wittmann, Tongewölbe T25, Ingolstadt, DE

2012
Who does the earth belong to while painting the wind?! Kunsthalle Sankt Gallen, St. Gallen, CH

2011
Petrit Halilaj. Kunstraum Innsbruck, Innsbruck, AT; Katalog / catalogue

2009
Petrit Halilaj: Back to the Future. Stacion – Center for Contemporary Art Prishtina, Prishtina, KOS

1996
Shote Galica, Grundschule / Primary School, Runik, KOS

Ausgewählte Gruppenausstellungen / Selected Group Exhibitions

2025
It's Just a Matter of Time. Palais Populaire, Berlin, DE
Ways of Knowing. Walker Art Center, Minneapolis, MN, US; Katalog / catalogue
Grey is the Cube, Blue the Ellipse. Maison de la Culture Amiens, Amiens, FR
Theatre of Speaking Objects: Works from the Wilhelm Otto Nachf. Collection. Kunsthalle Nürnberg, Nürnberg / Nuremberg, DE
Les étoiles se refroidissent aussi. La Condition Publique, Place du Général Faidherbe, Roubaix, FR
Art Encounters. Biennial Timisoara, Timisoara, RO

God, Human, Animal, Machine. Kunstall 44 Møen, Fanefjordgade, Askeby, DK

2024

Displacements and Torrents. Galerie – Cité internationale des arts, Paris, FR
The Bird Show: Vögel zwischen Freiheit, Krieg & Quantenmechanik. Eres-Stiftung für Kunst und Naturwissenschaft, München / Munich, DE; **Katalog** / catalogue
Italia 70 – I Nuovi Mostri (The New Monsters). Fondazione Nicola Trussardi, Mailand / Milan, IT; **Katalog** / catalogue
We Move as a Murmuration. Timespan, Helmsdale, GB; **Katalog** / catalogue
Sounds like a Whisper (Poetically Political). Städtische Galerie / City Art Gallery **Sofia, BG**
Performer and Participant. Tate Modern, London, GB
Ten Thousand Suns. Biennale of Sydney, White Bay Power Station, Sydney, AU; **Katalog** / catalogue

2023

NGV Triennial, Melbourne, AU; **Katalog** / catalogue
En el jardín. Museo de Arte Contemporáneo, Monterrey, MX; **Katalog** / catalogue
COSMOS: The Volcano Lover. Villa Olmo, Como, IT
Hope. Museion, Bozen / Bolzano, IT
#nichtmuedewerden – Felix Nussbaum und künstlerischer Widerstand heute. Museumsquartier Osnabrück, Osnabrück, DE
Thus waves come in pairs. Ocean Space, Venedig / Venice, IT; **Katalog** / catalogue
Lo que pesa una cabeza. TEA, Teneriffa / Tenerife, ES

2022

Wie geht es jetzt weiter? Zwölf Erzählungen aktueller Kunst aus Spanien. Frankfurter Kunstverein, Frankfurt a.M., DE
Breathing Water, Drinking Air. Philara Collection, Düsseldorf, DE
It matters what worlds world worlds: how to tell stories otherwise. Manifesta 14, Prishtina, KOS; **Katalog** / catalogue

Evidence. Mercer Union, Toronto, CA
Macht! Licht! Kunstmuseum Wolfsburg, Wolfsburg, DE
Adjustable Monuments. Sammlung Philara, Düsseldorf, DE; **Katalog** / catalogue

2021

Tremblements. Nouveau Musée National de Monaco, Monaco, MC
Kaunas Biennial, Kaunas, LT; **Katalog** / catalogue
The point of sculpture. Fundación Joan Miró, Barcelona, ES; **Katalog** / catalogue
Mother! Louisiana Museum of Modern Art, Kopenhagen / Copenhagen, DK (weitere Station / travelled to: Kunsthalle Mannheim, Mannheim, DE); **Katalog** / catalogue
In the Pupil of the Panther. Lundskonsthall, Lund, SE; **Katalog** / catalogue
Flowers in Art. Arken Museum, Kopenhagen / Copenhagen, DK
How Long is Now? The Israel Museum, Jerusalem, IL
Autostrada Biennale, Biblioteka Kombëtare e Kosovës Pjeter Bogdani, Prishtina, KOS; **Katalog** / catalogue
EVROVIZION: Crossing Stories and Spaces. Historijski muzej Bosne i Hercegovine, Sarajevo, BA (weitere Stationen / travelling to: Muzej savremene umetnosti Vojvodine, Novi Sad, RS; Goethe-Institut Athen, Athen / Athens, GR; NiMAC, Nicosia, CY; Tbilisi Photography & Multimedia Museum, Tbilisi, GE; Städtische Galerie / City Art Gallery Boris Georgiev, Varna, BG; Chişinău, MD; Krakau / Cracow, PL; Vilnius, LT; Königsberg / Kaliningrad, RU; Berlin, DE; Brüssel / Brussels, BE)
Diversity United: Contemporary Art from Europe. Flughafen Tempelhof, Berlin, DE (weitere Station / travelled to: New Tretyakov Gallery, Moskau / Moscow, RU); **Katalog** / catalogue
Jardin Secret. Palais des Beaux-Arts, Paris, FR

2020
Fuori. Quadriennale d'arte, Palazzo delle
Esposizioni, Rom / Rome, IT;
Katalog / catalogue
Ulrike Müller: The Conference of the Animals.
Queens Museum, New York City, NY, US
Biennale Gherdëina, Ortisei, IT
Studio Berlin. Berghain, Berlin, DE;
Katalog / catalogue
*A Breath? A Name? The Ways of
Worldmaking*. Biennale Gherdeina,
Ortesei, IT

2019
*You: Works from the Collection Lafayette
Anticipations*. Musée d'art moderne de
la ville de Paris, Paris, FR; Katalog / catalogue
Infancy and History. OCAT Institute,
Peking / Beijing, CN
The Garden Bridge. Brücke-Museum,
Berlin, DE
Homeless Souls. Louisiana Museum of
Modern Art, Kopenhagen / Copenhagen, DN
*Where Water Comes Together with
Other Water*. Lyon Biennale, Lyon, FR;
Katalog / catalogue
The Palace at 4 A.M. Archäologisches
Museum / Archaeological Museum,
Mykonos, GR; Katalog / catalogue
*G2 #15 WEGE ZUR WELT: Sammlung
Hildebrand*. G2 Kunsthalle, Leipzig, DE

2018
New Materialism. Bonniers Konsthall,
Stockholm, SE; Katalog / catalogue
*CHILDHOOD. Another Banana Day for the
Perfect Fish*. Palais de Tokyo, Paris, FR;
Katalog / catalogue
That's it! Museo d'Arte Moderna di Bologna,
Bologna, IT; Katalog / catalogue
When Animal Talked to Human.
Traversía Cuatro, Madrid, ES
Una vida domestica. Salon Acme,
Mexico City, MX

2017
*Mit den Händen zu greifen und doch nicht
zu fassen*. Kunsthalle Mainz, Mainz, DE

Art and Alphabet. Hamburger Kunsthalle,
Hamburg, DE
Friends of Birds. DOC!, Paris, FR
Viva Arte Viva. La Biennale di Venezia,
Venedig / Venice, IT; Katalog / catalogue
Final Projects: Group XLIV. MAK, Mackey
Apartments, Los Angeles, CA, US

2016
To Walk a Line. Akademie der Künste der
Welt, Köln / Cologne, DE
Triennale Kleinplastik, Alte Kelter, Fellbach,
DE; Katalog / catalogue
Par tibi, Roma, nihil. Nomas Foundation,
Palatino, Rom / Rome, IT
The Natural Order of Things.
Fundación Jumex Arte Contemporáneo,
Mexico City, MX
Shaping Ideas: Sculptures.
Noewe Foundation, Vilnius, LT
Cold Wind from the Balkans. Pera Museum,
Istanbul, TR
*The Distance of a Day: New in Contemporary
Art*. The Israel Museum, Jerusalem, IL

2015
*radical art and architecture: SUPER
SUPERSTUDIO*. Padiglione d'Arte
Contemporanea, Mailand / Milano, IT;
Katalog / catalogue
Alfred Jarry Archipelago: 'HA 'HA. Museo
Marino Marini, Florenz / Florence, IT
Appearance & Essence: Art Encounters.
Art Encounters Foundation, Timișoara, RO
Thirty One. Galeria Kombëtare e Kosovës,
Prishtina, KOS
WLGTDWI (What's Love Gotta Do With It).
SALTS, Birsfelden, CH
Ärger im Paradies. Bundeskunsthalle, Bonn,
DE; Katalog / catalogue
Slip of the Tongue. Pinault Collection,
Punta della Dogana, Venedig / Venice, IT

2014
Shit and Die. Palazzo Cavour, Turin, IT
DeGeneration of Painting. Fondazione 107,
Turin, IT; Katalog / catalogue
Fragile Sense of Hope: Telekom Collection.
me Collectors Room, Berlin, DE

2013
SUPER Visions: Zeichnen und Sein. Museum Schloss Moyland, Bedburg-Hau, DE; Katalog / catalogue
Zweiter Streich. Fürstenberg Zeitgenössisch, Donaueschingen, DE

2012
FUORICLASSE: 20 anni di arte italiana nei corsi di Alberto Garutti. Galleria d'Arte Moderna, Mailand / Milan, IT
It doesn't always have to be beautiful, unless it's beautiful. Muslim Mulliqi Preis / Prize, Galeria Kombëtare e Kosovës, Prishtina, KOS
The New Public: Von einer neuen Öffentlichkeit und einem neuen Publikum. Museion, Bozen / Bolzano, IT; Katalog / catalogue
Lost and Found. ERROR ONE, Antwerpen / Antwerp, BE
30 Künstler / 30 Räume. Kunstverein Nürnberg – Albrecht Dürer Gesellschaft, Nürnberg / Nuremberg, DE; Katalog / catalogue

2011
Temporaneo 2011: Contemporary Art in the Evolving City. IMF Foundation & Nomas Foundation, Auditorium – Parco della Musica, Rom / Rome, IT
Ernste Tiere: Petrit Halilaj, Judith Hopf, Bedwyr Williams. Bonner Kunstverein, Bonn, DE
Ostalgia. New Museum, New York City, NY, US; Katalog / catalogue
Based in Berlin. Atelierhaus Monbijoupark, Berlin, DE; Katalog / catalogue
Struktur & Organismus: Max Frey, Tue Greenfort, Petrit Halilaj, Rita Vitorelli. Marillenhof – Destillerie Kausl, Ötz, AT; Katalog / catalogue
You don't love me anymore. Westfälischer Kunstverein, Münster, DE

2010
Maladresses ou la figure de l'idiot. The Institute of Social Hypocrisy, Paris, FR

what is waiting out there. Berlin Biennale, KW Institute for Contemporary Art, Berlin, DE; Katalog / catalogue

2009
Melancholy of Compassion. Siemens Sanat, Istanbul, TR
Time Machine. Kunstverein Arnsberg, Arnsberg, DE

2008
Art is my Playground. Tersane, Istanbul, TR

2006
Mediterraneo Contemporaneo: Diciannove artisti tra identità e differenze. Castello Aragonese, Taranto, IT; Katalog / catalogue
De Portesio – Corpo Urbano. Fondazione Cominelli, San Felice del Benaco, IT; Katalog / catalogue
Migre. Careof, Mailand / Milan, IT
Open Air. Orto Botanico, Parma, IT

1999
Bambini di Kukës. Palazzo Municipale, Cremona, IT
Kosovë 1999. Lezhë, AL

Performances

2026
Syrigana. Hamburger Bahnhof – Nationalgalerie der Gegenwart, Berlin, DE

2025
Syrigana. Syrigana, KOS

2018
Shkrepëtima. Runik, KOS

Auszeichnungen und Stipendien /
Awards and Residencies

2024
Premio Stromboli, Stromboli, IT

2023
Kunstpreis Berlin (Bildende Kunst / Fine Art),
Akademie der Künste, Berlin, DE

2018
Smithsonian Artist Research Fellowship
(SARF), Washington, D.C., US

2017
Mario Merz Prize, Turin, IT

2016
MAK Schindler Scholarship, Mackey
Apartments, Los Angeles, CA, US

2014
Artist-in-Residence, Villa Romana,
Florenz / Florence, IT

2013
Artist-in-Residence, Fürstenberg,
Donaueschingen, DE

Ausgewählte Publikationen /
Selected Publications

Petrit Halilaj & Catherine Nichols (Hg. / eds.),
Syrigana, Prishtina: self-published, 2025.

Klaus Biesenbach et al. (Hg. / eds.),
KW: A History, Berlin: Distanz Verlag, 2021.

Petrit Halilaj & Álvaro Urbano (Hg. / eds.),
Kushtetuta? #3, Berlin: Motto Books, 2021.

Kit Hammonds & Patricia Marshalln
(Hg. / eds.), *On the Razor's Edge: Jumex
Collection #22*, Mexico City: Fundación
Jumex Arte Contemporaneo, 2020.

Petrit Halilaj, *Shkrepëtima*, Turin: Hopeful
Monster, 2018.

Stephan Berg et al., *Deutschland ist
keine Insel: Sammlung zeitgenössischer
Kunst der Bundesrepublik Deutschland*,
Cologne / Köln: Wienand Verlag, 2017.

Jen Hoffmann, *Animality*, London:
Marian Goodman Gallery, 2017.

Maurizio Cattelan, Marta Papini & Myriam
Ben Salah, *Shit and Die*, Bologna:
Damiani, 2014.

Boris Buden et al., *Il Piedistallo Vuoto /
The Empty Pedestal*, Mailand / Milan:
Mousse Publishing, 2014.

João Mourão and Luis Silva (Hg. / eds.),
Performing the Institution(al), Bd. / vols. 4 & 5,
Lissabon & Mailand / Lisbon & Milan:
Kunsthalle Lissabon & Cura Books, 2014.

Petrit Halilaj, *of course blue affects my way
of shitting*, Berlin: Chert & Motto Books, 2014.

Petrit Halilaj & Álvaro Urbano (Hg. / eds.),
About Mums & Dads – Kushtetuta #2, Berlin:
Eigenverlag / self-published, 2014.

Petrit Halilaj & Álvaro Urbano (Hg. / eds.),
Kushtetuta #1, Prishtina: KOSOVO 2.0, 2013.

Bonner Kunstverein (Hg. / ed.), *Kostërrc (CH)*,
Berlin: Chert & Motto Books, 2011.

Susanne Pfeffer (Hg. / ed.), *My work and me*,
Köln / Cologne: Walther König, 2011.

Simon Denny, Petrit Halilaj, Klara Lidén &
Nora Schultz, *shortlist. blauorange 2010:
Kunstpreis der Deutschen Volksbanken
und Raiffeisenbanken*, Wien / Vienna:
SFKB, 2010.

Drinnen & Draussen, Berlin: Chert &
Motto Books, 2010.

Lehre / Teaching

Seit / Since 2019
Studio Professor (mit / with Álvaro Urbano),
École Nationale Supérieure des Beaux Arts,
Paris, FR

Öffentliche Sammlungen / Public Collections

Art Collection Telekom, Lohmar, DE
Berlinische Galerie, Berlin, DE
Bundeskunstsammlung, DE
Centre Pompidou, Paris, FR
Colección Adrastus, Arévalo, ES
Colección Jumex, Mexico City, MX
Collection Fonds de dotation Famille Moulin,
Galeries Lafayette, Paris, FR
FRAC Champagne-Ardenne, Reims, FR
FRAC Grand Large, Dunkerque, FR
Fries Museum, Leeuwarden, NL
Fürstenberg Zeitgenössisch,
Donaueschingen, DE
Kölnischer Kunstverein, Köln / Cologne, DE
Museo Ettore Fico, Turin, IT
Museum of Contemporary Art, Chicago, IL, US
Muzeum Sztuki Nowoczesnej,
Warschau / Warsaw, PL
Noewe Foundation, Vilnius, LT
Nomas Foundation, Rom / Rome, IT
Nouveau Musée National de Monaco,
Monaco, MC
Sammlung Philara, Düsseldorf, DE
The Israel Museum, Jerusalem, IL

Impressum / Imprint

Diese Publikation erscheint anlässlich der Ausstellung /
Published on the occasion of the exhibition
Petrit Halilaj. An Opera Out of Time
11. September 2025 – 31. Mai 2026 /
11 September 2025 – 31 May 2026
im / at Hamburger Bahnhof – Nationalgalerie der
Gegenwart, Staatliche Museen zu Berlin
Direktoren / Directors: Sam Bardaouil & Till Fellrath
smb.museum/hbf

Ausstellung / Exhibition

Kuratorin / Curator: **Catherine Nichols**
Assistenzkuratorin / Assistant Curator:
Emily Finkelstein
Restauratorische Betreuung / Conservation:
**Elisa Carl, Tine Lippert, Thuja Seidel,
Johanna Wienert, Leon Wilke**
Ausstellungskoordination / Exhibition Coordination:
Elena Montini, Sophie Schattner
Kommunikation / Communication:
**Fiona Geuß, Anna Nike Sohrauer, Lorenz Dünges,
Nada Hussein, Theo Lemaire**
Kunstvermittlung / Mediation:
**Claudia Ehgartner, Sonja Azizaj,
Miriam Elisa Heidenreich**
Sekretariat / Office:
Katrin Berendsen, Katherine Israel-Koedel
Veranstaltungen / Event Management: **Eliette Cannici**
Sammlungsverwalter / Collection Management:
Jörg Lange, Thomas Seewald
Hauselektrik / Inhouse Electrics: **Garry Rogge**
Haustechnik / Maintenance:
Dirk Wagner, Stefan Gösche, Frank Wloka
Praktikant*innen / Interns:
Lisa Bockius, Hyunkyung Kim

Studio Petrit Halilaj:
Leiterin des Ateliers / Studio Manager: **Serena Rota**
Leiter Design / Head of Design: **Ferdinand Pechmann**
Entwicklung und Installation von Kunstwerken /
Artwork Development and Installation:
Martina Pelacchi & Hugo Larquè
Bildmaterial, technische Zeichnungen,
Ausstellungsentwurf /
Visualisations, Technical Drawings, Exhibition Layout:
Christina Stathakopoulou & Laura Roi
Archiv und Publikationen / Archive and Publications:
Sholem Krishtalka
Assistentin / Studio Assistant: **Mirjam Khera**
Produktion / Production: **Mattia Bertolo, Fritz Rahne,
Federica Partinico, Avantika Khanna, Marta Orlando,
Anna Berlin, Paydn Humble, Hannah Lee Jones,
Anky Coelen, Almost Alive**
Art Handling & Ausstellungsbau /
Art Handling & Exhibition Construction: **Kruse AT**
Medientechnik / Audiovisuals:
LICHTblick Bühnentechnik
Licht / Lighting Designer: **Josep Maria Comas Jorda**
Ton / Sound Designer: **Lugh O'Neill**
Malerarbeiten / Painting: **LIQUID PAINT**
Ausstellungsgrafik / Exhibition Graphics: **Eps51**
Produktion Ausstellungsgrafik /
Production of Exhibition Graphics: **Annette Herwegh**

Publikation / Catalogue

Für die / For the **Nationalgalerie –
Staatliche Museen zu Berlin**
herausgegeben von / edited by
Sam Bardaouil & Till Fellrath
Autor*innen / Authors:
**Petrit Halilaj, Lura Limani, Catherine Nichols,
Amy Zion**
Redaktion / Editing: **Lisa Hörstmann**
Übersetzungen / Translations:
**Tim Beeby & Sabine Bürger, Anne Diestelkamp,
Catherine Nichols**

Visuelles Konzept und Design /
Visual Concept and Design: **Eps51**
Druck und Bindung / Printing and Binding:
Tipostampa, Moncalieri
Papier / Paper: **Fedrigoni Arena White Rough**
Schriften / Fonts: **HB Bagoss (Displaay)**

Cover:
Petrit Halilaj. An Opera Out of Time,
Ausstellungsansicht / exhibition view
Hamburger Bahnhof – Nationalgalerie der
Gegenwart, Berlin, 2025

Erschienen bei / Published by
Silvana Editoriale S.p.A., Cinisello Balsamo
www.silvanaeditoriale.it

Silvana Editoriale

Hauptgeschäftsführung / Chief Executive:
Michele Pizzi
Verlagsleitung / Editorial Director: **Sergio Di Stefano**
Art Director: **Giacomo Merli**
Redaktionskoordination / Editorial Coordinator:
Maria Chiara Tulli
Korrektorat / Copy Editor: **Cristina Pradella**
Produktionskoordination / Production Coordinator:
Antonio Micelli
Redaktionsassistenz / Editorial Assistant:
Giulia Mercanti
Bildredaktion / Photo Editor: **Silvia Sala**
Pressestelle / Press Office: **Lidia Masolini**

Abbildungs-
verzeichnis / Photo Credits

Dank/ Acknowledge-ments

Die Ausstellung wird gefördert von /
With the support of
Hamburger Bahnhof
International Companions e.V.
Italian Council – Direzione Generale
Creatività Contemporanea del
Ministero della Cultura

Die Publikation wurde ermöglicht durch /
The publication was made possible by
Philipp und Kartika Laura Solf
Hamburger Bahnhof
International Companions e.V.

Der Hamburger Bahnhof dankt für
die enge Zusammenarbeit mit dem
Studio des Künstlers sowie ChertLüdde,
kurimanzutto und Mennour. /
Hamburger Bahnhof would like to thank
the artist's studio as well as ChertLüdde,
kurimanzutto and Mennour for their
close collaboration.

Hamburger
Bahnhof
International
Companions e.V.